T0365379

THE MILITARY
AND
PUBLIC RELATIONS

Issues, Strategies and Challenges

THE MILITARY
AND
PUBLIC RELATIONS

Issues, Strategies and Challenges

Col. (rtd) John Adache PhD

Research Fellow, Centre for Strategic Research and Studies
National Defence College, Nigeria (2006-2012)

authorHOUSE®

AuthorHouse™ UK Ltd.
1663 Liberty Drive
Bloomington, IN 47403 USA
www.authorhouse.co.uk
Phone: 0800.197.4150

© 2014 Col. (rtd) John Adache PhD. All rights reserved.

Cover Concept: John Adache
Cover Design by Eneojo Gabriel Adache

No part of this book may be reproduced, stored in a retrieval system, or transmitted
by any means without the written permission of the author.

Published by AuthorHouse 07/02/2014

ISBN: 978-1-4969-8235-3 (sc)
ISBN: 978-1-4969-8236-0 (e)

Library of Congress Control Number: 2014910040

Any people depicted in stock imagery provided by Thinkstock are models,
and such images are being used for illustrative purposes only.
Certain stock imagery © Thinkstock.

This book is printed on acid-free paper.

Because of the dynamic nature of the Internet, any web addresses or links contained in
this book may have changed since publication and may no longer be valid. The views
expressed in this work are solely those of the author and do not necessarily reflect the views
of the publisher, and the publisher hereby disclaims any responsibility for them.

Dedication

Dedicated to Sidney and to Faith,
Two children of mine,
Duo of whom despite personal circumstances
Admirably, best epitomize
Public Relations Hallmarks namely
Civility, Quiet Confidence, Warmth and Friendliness

Contents

Part One
Background and Historical Development

Part Four
Issues, Challenges and Conclusion

Acknowledgements

This work owes its successful completion to the encouragement and inspiration which I drew from many people foremost of which is Dr Martin Edmonds, my lecturer, Professorial Fellow and Director, Centre for Defence and International Security Studies, Lancaster University, United Kingdom. During 1991-92 as an MA student in Defence and Security Analysis, the idea which first motivated me to seriously consider doing a research on public relations in the military partly occurred from the reading of his work, **Armed Services and Society.** In this interesting book, he among others fathoms a general theory encompassing the many facets of the relationship between the Armed Services and Society in the political, economic, social and cultural realms at both the domestic and international arena. He therein outlines the need for constant public support for armed services roles as members of the National Security System. His discourse furthermore on the role of the military, also highlighted crucial areas requiring focus by military public relations and information branches outside their traditional function of providing information that will facilitate public understanding of defence aims in recruitment, and in community relations. I thank also my class mates and the many friends and acquaintances that I made in Lancaster including Dr Remi Ajibewa of ECOWAS and Dr Mohammed Salisu.

The curiosity and determination to venture further into academics after disengagement from the Army in 2000 impelled my enrolment for Doctorate Degree in International Relations at the University of Abuja, which I completed in July 2006. Engaged as a Research Fellow at the Africa Centre for Strategic Research and Studies, National Defence College, Abuja same year, I resolved from that onset to take advantage of that setting to make a contribution to knowledge by writing a book. This book being that outcome, it is a contribution which I earnestly believe will be valuable to my erstwhile constituencies namely, the Nigerian Military Public Relations Branch, the Nigerian Military and Defence establishment as well as Military Public Relations Branches across the world. Indeed from my days in Lancaster in 1991, I have been seeking out texts with specific and detailed focus on military public relations and its practice. The nearest I have come across have been pages or at best a chapter devoted to public relations practice in the military tucked away as part of general public relations texts encompassing practices in other sectors.

This is to further register my appreciation to many other personalities, individuals and friends whose tremendous kindness I hereby acknowledge. First, my appreciation goes to Late General Sani Abacha, former Head of State and Commander in Chief of Nigerian Armed Forces whom as Army Chief, I served as Public Relations Officer during which period I had tremendous exposure to PR activities. I register also my appreciation to Dr (Mrs) Maryam Sani Abacha, former First Lady, in whose office I had served in the State House, Abuja as Public Relations and Research Officer. My appreciation goes equally to General Abdulsalami Abubakar and Justice Fati Lami Abubakar, former President and First Lady respectively, whom I had privilege of equally working with. My appreciation also goes to my late bosom friend, Mallam Mamman Nassir, who as Chief Press Secretary to the First Lady, I had worked closely with.

I thank immensely Brigadier General Fred Chijuka rtd, a very amiable Director of Army Public Relations and later, of Defence Information; an eloquent PR practitioner under whose tutelage I not only cut my teeth in Public Relations practice but sharpened them as well. I also thank Commodore Olutunde Oladimeji rtd, a doyen of Military Public Relations practice and a long standing Director of Naval Information and Public Relations. He was very kind to have found time to go through this work and provided some guidance and useful suggestions. To Generals O.E. Okon rtd, Brigadier Generals G.I. Ugbo, F. Chukwuma, G. Adewale, M.D. Yusuf, A.C. Olukolade, and Col O. Olaniyan, all former Directors of Army Public Relations, I am equally grateful. Equally to Commodore Aliyu, Director Naval Information, Air Commodore Y. Anas, Director NAF Public Relations and Information, Col M.M. Yerima, Director Defence Information and all other officers of Army Public Relations – past and present, I thank immensely. I thank equally Prof Inno Ukaeje, Professor O.B.C. Nwolise, Dr Kabir Mato, Dr Chris Iyimoga, Dr and Mrs A.D. Abbah.

To the entire National Defence College Community I register immense thanks. To especially Rear Admiral TJ Lokoson, I am grateful for his support, advice and encouragement. I thank Major Gen M.I. Idris, Dr Istifanus Zabadi, Dr Gani Yoroms, Ms Julie Sanda, Dr Emeka Okereke, Dr (Mrs) Blessing Gaiya, Dr H. Abdullahi, Dr O. Nwankwo, Mr C.S. Udeh, Danladi Bot, Mrs Rhoda Namiji, Mrs Aisha Yanet and Mrs Habiba Decker, Isaac Terwase, Dr Freedom Onuoha, Danjuma Aku and Moses Owolabi. I thank also Mr Emma Unuakpo and Reginald Nwokedinobi for their support.

To the following great friends and colleagues – Ex Boys of the Nigerian Military School, I owe much appreciation namely, Generals L.P. Ngubane, S.O. Idoko, D.M. Chong, A.I. Muraina, O.A.C. Ariahu, L.M.K. Banjiram, G. Audu, P. Isang and S.Y. Audu P.T. Boroh; AVM J.O. Oshoniyi, M. Oladuni and Rear Admiral A. Seleh, Col and Mrs MJA Agbah-Attah rtd, Col D. Abel rtd, Group Capt JM Alagoka rtd, Major D Idoko rtd, Ode Ikwue and all my other Ex Boy Class mates, my deep and special thanks. I thank also Brigadier General and Mrs James Adejoh, Maj Gen Gen Okoh, Col D. Apochi rtd, and Major Sunday Orokpo.

I thank equally Chief Robert Usman Audu, Mr Sani Adeyi, Flight Engr Sunny Abutu, Rev Alex Odiniya, Alphonsus Okoliko, Barrister Joe Abrahams, Thompson and Mrs Eugenia Abuh, Ejike Eze, Adelabu Morebishe, Mr Frank Onojah, Mr Aurelius Adejoh, Titus Akoh, James Adah, Hon Emmanuel Odiniya, Paul Yahaya, Felix Idakwo, Mr Ochapa Ogenyi, Lawrence Ojabo, Hon Adu–Ojo Ebute,, Emma Ekele, Hon Obida, Godwin Yakubu, Gabriel Ochai, Hon Pius Ikwuje, Silas Ammeh, Alhaji Danjuma Ibrahim, MWO Edwin Orokpo, Joseph Erico, Simon Echofu, Silas Iyaji, Abutu Okoliko, Mathew

Onoja, Mathew Attah, and Barrister Ameh Adejoh. I equally thank my 'Summer' friends and associates, namely, Mr Danjuma Lar, Mr Sunday Adejoh, Philip Ibrahim, Arch Ali, Francis Amanabo, Yahaya Mohammed, Alhaji Bello Dange, Alhaji Aminu, and all others not mentioned here. I equally express appreciation to To Godwin and Mrs Rebecca Zekeri, Emmanuel Simon and all other staff of Summer Guest Inn, I say thank you immensely.

To the following relations and friends, I equally offer my thanks namely, Gabriel and Mrs Victoria Ojile, Emmanuel and Mrs Ojoma Onoja, Godwin and Mrs Omojo Obla, Linus Eneche and family, Abel Eneche, Sunday Egwu, Usman Jacob Adache, Sunday Adache, and Mike Egwu, Monday Onoja, Ojoniko Adache, Sunday Jacob Adache, Ugwa Egwu, Ojoniko Odiniya, Hajia Fati Abubakar, my elder brothers Jacob Adache, Mathew Adache, James Odiniya, Gabriel Odiniya, Peter Abutu, Joseph Abutu, and Jacob Diploma Odiniya. There are many others of my relations and friends who deserve my deep appreciation. However, it is not possible to list all the names here as it will be invidious to single out just some. To "you all" therefore, I give my many thanks.

I very warmly on final note thank my dear wife, Grace Eleojo Adache, and my dear children Eneojo, Marshal, Mercy, Joy, Freda, and Marvin for their fervent prayers and support. To Sidney and Faith, I deeply appreciate them both and give special thanks to God for their lives. Finally, I thank God Almighty for his many years of guidance upon my life and those of my family, for sustaining and steering me across difficult storms and, for providing the strength and the wherewithal in putting this work together.

Colonel (rtd) JOHN ENEMONA ADACHE, PhD

Preface

Morris Janowitz, American Professor, Sociological theorist and co-founder of Military Sociology who, along with Samuel Huntington, made enormous contributions to establishment of contemporary civil military relations, aptly stated that the professional military remarkably, has been object of sociological investigation such that there has continued to be marked increase in scholarly work relating to the sociology of military institutions and militarism. It is probably from this premise that the role of the military and its relationship to society in a number of ways have from time, been generally a focus of great interest. Ample literature testify to this with increased intensity especially from about the late sixties to the seventies when there began a worldwide and rapidly increasing phenomenon of "The Man on Horseback", an interesting euphemism then for the increasing involvement of the military not only in politics but in direct governance of nation states as well.

The phenomenon was prevalent in especially the developing nations of Africa, Asia and Latin America and is not surprising going by the observation that stable democracy is a relatively recent phenomenon in these countries. No doubt in such countries, nascent democratic institutions as well as the military especially, is confronted with the challenge of gaining consensus and of identifying with public interest. This is not the case with the advanced democracies of the west especially the United States of America and Britain where high premium is accorded unrestricted flow of information as critical catalyst to the growth and sustenance of democracy. Recognising the power of public opinion and of the need to continue to maintain public support, it follows logically that public control of government institutions, including the military, should depend particularly on truthful account of activities that are carried out in the name of the people. With focal attention on military involvement in politics, an anathema of sort that should be discouraged in consonance with democratic tenets of military obeisance to civil and democratic control, no thought seemingly was given to public relations, a discipline whose effective practice in the military could be used to achieve the broader goals of civil military relations which amongst others seeks to regulate the military institution and its role in society.

Military public relations is a discipline whose practice has direct bearing and impact on military civilian relationship; relevance of which hitherto was neglected. Public relations could be strategically positioned as vehicle through which government institutions could seek to identify with the peoples interest, render accounts of their performances and seek informed support. The recognition which western democracies accord these concepts including detailed academic and professional focus is sadly not the same in developing and emerging democracies. Further analyses of existing literature on Public Relations suggest that there have been no appreciable focal or in-depth study into this vital subject as catalyst to effective civil military relations either from within or outside military establishments. Such a study and indeed focus is therefore highly desirable. No doubt the military as Martin Edmonds noted, has evolved through various statuses in society: warriors, crusaders, mercenaries, praetorian guards, *condotierri*, guerrillas, commissars, braves, etc, to being the modern military that it is with a unique nature and position in society.

My decision and resolve to make this contribution to the subject of military public relations from a global perspective, not only stems from a desire to stimulate discourses on this aspect of armed services-societal relationships per se, but also by the belief that public relations does hold a vital role in smoothening the relationship between members of society and the military, - a profession I have been privileged to have been part of. The recurring theme deriving from the contents of this text strongly infer and indeed reiterate that public relations with all its potential could be a tool of civil military relations.

By its nature, public relations has become a discipline whose principles are not being only appreciated, applied and practiced by its practitioners but by virtually every one. This book therefore aims to not only be a contribution in general terms to the discipline but seeks in particular to being a useful source of reference to especially military public relations officers and indeed all military officers for teaching and as a guide for its practice to enhance cordial relationship between the civil populace and the military in especially Nigeria's democratic polity.

Col (rtd) John Enemona Adache PhD
Defence, Security & Communications Consultant
50, Birnin Kebbi Crescent, Garki 2
Abuja - Nigeria

ForeWord

Public relations and indeed its practice in today's world has generally become a global imperative. Widely acknowledged as one of society's fast emerging professions, it is contemporary and dynamic in its expression and utilises among others, the critical tools of information, persuasion, lobby, reconciliation, as well as cooperation. These elements are today vital and intrinsic to its practice as they have been many years back into history. The modern world especially with increasing democratization has compelled most organizations in society to give greater impetus to public relations and communications management. It is to that extent that the scholarly body of knowledge of public relations has grown significantly in especially the last 25 years. Aided by the rapid expansion of new communication technologies such as satellite television and the internet, it continues to evolve towards establishing itself as a strong discipline. The acceptability of public relations and its approaches and methods have become deeply entrenched in business, government and in many other complex organizations. In the same manner, its utility and relevance have become widely instituted in the Armed Forces of many nation states even as its growth and development keeps improving in the militaries of developing nations.

The Military and Public Relations – Issues, Strategies and Challenges, is a text which broadly articulates and highlights in-depth, the many aspects to public relations practice in the military. It also broaches very salient issues relating to public relations practice in the military. The military is a unique public institution that performs a legitimately privileged role in society and has over time, come to reckon with the immense institutional image-making potential of public relations as exemplified by its utility in many civil organizations. The necessity thus arises for the development of organisational mechanisms and channels in the military through which to constantly `keep the military in the public eye', through military public relations activities. Such a need is further reinforced by the fact that within the overall framework of a country's security system are also public relations roles in the promotion of military interests as they relate to the performance of their specified constitutional roles. It is therefore appropriate that public relations be properly positioned as the strategic machinery through which the military could seek to identify with the people and invariably, national interest in order to render accounts of their performances and seek informed public support as obtains in developed democracies.

The text is logically structured into four parts. Part One under the broad title, Background and Historical Development x-rays the military as an institution of society, delineates and traces the evolution and development of public relations into history and furthermore, its historical development in the military. Part Two under the heading, Public Relations Principles, Approaches and Practice, fundamentally examines the subject of Public Relations and its Role and Function, in the Interface of Military and Society. There is an analysis of the `Competence' of the Military to Conduct Public Relations, a legal perspective which interrogates the authority of military institutions to conduct public relations without due political authorization. It is an issue that is prevalent mainly in liberal democratic nations especially the United States where, against demands of the concept of "civil control", the authority of the military to conduct public relations outside government framework is put to question. The text further highlights the Purpose, Targets, Strategies and Tactics of Military Public Relations.

Part Three titled Public Perception and the Nigerian Military, Public Relations Practice and Training begins with analysis of Public Perception and its Management in the Nigerian Military. It dwells extensively on Public Relations Practice in the Nigerian Military, highlighting its practice in the respective Services – Army, Navy, Air Force and their coordinating higher authority, the Defence Headquarters. Military Public Relations Training and Professionalization is an imperative which the book also strongly advocates in this section.

Part Four titled Issues, Challenges and Conclusion analyses some current and emerging issues in military public relations. Such issues as Technology, Public Relations and the Military; Public Relations, Social Media and the Military; and Negative Connotation of Public Relations: The Nigerian Dimension. There is also a topic on How to Foster Cordial Civilian – Military Relationship. Another chapter focuses on Security Threats, Crisis Management and the Role of Communication. Another chapter equally brings into focus, the need for Effective Communications and Interpersonal skills by Military Public Relations Officers. The book further analyses the Challenges to Military Public Relations Practice and concludes with an examination of its overall Importance in a Democratic Society.

By its nature, public relations have become a discipline whose principles are not reckoned with and applied by its practitioners alone but by virtually every one in society. This book, written by a long standing veteran military public relations professional and practitioner is no mean contribution to the field of public relations generally, but especially to the military public relations branch. The book no doubt, should bring forth better insight to the understanding by the civilian populace of public relations practice in the military. The publication should prove beneficial as a source of knowledge to public relations and communications professionals operating in diverse regions of the world. In the same manner, it should prove useful to students and research scholars specializing in military public relations or public affairs. It certainly should be a useful source of reference to especially military public relations officers and indeed all military officers. Above all, it would also be relevant for teaching, and as a guide for its practice to foster sustainable cordial mutual relationship between the civil populace and the military in especially Nigeria's democratic polity.

I commend and recommend this interesting and worthy text to military public relations practitioners, all public relations experts and professionals as well as the general public.

Brig Gen Frederick Bini Chijuka (Rtd)
Former Director Army Public Relations Dept &
Pioneer Director of Defence Information
Defence Headquarters, Abuja – Nigeria.

Index of Abbreviations

ADAPR	Assistant Director Army Public Relations
AFRICOM	Africa Command
AFSC	Armed Forces Command and Staff College
AHQ	Army Headquarters
AMG	Air Mobility Group
AWS	Advanced Weapons School
APRD	Army Public Relations Department
APRO	Army Public Relations Officer
BBC	British Broadcasting Corporation
BCE	Before Christian Era
COAS	Chief of Army Staff
CDS	Chief of Defence Staff
CNN	Cable News Network
DAPR	Directorate of Army Public Relations
DCAF	Geneva Centre for Democratic Control of Armed Forces
DHQ	Defence Headquarters
DINFOS	Defence Information School
DOPRI	Director of Public Relations and Information
DoD	Department of Defence
DPR (A)	Director of Public Relations (Army)
ECOMOG	Economic Community Monitoring Group
EUCOM	European Command
FAPRA	Federation of African Public Relations Association
FTS	Flying Training School
GAF	Ghana Armed Forces
GSM	Global System for Mobile Communication
GOsC	General Officers Commanding
HMOD	Honourable Minister of Defence

IDP	Internally Displaced Persons
IMT	Institute of Management and Technology
IPR	Institute of Public Relations
KAPE	Keeping the Army in the Public Eye
KAIPTC	Kofi Anan Institute of Peace Training Centre
LSPR	London School of Public Relations
MACA	Military Aid to Civil Authorities
MACP	Military Aid to Civil Power
MPB	Military Pensions Board
MPRD	Military Public Relations Department
MPRI	Military Professionals Resource International
MOD	Ministry of Defence
MOG (v)	Media Operations Group (volunteer)
NA	Nigerian Army
NATO	North Atlantic Treaty Organization
NAF	Nigerian Air Force
NDA	Nigerian Defence Academy
NDC	National Defence College
NDC	National Defence Council;
NIPR	Nigerian Institute of Public Relations
NN	Nigerian Navy
NNDC	Nigeria National Defence Policy
NSC	National Security Council
NAFRC	Nigerian Armed Forces Rehabilitation Centre
NASPRI	Nigerian Army School of Public Relations and Information
NIPRNET	Non Classified Internet Protection Reuter Network
NMS	Nigerian Military School
NOK	Next of Kin
ORBAT	Order of Battle
PAOs	Public Affairs Officers
PK	Peace Keeping
PRISA	Public Relations Institute of South Africa
PR	Public Relations
PRO	Public Relations Officer
PRSA	Public Relations Society of America
PSO	Peace Support Operations

QONR	Queens Own Nigeria Regiment
RNA	Royal Nigerian Army
RNC	Royal Niger Company
RNN	Royal Nigerian Navy
RWAFF	Royal West African Frontier Force
SHAPE	Supreme Headquarters Allied Powers Europe
SOPs	Standing Operational Procedures
TAPIOS	Territorial Army Pool of Information Officers
UK	United Kingdom
UN	United Nations
UNILAG	University of Lagos
UNN	University of Nigeria
US	United States
WAFF	West African Frontier Force
UNIFIL	United Nations Interim Forces in Lebanon

Part One

Background and Historical Development

CHAPTER ONE

INTRODUCTION:
THE MILITARY IN SOCIETY

The military globally are critical national defence institutions reputed to be older than recorded history itself. Diverse studies on the military institution ranging from its evolvement, nature and role in society have severally been undertaken. It is thus pertinent that a discussion such as this of the military within the context of civil military relations requires proper delineation of the term `military.' As Martin Edmonds rightly pointed out, a clear and adequate definition is required in view of the fact that reference to the term most of the time has often been used to denote uniformed personnel who are in enlisted service in the armed forces of nation states. It is also important according to him for a clear distinction to be made between those actually recognized as members of the military and other uniformed personnel in society who are equally involved in the performance of ancillary security duties. Furthermore, some people use the term `military', when they meant to refer to the army, when in fact they meant to refer to the combination of the three branches of the armed forces namely, the Army, Navy and Air Force.

While this text recognizes that quite a number of definitions exist, the definition of the term, military, adopted in this discourse is that provided by Martin Edmonds which defines the military as "that state organisation or group of organisations permanently established by constitutional law, enjoys a monopoly of certain categories of weapons and equipment, and is responsible for the constrained application of violence or coercive force to eliminate or deter anything or body that is considered to threaten the existence of the nation state and the interests, simply or collectively of its citizens"[1]. In addition to this precise and stipulative definition of the `military', for which the author substitutes the term `armed services', a further dimension to the definition provided is the categorisation of the military on the basis of the "environment within which they predominantly operate: land, sea, air or space"[2]. The reason behind this categorisation, he explains, is due to technological developments in the modern artefacts of warfare, and the range of uses to which these implements of war could be put.

It is, however, essential that in so defining and delineating the term military, he also pointed out that in addition to the essential members of the `military', whose specialty, according to Harold Lasswell, is the "constrained management of violence"[3], there are other large groups and organisations working within a military environment who in various ways provide direct and indirect assistance to the military. These include a large number of skilled civilian staff of both members and non-members of Defence Ministries who are either engaged in providing administrative support, policy formulation, and weapons research and production, or working in organisations that provide ancillary and essential logistic support services for the military. This recognizes that within the context of modern day defence organisations, there has emerged an overlapping of functions between members of the Armed Services and those civilians who provide essential support services either through policy formulation or execution. A further important point to note from the above definition of the military as provided is that it rests on legal framework which assigns to the military, the primary responsibility for the security of the nation state and its citizens against external physical threats. This function to Martin Edmonds thus provides the foundation upon which the issue of legitimacy and role of the military in society has always been predicated.

Legitimacy of the Military and Role in Society

The issue of legitimacy in relation to the military has many dimensions. In this text, however, the definition of the term and views enunciated on it by Jacques van Doorn are considered relevant. While he defines legitimacy as "the capacity of a social or political system to develop and maintain a general belief that the existing social order and its main solutions are generally appropriate"[4], he also noted in relation to the position of the armed forces as the embodiment of a legitimate order, that no matter what the type of government or political system was, as a general rule of the thumb "the legitimacy of the armed forces was guaranteed as long as (1) the function of the military coincided sufficiently with what the political community defined as legitimate goals, (2) the military subculture coincided sufficiently with the political culture of the larger unit, and (3) the composition of the armed forces was sufficiently representative of the composition of the political community"[5]. On the basis of this definition, he noted that with the exception of a number of new nations, no serious tension existed between the political elite and the military establishment. "The armed forces accept their subordinacy to the political culture and regard themselves as the loyal executives of the political regime, regardless of whether the latter derive their legitimacy from traditional, legal or charismatically determined values"[6].

On the basis of the premise by which the legitimacy of the armed forces is based, most nations have come to attach much importance to the provision of national security and, further, as a function which the military are the proper agent of government to perform. This usually calls for their recognition as the institution of state with functions that are laid down within the national constitution whether this be written or established by convention. This point is further expanded by Samuel Finer who, using the term 'army' for the military, noted that the "the army is a purposive instrument. It is not a crescive institution like the church; it comes into being by a fiat. It is rationally conceived to fulfil certain objects... the principal object is to fight and win wars"[7]. It is in consonance with such legalistic provision for the roles of the military that the Constitution of the Federal Republic of Nigeria (1999), chapter V1, part III c section 217(1) states that there shall be an armed forces of the Federation which shall consist of the Army, a Navy, an Air Force and such other branches of the armed forces of the Federation as may be established by an Act of the National Assembly[8]. Section 2 goes further to say that the Federation shall, subject to an Act of the National Assembly made in that behalf, equip and maintain the armed forces as may be considered adequate and effective for the purpose of:

(a) Defending Nigeria from external aggression;
(b) Maintaining its territorial integrity and securing its borders from violation on land, sea or air;
(c) Suppressing insurrection and acting in aid of civil authorities to restore order when called upon to do so by the President, but subject to such conditions as may be prescribed by an act of national assembly.
(4) Performing such other functions as may be prescribed by an act of the national assembly"[9].

From the position of such legal provision, Martin Edmonds further highlights the constitutional position of the military in which he notes that "the basis of legitimacy for the armed services rests in part upon their constitutional position (for they need to be seen to have legal authority) and in part upon the public's acceptance first, of the essential function they are supposed to perform on behalf of society to defend and protect it, and, second, their manifest competence at fulfilling that function together with their profesionalism"[10]. Any assessment of the place and role of the military in society would therefore invite attention to the phenomenon of war and conflict to which the interrelationship between the military and society has often been associated.

War is defined as the use of violence, or physical coercion, by a state, a society or a group against another to achieve a desired objective. It has been posited that war needs to be understood as an actual, intentional and widespread armed conflict between political communities. Thus, fisticuffs between individual persons do not count as a war, nor does a gang fight. War is thus a phenomenon which occurs only between political communities, defined as those entities which either are states or intend to become states (in order to allow for civil war). Classical war is international war, a war between different states, like the two World Wars... and war within a state between rival groups or communities in a state, like the American Civil War. Certain political pressure groups, like terrorist organizations, might also be considered "political communities," in that they are associations of people with a political purpose and, indeed, many of them aspire to statehood or to influence the development of statehood in certain lands[11].The mere threat of war, and the presence of mutual disdain between political communities, does not suffice as indicators of war. The conflict of arms must be *actual*, and not merely latent, for it to count as war. Clausewitz famously suggested that war is "the continuation of policy by other means".

Martin Edmonds explains the interconnection between war, society and the military by stating that war is intrinsic to a society's internal affairs since it is a means employed by one society against another. As he put it: "a decision whether or not to resort to war, or to use violent means for whatever reason, rests to a high and significant degree on that society's own nature and values. Some societies or their governments have, over time, displayed a greater propensity than others to resort to violence to achieve their objectives for any number of ideological, geopolitical and cultural reasons. Others, which might be considered more pacific in their approaches to their relations with outside bodies, have demonstrated nonetheless a resolute determination to protect and defend themselves by physical means against real or perceived predators. In either case either for offence or defence, the organized use of force and violence against outsiders is the principal, if not exclusive function of the armed forces of society, or today, of the nation-state"[12]. Apart from functions that are constitutionally provided, the military have come to acquire other roles which they have performed very usefully in many nations. Some of these are self-initiated in aid of the society, but mostly they are at the behest of the civil authority or government in power. These include the protection and promotion of vital national interests and values; advising government on military matters; executing government policies; promoting national unity; being delegated greater responsibility in national decision making in war time; providing aid to civil authorities in times of national emergencies or when necessary; honouring international political commitments and obligations; promoting education where necessary; and acting as agents of political values such as security, public order and national prestige, amongst others. Military aid to the civil power (MACP) (sometimes to the Civil Authorities) is assistance by the armed forces to the police in maintaining law and order. It is used in many countries, of the west including the United Kingdom and Canada. MACP in Britain is a fundamental military task carried out by the army which like all deployments in the armed forces its use is authorized by the defence minister. It is essentially the operational deployment of the armed forces of the United Kingdom in support of the civilian authorities, other government departments and the community as whole[13]. The most prominent example of MACP in Britain was the long standing use of British security forces in Northern Ireland.

Similarly in Canada, the Canadian forces play an important role in supporting civil authorities charged with enforcing Canadian laws. For example, they assist the Department of Fisheries and Oceans in the surveillance of the 200-mile Extended Fishing Zone and the enforcement of Canadian fisheries laws in that zone when coercive assistance is required. The Canadian forces are also called upon to provide emergency assistance to Canadians in cases of disasters such as floods, forest fires and landslides. The Department of National Defence works with other Departments to improve the availability and effective employment of the Canadian Forces in these roles[14]. Nigeria's national constitution under section 217 also has similar provisions of Military Aid to Civil Power as provided specifically under section (c) namely, suppressing insurrection and acting in aid of civil authorities to restore order when called upon to do so by the President, but subject to such conditions as may be prescribed by an Act of the National Assembly[15].

The Nature of the Military

It is helpful to understand the nature of the military as a necessary follow-up towards a proper appreciation of the roles of the military in society. Such an understanding would not only shed light on peculiar characteristics of the military but would also provide insight into the manner in which the military organizes itself for the efficient performance of its assigned roles. Samuel Huntington in his pioneering work on the military, "The Soldier and the State", provides an insight into the nature of the military when, in his analysis, he concludes that the US military meets the criteria of professionalism, namely: "expertise, social responsibility and corporateness"[16]. The professional man is an expert with some form of specialised knowledge and skill in a significant field of human endeavour. This is acquired after prolonged education and training backed by experience. Identifying military officers as the main embodiment of professionalism within the military, Huntington noted that the US officer corps appears to contain many varieties of specialists including large numbers which have civilian counterparts - engineers, doctors, pilots, administrators, personnel managers, intelligence analysts, and communicators. He pointed out that the officer's prime responsibility is the defence and security of the state, bearing in mind that the military is also a profession that also comes under the purview of the state. Within this context, he identifies the duties of the military officer to include "organising equipping and training of the military force; the planning of its activities; and the direction of its activities in and out of combat"[17]. The corporate nature of the military as outlined by Huntington is echoed by James Clotfelter who observed that "the military is corporate in several senses. It regulates its own affairs through a system of internal administration which formalizes and enforces the standards of professional entrance, performance and advancement. It has a body of ethics and a solidarity and cohesion based on the vestiges of the gentleman officer's code and the management of a large proportion of the officer's activities by the profession itself. The uniform and a shared sense of group identity help to distinguish the military man from the civilian"[18].

Another aspect of the military that is highlighted by Huntington which sheds further light into the nature of the military is in relation to specialisms within the organisation. These subcategories of role he likens to specialists in the medical profession such as cardiologists, obstetricians, and oculists. As he noted, the variety of conditions under which violence may be employed and the different forms in which it may be applied form the basis for sub professional military specialisation. This brings to mind the element of distinction between the fighting sides of the military referred to as the "teeth arms", and those sections that provide the logistic and administrative back-up, known as the "tail". The provision of operational logistical back-up in peace and in war is provided by the military themselves, though civilians are increasingly being subcontracted in some areas.

Transformation within military circles over the years in many nations has seen other categories and branches added to the military services who are specialists and professionals in their own right. Within this group as rightly delineated by Martin Edmonds are the chaplains, teachers, lawyers, public relations experts and nurses. The job of the public relations branch within the military, which is the focus of this work, as he pointed out has become very essential to the armed forces as a result not only of changes in the nature and conduct of war but also as a result of increased societal awareness and other evolving dimensions that play on the interrelationship between the military and society. Civil military relations is an interrelationship which is on-going and calls for military `image making' not just from the point of view of the professional interests of the military but more especially from their increased involvement in government policies, politics and in dealings with various sections of the society. Henry Stanhope emphasised the importance of `image making' for the military whereby in respect of the British Army, he noted that "the hardest post war battle for the Army has been to establish a new identity for itself in a changing world... Not only has the chance of travel diminished, but so has the soldier's place in the scale of importance... at home defence has dropped several places in the order of priorities..."[19]. The military through historical evolutionary processes as well as transformation has become not only a visible institution of state but an enduring and indispensable part of society given especially the ever unfolding dynamics of global security challenges.

References

1. Edmonds, M. (1988) **Armed Services and Society**, Leicester University press, p.26
2. Ibid
3. Lass well, H. cited in Huntington, S. (1957) **The Soldier and the State**, Cambridge, Massachusetts, p.8
4. Harries Jenkins and Jacques van Doon, (1976) **The Military and the Problem of Legitimacy**, Sage pub Inc. p.20
5. Ibid
6. Ibid
7. Finer, S. **The Man On Horseback**, 2nd ed Westview pub. P.6
8. Constitution of the Federal Republic of Nigeria 1999
9. ibid
10. Edmonds, M. (1988) **Armed Services and Society**, Leicester University press, p.97
11. Orend Brian, "War", http://plato.stanford.edu/entries/war/
12. Edmonds, M, op cit
13. http://en.wikipedia.org.wiki/Military_Aid_to_the
14. **Challenge and Commitment – A Defence Policy for Canada** (Ottawa, Canadian Govt Pub 1987) P. 87
15. Constitution of the Federal Republic of Nigeria, op cit
16. Huntington, S. **The Soldier and the State,** Cambridge, Massachusetts 1957 p. 8
17. Ibid
18. Clotfelter, J. (1976) **The Military in American Politics** Harper and Row pub. New York p.30
19. Stanhope, H. (1979) **The Soldiers**, Hamish Hamilton, London, P. 294

CHAPTER TWO

PUBLIC RELATIONS: DELINEATION, EVOLVEMENT, GROWTH AND DEVELOPMENT

Delineation

The field of Public Relations is replete with so many definitions as there have been several attempts at definition of the concept. Some definitions are examined here as being of analytical relevance. The Institute of Public Relations, (IPR) in the United Kingdom in February 1948, defines Public Relations as "the planned and sustained effort to establish and maintain goodwill and mutual understanding between an organisation and its publics"[1]. Critical in this definition are two components namely, mutual understanding and goodwill which must be created or established in a deliberate manner between an organisation and its publics. The planning process by the organization in this case requires that it pays serious attention to details through proper analysis, anticipation and research. Emphasis here is that a mutually complementary process of understanding between the organization and its public(s) must be established and sustained in the interest both of the organization and its clientele publics.

A second definition, which is recognized as one of the most persistent, was that given by *Public Relations News*, one of several commercial newsletters serving the profession. It defines public relations as "the management function which evaluates public attitudes, identifies the policies and procedures of an individual or an organisation with the public interest, and plans and executes a programme of action to earn public understanding and acceptance"[2]. The role of management as espoused in this definition is very crucial as management at its level requires proper evaluation of public perception and attitude towards an organization by whatever measure to be able to plan and actualize programmes of action that will enable the public to properly identify with its goals, policies, and even products in a positive and friendly way. Research and analysis are again very crucial here.

A third definition is that provided by Rex F. Harlow, a long time public relations scholar. From an analysis of 472 references he produced a working definition that is regarded as both conceptual and operational. It is that: "public relations is a distinctive management function which helps establish and maintain mutual lines of communications, understanding, acceptance and cooperation between an organization and its publics; involves the management of problems or issues; helps management to keep informed on, and responsive to public opinion; defines and emphasizes the responsibility of management to serve public interest; helps management to keep abreast of and effectively utilize change, serving as an early warning system to help anticipate trends; and uses research and sound and ethical communication as its principal tools"[3]. The application of public relations deriving from this analysis would be useful to many establishments and agencies in society including enterprises, trade unions, and government agencies, the military, voluntary associations, hospitals, religious and non-governmental organizations among others. To be able to achieve their goals, such institutions must of necessity be able to develop effective linkages and relationships with different audiences and publics. The management of these institutions need to understand the attitudes and values of their publics with a view to achieving ultimate institutional goals[4].

The Nigerian Institute of Public Relations equally defines the concept as the discipline which looks after reputation with the aim of earning understanding, support, influencing opinion and behaviour. It is the planned and sustained effort to establish and maintain goodwill and mutual understanding between an organization and its publics[5]. All of the above definitions are useful in their respective approaches and in the manner by which they respectively relate its application to various organizations in society.

Evolvement, Growth and Historical Development

The beginnings of public relations and its evolvement as a discipline is deeply rooted into history. A natural and recurring element of human social interaction, it is ancient in its foundations, rooted in the earliest interactions of people in societies long gone. It is contemporary in its expression as one of society's emerging professions[6]. Elements of Public relations approaches such as information, lobby, persuasion, reconciliation and cooperation are today aspects of its practices as they have been many years ago. All phases of human history have no doubt been associated with one aspect or other of public relations practices. Ancient civilizations and medieval society thus offer glimpses of public relations-like activities for example, Ptah-hotep, an adviser to one of the ancient Egyptian Pharaohs wrote at about 2,200 BCE of the need for communicating truthfully, addressing audience interests and acting in a manner that is consistent with what is being said[7].

Evidences of ancient origins of Public relations include bulletins and brochures in ancient Mesopotamia (present day Iraq) dating to about 1,800 BCE. Philosophers that include Socrates, Aristotle, Philip of Macedonia, Alexander the Great and the Roman General Julius Caesar among others all recognized the importance of public relations with their recognition and application of its tenets. Religious history is also replete with many instances of the application of rudiments of public relations. John the Baptist for example, is recognized in the social history of Christianity as the precursor or advance-man who was effective in generating among his publics an anticipation and enthusiasm for Jesus Christ[8]. In the mid-first century, Peter and Paul led the Christian Apostles in their use of many persuasive languages, such as speeches, staged events, letters and oral teaching. Their aim was to increase interest in Jesus and his message, to increase membership in the new religious movement, and to maintain morale and order among church members[9]. The Islamic faith equally found useful, the application of public relations methods. It was revealed that the Prophet Mohammed in the early days sometimes retired to an out-of-the-way-place to ponder about problems facing his people, eventually to emerge with writings that he identified as the word of Allah. These writings, eventually assembled as the Koran (right), thus received a credibility that led to easy acceptance by his followers[10].

Many notable Christian personalities applied the principles of persuasive communication, the courting of public opinion and the tactics of lobbying in their dealings with the public and their followers. Some of these include Pope Urban II in 1095, Stephen Langton, the Arch Bishop of Canterbury in 1215, Thomas Aquinas, the 13th Century Philosopher, John Wycliffe of England, Martin Luther, Ignatius of Loyola, and Pope Gregory XV who popularized the word 'propaganda' in 1622 when he established the Congregation of the Propagation of the Faith to spread the church's message into non-Christian lands. Presently even in the 21st Century, religious organizations continue to use public relations strategies and tactics. Groups translate the Bible and other religious books into the language of the people, often paraphrasing the message or revising it with contemporary experiences. Churches and Synagogues, as well as religious organizations such as dioceses and districts, employ their own public relations people, have interactive web sites, and function at a very high level of professionalism. The Religion Communicators Council (formerly, three Religious Public Relations Council) is the oldest association of public relations practitioners in North America, older even than the Public Relations Society of America.[11]

Beginnings in the United States of America

Tracing its American beginnings, Cutlip, Center and Broom averred that the tools and techniques of public relations have long been an important part of political weaponry. Sustained campaigns to move and manipulate public opinion they asserted go back to the Revolutionary War and the work of Samuel Adams and his cohorts. These revolutionaries understood the importance of public support, and knew intuitively how to arouse and channel it. They used pen, platform, pulpit, staged events, symbols, the leak and political organization – in an imaginative, unrelenting way[12].

The beginnings equally of Public relations Education could be traced to the United States with Scott M. Cutlip, a central figure to it. Occupying a prominent place in the U.S. Army Public Affairs Hall of Fame, Major Scott M. Cutlip is regarded as the father of Public relations education in the United States of America. He began his military career as a private soldier in May 1942. At the end of 1945, Cutlip left military service as a Major having made a significant contribution to Army Public Affairs programme in its early stages of development. Following the end of World WarII, General Dwight D. Eisenhower, Chief of Staff, and other senior officers were concerned about the status of U.S. Army Public Affairs especially about explaining military programmes to the public and the lack of military expertise in Public Affairs. One of the steps taken to improve military public affairs was the establishment of what became the Defence Information School. The second step was the assignment of senior public officers to graduate school to prepare them for assignment into public affairs. Cutlip made several outstanding contributions to public relations as well as public relations education. He was co-author of the book, "Effective Public Relations" which has been published in seven editions and is one of the best-selling books in the field. He was awarded the Department of the Army's Commander's award for public service in 1984 for "more than 25 years of outstanding service to the Department of the Army and its public affairs programme"[13]. The use of sustained campaigns to move and manipulate public opinion as earlier stated, go back to the Revolutionary War and the work of Samuel Adams and others. This was equally effectively put to use by America's first President, George Washington who, following American Independence, toured the colonies from north to south soliciting public views. Such a tradition still exists today in America as its chief executives have continued to carry on the tradition of collecting feedbacks and representing the government in the form of town hall meetings and press conferences.

The European Influence

Although the history of the early beginnings as well as the growth of public relations are traced to the United States, Europe equally played very significant role in its growth and development as professional public relations mushroomed after World War II when diplomacy and mass communications became central to the stability and reconstruction of scores of countries. In the post-war era, the great powers in the ideologically charged atmosphere resorted to propaganda to relay their views across through a host of intermediaries especially the media, domestically and globally, to further their aims. The struggle between the two ideological arrowheads, the United States and Russia respectively, dominated the headlines for nearly 50 years. Even with ideological differences that were particularly manifest in the period of the cold war, public relations flourished with formation of national professional associations in Western Europe. European nations in various ways impacted on the development of Public relations. Nations such as Germany, France, Belgium, and Holland among others all made their contributions to its development. Elements of public relations practice can also be identified in socialist communist nations of former Union of Soviet Socialist Republic nations, including its Eastern Bloc nations as well as China. In these countries according to Nwolise, soldiers are not separated from the people as in the western or bourgeois societies. However, the communist parties in these socialist societies still carried out certain actions and programmes geared towards making the people love, respect and support their forces. However, in the modern era of liberal open market economy and democratic practice to which all these nations are embracing, the need for public relations in all sectors of their societies including the military are becoming very visible.

British Influence and Impact

The British influence on public relations in Western Europe is widely acclaimed especially its development and practice. Bates asserts that if any country could be said to rival the United States as a centre of professional public relations power and influence, it is England and by extension all the countries of the United Kingdom. The most important early influence came in the 1930s from local governmental authorities (not be confused with the separately elected governments in Scotland, Wales and Northern Ireland)[14]. These authorities were charged with providing a wide range of civic services such as fire, police and state education. Following social reforms in the 19th century, they were forced to give serious consideration to public communications. Then, in the early part of the 20th century, as their involvement in these initiatives grew, local government administrators, specialists in communication among them, began to "professionalize."

It was local government officials who were most responsible for founding the Institute of Public Relations (IPR) in the UK in 1948, the first organization of professional practitioners. Bates further recounts that as the communication role of the UK central government grew, particularly during the first and second world wars (1914-1918 and 1939-1945) when propaganda was in high gear, a small number of professionally oriented public relations practitioners began to emerge. The most notable of these was Maurice Buckmaster, head of Special Operations Executive (France), who was responsible for dropping agents into that country. He stated further that before the war, Maurice worked for the Ford Motor Company in Europe in a non-public relations capacity, then again after the war, later becoming a consultant for the French champagne industry. He was president of the Institute of Public Relations in 1955-1956.

Central government peacetime propaganda was also important to the development of public relations in the United Kingdom. Of note was the establishment of the Empire Marketing Board, which was designed to implement imperial preference through market research, supply chain management and publicity. Its secretary, Sir Stephen Tallents, had an enthusiasm for national propaganda that was best encapsulated in his pamphlet, "The Projection of England," published in 1932. Among others, he offered patronage to the leader of the British Documentary Film Movement, John Grierson, whose interests encompassed democratic education and public relations, and about which he wrote extensively between the wars. Grierson's ideas influenced a number of leading practitioners in the post-war era.[15]

The formation of the British Council as asserted was greatly motivated by the ideas of Tallent. Its formation for all intents and purposes, is till date the UK's largest public relations agency worldwide. Lesser influences during this period were publicity agents from theatre, film and sports, from the burgeoning design industry, and from the corporate sector. The post-World War II era left new challenges for the UK, most notably its relationships with other countries, and during the process of de-colonization, which stimulated the growth of public relations. In terms of domestic politics, the major policy shift was nationalization; whereby government took ownership of core industries from the private sector. The threat of nationalization led to the formation of organizations that could lobby on behalf of private enterprises. Subsequent UK governments as pointed out have engaged in both nationalization and privatization, necessitating substantial communication.

In the 1960s, following the delayed post-war economic recovery, public relations consultancies became a sector of great importance to the evolution and practice of public relations. Other key figures in the history of UK public relations prior to World War II included several individuals of note. Brebner had a distinguished career in the 1920s and 1930s at the Post Office and at the Ministry of Information where he was successively Director of the News Division, Special Overseas Operative and, at Supreme Allied Headquarters, Director of Press Communications. In 1949, he wrote the first British book that had "public relations" in its title, *Public Relations and Publicity*. This remained the only book on public relations until the IPR published its own edited volume some 10 years later. Basil Clarke, a former Daily Mail journalist, worked for central government at the Ministry of Reconstruction, the Ministry of Health and, finally, as Director of Public Information in Dublin[16].

Development in Africa and Nigeria

South Africa pioneered the development of public relations in the African continent as it was the first to evolve a body of knowledge for public relations[17]. The country set the pace as the first to establish a Public Relations Institute in the world - the Public Relations Institute of South Africa, (PRISA). Consequently it obtained certification for quality management from the International Standards Organisation. PRISA is the third largest Public Relations Institute in the world behind the Public Relations Society of America (PRSA) and the International Institute of Public Relations IPR in Britain. The first public relations officer in the country was appointed by the South African Railways in 1943, and the first public relations consultancy was established in Johannesburg in 1948[18].The South African PR and communication management industry has a turnover in excess of 4 billion Rand and employs an estimated figure of 10,000 people[19]. South Africa equally has been able to develop a virile Army Public Relations Department that is steadily projecting the good image of both the Army and the government[20]. Kenya in East Africa and Egypt in North Africa are countries where public relations have developed with flourishing practices.

In the West African sub region, Nigeria and Ghana pioneered the development and practice of public relations facilitated especially with their colonial linkages to Britain, as well as the growth of civilization, political development from the late 40s to the early 50s and the gradual processes of industrialization. Public relations in Nigeria, by historical development, dates back to 1948 when the colonial office established a public relations office in Lagos with similar offices in Ibadan, Kaduna and Enugu. A retired British Military officer was appointed with the brief to pacify Nigerian public opinion and make it receptive to imperialist propaganda thus making Nigeria safe for His Majesty's rule. These were the days of extreme nationalism, whipped up by the oratorical skills and activities of the Ziks, Enahoros, the Mokwugo Okoyes, the Aminu Kanos, and the Raji Abdallahs[21]. Subsequently, barons of industry and commerce responded to the initiatives of the Colonial government with the United African

Company, UAC leading the way with the appointment of Major Parker, a retired British Military Officer, as its PR Manager.

The success of Major Parker encouraged other British Multinationals notably Shell BP, to appoint their own Public relations executives with the appointment of Nigerian nationals. By 1960, Adekunle Ojora replaced Major Parker while Kanu Ofonry was in charge of public relations affairs at Shell BP. Theophilus Adetola Awobokun was another notable Public relations practitioner who had a stint with Shell BP. In the public sector were people like Bob Ogbuagu often referred to as the repository of the practice in Nigeria. There were also Olu Holloway of the Nigerian Railway Corporation, Chief Alex Akinyele of Nigerian Customs and Excise, Major Ibikunle Armstrong (rtd) with the Leventis Conglomerate, Segun Smith at the Nigerian Breweries and Alex Nwokedi at the defunct Electric Corporation of Nigeria. Other powerful practitioners of note were Scott-Emuakpor and late Sam Epelle who at one time or the other were responsible for the Federations Public Image[22]. Sam Epelle who is credited with having done a lot for the Federation was a one-time director in the federal Ministry of Information. Efforts at professionalization of Public relations in Nigeria started with formation of the Public Relations Association of Nigeria in 1963 with branches in Lagos, Benin, Ibadan, Kaduna and Enugu. In spite of initial teething problems usually encountered by every new organization, Bob Ogbuagu championed the establishment of a Public relations Institute in the tradition of the British Institute of Public Relations. The outcome was the formation of the Nigerian Institute of Public relations, NIPR in 1967.

References

1. IPR's definition in Black, Sam. (1989) **Introduction to Public Relations**, The Modino Press, P.3
2. *Public Relations News* quoted in Cutlip, S.M. et al (1985) **Effective Public Relations** New Jersey, Prentice Hall Inc. p.3
3. Ibid p.4
4. H. Childs, (1982) **An Introduction to Public Opinion**, New York: John Wiley and Sons Inc.,
5. Nigerian Institute of Public Relations, Lagos: Professional Development Programme, 2008 P.1
6. Ron Smith, PR History @ http:// faculty.buffalostate.edu/smith/PR/history.htm
7. Ibid
8. Ibid
9. Ibid
10. Ibid
11. Ibid
12. Cutlip, S.M. et al (1985) Op cit
13. US Army Hall of Fame @ http://www.army.mil/institution/armypublicaffairs/hof/
14. Don Bates, *"Mini-Me History"* @ www.instituteforpr.org
15. Ibid
16. Ibid
17. (Skinner *et al.*cited @ http://wiki.answers.com/Q/ What_is_the_history_and_evolution_of_public_relations#ixzz1aOE0KgjI
18. Ibid(Skinner*et al.*, 2001:22).
19. Brown, B. cited in Tokoya, OO Public Relations Practice in the Nigerian Army: Challenges and Prospects. (Research Project submitted to the National Defence College, Abuja, August 2009) P. 4
20. Falconi, cited in Tokoya, OO (Ibid)
21. Ogbomoh, V.L. "Acceptability of Public Relations Practice" in Report of Training Seminar organized by Nigerian Army Public Relations Department held at Command Officers Mess 1 Marina-Lagos, 29-30 December1987, P. 27.
22. Ibid

CHAPTER THREE

MODERN PUBLIC RELATIONS AND ITS DEVELOPMENT IN THE MILITARY

The history of modern public relations are divided into four phases namely, publicity which Grunig and Hunt equate to the Press Agentry model; others are information or public information model, advocacy or asymmetrical model, and the relationship or symmetrical model[1]. The publicity era dates to the 1800s and were devoted to dissemination and attention-getting, one-way communication with little emphasis on research. The Information era came about the early 1900s and was focused on honest and accurate dissemination of information, one way communication and elements of research devoted to readability and comprehension. It was mainly applied by governments as well as non-profit and business organizations.

The advocacy era dates to the mid-1990s and was focused on modifying attitudes and influencing behaviour. It also employed two-way communication and applied attitude and opinion research. It is employed mainly by competitive business organizations, including Causes and Movement Organizations. The relationship era spawns from the latter part of the 20th Century and the beginning of the 21st Century and is complementary to the earlier three approaches of publicity, public information and advocacy. It focuses essentially on mutual understanding and conflict resolution, two-way communications and employs research, based on perception and values. It is employed mainly by regulated business organizations, government, non-profit organizations and social movements. Practical applications of the relationship model in the civil world as demonstrated often are the use of détente and rapprochement modalities to settle conflicts. Public relations mechanisms have in today's world become very useful to conflict resolution across the world.

Bates deduction arising from the aforementioned approaches is that public relations is becoming more research based and moreover a function of the nature, management and leadership of an organization, rather than simply the resort to implementation of communication tactics. Meanwhile, new technologies such as the internet that allows organizations to communicate directly with their publics, combined with the fragmentation of the so-called mass media, are creating new opportunities for public Relations practitioners[2]. The tendency nowadays by many public relations firms and practitioners to use social media platform exemplify this. Indeed as a practitioner put it, the advent of social media represents a new era for PR and the way in which it should be practiced.

Development and Growth in the Military

The military across the world are recognized critical national defence institutions. Performance and indeed the effectiveness of a military is judged by its ability to deter incursion or attack on its national territory or if the nation is attacked, the ability to successfully prosecute a war and redeem the territorial integrity of such a nation. with such a critical role, it has been argued that public relations for the military needs to be conducted in a manner that is considerate of the obligations of a military force to its mother nation. This important need among others has been a guiding principle in the gradual evolvement and development of the discipline in the military. The military in many nations of the world today have functional public relations and information departments operating at single service or at unified command levels. The United States is however, one country that is pre-eminently recognized to have pioneered and championed the development of public relations in its Armed Forces. While remotely the development could be linked to the American Revolution, Stephen Johnson however, links the evolution of Military Public Relations in the Americas to culture and necessity. He avers that public relations as an institutional communication process is part of a tradition that has long supported an open market place of ideas and a high level of confidence between citizens who relate to each other based on a commonly accepted social contract[3].

However, as the art of public communication developed in American politics, it temporary lost its currency in the American military. It was to that extent that by the end of the civil war, official news from the battle field came from sporadic proclamations in Congress or by interviews infrequently granted to the Press. As a consequence, the public in both the north and south grew suspicious of the sacrifice it was asked to make. Correspondents roamed the fronts freely at will and provided stories of carnage and incompetence. Letters written by soldiers to families back home often wound up in local newspapers substituting for news accounts. American military public affairs as Stephen asserted, remained in such infancy until World War I when President Woodrow Wilson established the civilian Committee on civilian information to travel across the country to boost public support for the war effort by giving speeches in churches, schools and service clubs.

At the end of the conflict, a public information unit was organized in the Army's Military Intelligence Division. In 1929, it was renamed the Public Relations Branch and in 1940, was taken out of intelligence altogether and transferred to the office of the Deputy Chief of Staff and then to the War Secretary's office. At the beginning of World War II, its handful of personnel grew to more than 3,000 persons cranking out stories from the fronts, facilitating newsreel and radio coverage, and urging public support for the troops. The Navy and Army Air Corps also expanded their public relations staffs, providing information, censoring some news and helping war correspondents get their stories. When the war was over, military public relations had become part of the United States Armed Forces Mission in War and Peace[4].

Growth and Philosophy of US Military Public Affairs

"Public Affairs" is the military designation for public relations at the Department of Defence level. Under direction of an Assistant Secretary of Defence, trained information officers of the Army, Navy, Marine Corps and Air Force are assigned to the Office of Public Affairs at the Pentagon in Washington. Along with civil service public relations specialists, they are responsible for producing and releasing all military news at the seat of government. The office is a central point for handling public information and related activities concerning the department of defence, including the three military departments. Its basic function is to assure prompt and accurate responses to enquiries concerning the department of defence, DOD, to provide public understanding of DOD's aims, activities and needs; and to provide liaison and cooperation with information media representatives. With this as the main outlet to the public for national defence news, the operations function is as important as the advisory one. Facts must be released as soon as possible within the large general outline of national security. This top level direction and operations are handled by Public Affairs four offices – News Services, Public Services, Security Review, and Plans and Programmes. A fifth, Declassification Policy, also functions within the Office of Public Affairs but is not directly involved in the military public relations activity[5].

Public affairs are indeed a vital mission in the United States Armed Forces. It is supported by the notion that government must render accounts for the resources given to it by the people. Moreover, the military – which defends the nation from external enemies and occasionally puts American sons and daughters in the harm's way - is obliged to keep family members informed of the safety of the nation and their relatives in uniform. Undoubtedly, no other government department has such a responsibility other than the Presidency. And no other agency has such a well-oiled and efficient public communications machine as the Department of Defence and its three military branches[6].

There are two reasons to this, the first being that public affairs strengthens the armed forces ability to carry out its mission in war and peace by providing timely, accurate, information about the military to soldiers, their families, citizens and to the general public. At the core of public affairs mission is the concept that both soldiers and citizens should understand the role of the institution. Informed soldiers are more likely to survive and win if they know why they fight and how well they are doing it. Battles are won, disasters are averted, and rescues accomplished when there is favourable public opinion. When people don't understand what their soldiers do for them, there is scepticism and distrust. Rumour fills the vacuum when there are no facts[7]. The second reason is that public affairs help to prevent war. Deterring outside aggression is only possible when potential adversaries know that US Armed Forces are trained, equipped and prepared to defend their country, interests and friends[8] Stephen further asserts that the manner in which this is done has evolved along with technology, but that there is an overall guiding principle that the US military does not own a printing press to force feed the American public with propaganda. Internal television and radio networks exist, websites act as electronic bulletin boards, and base newspapers may carry news of the military community. But the primary channel for disseminating news to the public is the independent media as the independent media makes such news trustworthy. It is within such frame of reference, that military doctrine based on lessons learned defines public affairs philosophy and practice. It guides commanders and Public Affairs Officers (PAOs) on how they should treat information they collect and pass on to both the public and soldiers. Opposing forces or adversaries might lie or disinform, but the American military must speak only the truth. Information, whether complementary or embarrassing, is freely passed through internal channels and given to the news media for public dissemination within the constraints of military security and public law. Generally, four doctrinal concepts guide US military public affairs practice: These are – the public's right to know, Maximum disclosure with minimum delay; Information must come from a trusted source and Internal news come from the Commander first[9].

Public Relations in the United Kingdom Armed Forces

The principles of public relations and aspects of its practice have always been part of military public relations in the Armed Forces of the United Kingdom. Badsey contends that the importance of the media in warfare long predates the creation of the British Army, while the Army and its soldiers have always engaged with the media to seek publicity for themselves. He avers that for centuries, war reporting was largely the province of senior officers or their paid chroniclers. By such tradition which lasted well into the Second World War, important generals would take favoured journalists into their headquarters, to become their historians after the war.

Ever since then, there have been cases of successful officers and reporters establishing mutually beneficial working relationships, usually from very early in their respective careers. He stated further that for security considerations especially from the period of the First World War, reporters were excluded from the war zone under a censorship regime that was reflective of military posture on operational security at the time. The practice was on until the army approved the incorporation of uniformed war correspondents in 1915, based on assumption that the national media, without losing its independence, had become part of the war effort[10]. Badsey noted further that this system of military-media relations, whereby the national media was visibly incorporated into the war effort and reporters becoming part of the military, was successfully revived in the Second World War. Over time as a reflection of the increasing importance of the media, in 1937 the War Office instituted the post of Director of Public Relations (Army) or DPR (A). From this period, the application of public relations techniques has always been there with the UK armed forces in principle and by some measure, in practice. The UK forces for example, did not lose sight of its relevance during its involvement in the Suez crisis in 1956 and equally during the Falklands crisis in 1982. Badsey further attests to the fact that experiences derived from these conflicts helped to put the British ahead of their contemporaries in dealing with the media in the television age. Formal training in giving media interviews while on operations was introduced at the Royal Military Academy in the early 1970s, chiefly as a response to 'The Troubles' in Northern Ireland (1969-2007) As Badsey further put it, the Falklands war also revealed the need for trained soldiers rather than civilians as media escorts on operations, leading to the creation in the mid-1980s of the Territorial Army Pool of Information Officers (TAPIOs), later renamed the Media Operations Group (Volunteer) or MOG (v), and its equivalents for the other services[11].

Public relations awareness and its importance in the UK Armed Forces particularly heightened prior to the Gulf War in 1991 as emphasis was placed on spreading the theme of PR awareness throughout the Ministry of Defence and the command structure. Modifications were made to the reporting chain within the DPRS with the Chief of Public Relations reporting jointly to the chief of the Defence Staff and the Permanent Under Secretary of State. The DPRS was reinforced by the appointment of an Assistant Chief of Public Relations (Military), who was given specific responsibility as a serving officer at Captain RN/Colonel/Group Captain level for the co-ordination of contingency planning work[12]. That essentially is a tri-service appointment and its prime interface is with the MoD central commitments staff. His task is to ensure that MoD planning takes account of PR in operational circumstances, and in the context of a time of tension and war, to ensure that UK PR planning is harmonized with NATO PR planning. While the DPRS is staffed for peace time functions, attention is equally given to staffing implications of periods of tension and war[13].

The importance attached to PR from the period of the Gulf War lies in this underlining statement issued by the UK MoD in 1991 to the effect that 'public relations continues to be a vital aspect of our contribution to the multinational effort aimed at deterring further Iraqi aggression and ensuring that sanctions work... We must keep support of the media and the public. The maintenance of constructive relationships with the media now is crucial to our PR effort in the event of hostilities. Good PR also contributes significantly to the moral of our deployed force and their families[14].

Inter Services Public Relations (ISPR) Pakistan Armed Forces

Pakistan, India, Bangladesh and Indonesia are some of the Asian nations with flourishing Public relations and information outfits in their Armed Forces. The Pakistani Armed Forces operates a unified public relations system for its Defence Forces as the public relations requirements of the Armed Forces are looked after by the ISPR Directorate. The Directorate was established in 1949 with Army's Colonel Shabaz Khan as its first Director-General. The ISPR Directorate is staffed with combined military of Pakistan Defence Forces alongside a large number of civilian officers. It functions as a part of the Joint Chiefs of Staff Secretariat and its purpose is to garner national support for the Armed Forces and strengthen their resolve to accomplish the assigned mission while undermining the will of the adversary. It also acts as an interface between the Armed Forces, the media and the public. It formulates much of the media policy of Pakistan's military, safeguards the Armed Forces from negative influences and monitors both international and domestic media. The ISPR also issues notices regarding military exercises and notifies relevant parties and the public media about Pakistan's indigenous ballistic missile testing program.

In Pakistan's military staff appointments and assignments, the ISPR is one of the most prestigious Directorate of Pakistan Armed Forces. Its Executive Officer is the Chief Military Spokesperson of the Pakistan Armed Forces. The director-general directly reports to Chairman Joint Chiefs of Staff Secretariat, Chief of Pakistani Army. He is also responsible to the Chief of Air Force, Commandant of the Marines, the Chief of Naval Staff and of the Coast Guard. The Army has dominated its Command over time but the Navy has had the privilege once of commanding the Directorate which currently is headed by an Army Two-Star General[15].

African Armed Forces and Public relations

Research findings reveal the existence of public relations and information departments in many African national Armed Forces. However, their institutional development, structure and growth are very minimal except for a few countries like Nigeria, Ghana and South Africa. These nations especially have somewhat elaborate public relations outfits following from similar traditions of its growth in the civil sector in these countries. The Ghana Armed Forces (GAF) has a full-fledged Directorate of Public Relations while South Africa similarly has a well-developed Public Relations Branch. As pointed out earlier in this text, South Africa has been able to develop a virile Army Public Relations Department that is steadily projecting the good image of both the Army and the government. The importance attached to the relevance of public relations in African Armed Forces has continued to increase especially with pervasiveness of Peace Support Operations activities across the globe and in especially troubled spots in Africa.

Beginnings and its Development in Nigerian Military

The entry of Public relations practice into the Nigerian military started with the Nigerian Army. Ogbomoh asserts that public Relations practice started in the Nigerian Army through a combination of fortuitous circumstances. One was the realization that dawned on the British towards the end of the fifties, a realization fuelled by the new age of global information explosion that even colonists have a right to know about their defence outfit. Another was the Congo experience. It was necessary to build a bridge between the peacekeeping Nigerian troops in that strife-torn territory and their relatives at home. Major R.C. Irving, a retired British Officer, had the distinction of being the first Nigerian Army public relations man. His brief was specifically the production of the Nigerian Army Magazine as he was never attached to any formation but occupied a seat at the Geneva section of the Ministry of Information[16]. To Reuben Fashina, a long-time Director of Army Public Relations, the introduction of public relations practice in the Army evolved from many reasons both remote and immediate. One of the reasons according to him was to meet the ever increasing and long standing demands of a new age which could be described as an age of information explosion and thirst for knowledge. This according to him refers to a situation whereby the ordinary man wants to be informed about almost all fields of human activities vis-a-vis their significance and relevance in society locally, nationally and internationally. Another reason, he traced to the relationship of the Nigerian Army with some foreign armies which have elaborate public relations departments. Examples include the United States Army and the British Army[17].

In his reflections on Army public Relations Department, Major Giwa, the first indigenous Director of Army Public Relations said he was drafted from his post as a Publicity Officer in the Federal Ministry of Information in 1961 in the rank of Captain to boost the part of the Nigerian Contingent in the peace keeping operation in the strife-torn Congo. The period of his entry into the Army he said, witnessed the beginning of the exodus of the British officers from the Nigerian Army and the taking over of the various units and services by the Nigerian Officers. Regarded as an intruder by both the British and indigenous officers, he asserted that it took the greater part of his early days in the Army to explain his mission to the Nigerian troops both at home and abroad. Working under Brigadier Ogundipe in Kasai Province of the Congo, his job as public relations officer revolved around filing stories about the peace-keeping activities of the Nigerian troops that were scattered all over Congo[18].

On his eventual return home, the Nigerian Army authorities, impressed with his performances made a request to the Federal Ministry of Information for his secondment into the Army and attached to the Education Corps under the command then of General Olutoye. There, he started the revival of the Nigerian Army Magazine and was later posted to the Administrative Branch, ('A' branch) as one–man unit under Command of the first Nigerian Adjutant General, General Yakubu Gowon. Major Giwa worked tirelessly to publicize the Nigerian Army as well as educate the Nigerian media and public what the Army stood for in the development efforts of Nigeria's First Republic. With cessation of hostilities at the end of the Nigerian civil war, the army authorities felt the need for expansion of its publicity and public relations activities to meet the challenges of the transition period to civilian rule after the end of the second military regime. Proposals were made and the first group of Military Public Relations Officers were commissioned[19]. He retired from the Army in 1972, succeeded by Brigadier E F Sotomi as the Director of the newly established Military Public Relations Department, MPRD which was however, short-lived. Brigadier Sotomi as Director indeed had robust plans for the development of public relations in the Nigerian military. As Commodore Oladimeji testified, it was uunder the leadership of Brigadier General Sotomi, that a grand plan was laid to establish a very powerful Military Public Relations Corps [like the then Armed Forces Medical Corps]. However, the idea of a separate corps did not go down well in high military quarters then. When Brigadier General Sotomi retired in 1977, the idea of a Military Public Relations Corps was shelved. It was renamed Army Public Relations Department under the Adjutant-General office[20].

References

1. Grunig and Hunt (1984) cited in Olutayo Otubanjo, "150 Years 0f Modern Public Relations Practices in Nigeria" at http://ssm.com/abstract=13727042
2. Ibid
3. Stephen Johnson, "Military Public Relations in the Americas: Learning to Promote the Flow www.au.af.mil/au/awc/awcgate/ndu/military_media_in_americas.doc
4. ibid
5. Arthur Dreyer, "Functions and Responsibilities in the Departments of Defense, Army, Navy, Marine corps and Air Force Information Services in Military Public Affairs" in Stephenson, H. (1960) **Handbook of Public Relations** New York, McGraw-Hill p.775
6. Stephen Johnson, "Military Public Relations in the Americas…, Op cit
7. Ibid
8. Ibid
9. Ibid
10. Stephen Badsey, "In the Public's Eye: The British Army and Military-Media relations @ http://RUSI.org
11. Ibid
12. ibid
13. ibid
14. H.H. Pyper, The media in Modern Warfare – Friend or Foe?, in the Sunday Times (of London) 24 February 1991
15. http://en.wikipedia.org/wiki/Inter-Services_Public_Relations
16. V.L. Ogbomoh, "Acceptability of Public Relations Practice", op cit
17. Fashina, R. "Reflections on Army Public Relations Department Since its Inception" in Report of Training Seminar organized by Nigerian Army Public Relations Department held at Command Officers Mess 1 Marina-Lagos, 29-30 December1987, P. 2
18. Giwa, A. "Reflections on Army Public Relations Department Since its Inception" in Report of Training Seminar organized by Nigerian Army Public Relations Department held at Command Officers Mess 1 Marina-Lagos, 29-30 December1987, P. 49
19. Ibid
20. Oladimeji, O.A. Naval Public Relations Notes

Part Two

Public Relations Principles, Approaches and Practice

CHAPTER FOUR

THE ROLE AND FUNCTION OF PUBLIC RELATIONS IN THE INTERFACE OF MILITARY AND SOCIETY

Introduction

A reflection back to the definitions of public relations examined in chapter 2 and their dissection further highlighted the essential functions of public relations in an organisation. Such broad functions of public relations are indeed vital and relevant to the public relations operations of many complex organisations and institutions in society especially in relation to enhancing their success. As Roger Haywood, an author and PR practitioner pointed out, an organisation that succeeds without public relations is as likely as, say, a salesman, a politician, a lawyer or any other professional persuader succeeding without a personality. The importance of personality or good image is such that according to him, "...there are a few organisations that have such a revolutionary product or unassailable monopoly or privileged role in society that they can afford not to bother about making friends and influencing people"[1].

The military is one such unique public institution that is recognized as performing a legitimate and privileged role in society. Thus the armed forces of many nations have for long recognized the immense image making potential of public relations through a myriad of approaches, strategies and tactics. The necessity therefore, further arises for the development of organisational mechanisms and channels in the military through which to constantly `keep military institutions in the public eye'. Such a dimension in relation to the British Army was pointed out by Henry Stanhope in stating the essence of the British Army's deliberate effort to strengthen its links with its civilian society. As he put it, "it has to do so, or civilians would know nothing of the Army outside those glossy recruiting advertisements which few people seriously believe. If it did not bother to cultivate these contacts, it would be forgotten until the next war broke out"[2]. Pockock corroborates this position through his assertion also in relation to the British Armed Services that: "nowadays the services take public relations very seriously. It is subject for study and debate at the Staff Colleges; its skills are taught to young officers as integral part of their professional training; above all, it is recognized as being of extreme importance"[3]. Similarly Brigadier Sotomi, the first Director of Military Public Relations in Nigeria amplified such relevance in relation to the establishment of the Directorate of Military

Public Relations in the Nigerian Army. According to him the establishment of the Directorate is recognition of the need to bring the Army closer to the public so as to enable civilians have clearer understanding of what the Army is doing for the nation. Besides, it also underscores the Army awareness of the influence of public opinion on human endeavour and behaviour. He opined further that it is part of military public relations functions to evaluate this public opinion and identify the policies and procedures of the army with public interest[4].

Military and Civil Public Relations: The Difference

Although broad public relations functions are applicable to most organisations, aspects of some of the functions may differ slightly in their application to an institution. The military, for example, has some basic differences from civilian ones and correspondingly, differences exist between military public relations and public relations for civil or commercial organisations. Whereas commercial, corporate and institutional public relations are based on the free enterprise concepts of marketing a product or service for a private organisation, military public relations programmes are not. Among other reasons, they are meant to provide information and maintain awareness and concern for public opinion regarding an organisation that is owned and operated in the overall security interests of a nation.

In the same vein, while a civil public relations officer is answerable to the management of his or her company, consumers of the company products and to some extent the shareholders, a military public relations officer is immediately responsible through his immediate command to his service, to the Defence Ministry and ultimately, to government, on behalf of the people. When a unit commander's actions or those of his public relations functionaries produce negative results, its unfavourable effects have national and international implications that could cause serious damage to national defence postures and objectives. This, perhaps, explains the precautionary measures of being less open with information and comment by senior military officers especially at high level military commands when dealing with military matters. They have an interest not to be misquoted or misrepresented by the media on issues with political or security implications[5].

Role and Functions

It is relevant to examine the basic roles and functions of the military in the interface of the military and society from its legitimate constitutional position in society. Such a position logically provides the basis for the existence of the military and defines its functions. Legitimately, the military in countries with democratic traditions are, by civil military relations concepts of "civil control" of the military, subject to constitutional "checks and balances" and are both responsible and accountable to the society through government and parliament. This calls for accountability of the military to society on the legal performance of its roles. The military, through public relations, can provide society with elaborate information on their roles especially as these relate to the part played by the various services in the scheme of national defence and security. To carry out such roles, the Pentagon in the United States has elaborate public relations and information machineries for the services and marines. It regularly provides updates and briefing to the American public. One such briefing provided by the United States Air Force was conveyed under the title, "informing the general public on national security" in which "what began as a routine comment at an Air War College on National Security forum at Air University mushroomed into a National Air Force briefing team constantly in demand and travelling from coast to coast informing the public about the threat and discussing today's complex defence issues in depth... one perception appears overriding: the team noted what is termed an intense thirst by the US public for information on defence related matters - the budget, nuclear war, the Soviet threat and modernisation."[6]. Other US armed services equally carry out such functions intermittently.

Another aspect to the role and function of military public relations has to do with the notion in civil military relations by which the military, though established constitutionally and entrusted with national defence duties is frequently looked upon in many societies as a threat to popular national governments and to individual liberty. Such feelings have always heightened anxieties as a result of the supplanting of democratic rules through military coups, especially though not exclusively in the developing nations. Although such fears are a little less in the developed countries of the Western World, the situation as experienced in Portugal in the past and in France in the 1950s, where there had been a prospect of a military intervention, did give some credence to the genuineness of such fears.

In spite of such position, arguments as to the fears of a "man on horseback" threat is ruled out in a country like the United States as a result of the firm entrenchment of military professionalism and the political tradition of "civil control" of the military in that country. But John P. Lovell's reappraisal of traditional and modern concepts of civil military relations suggests the relevance of the prospect of such a threat in almost all political systems. As he put it, "clearly, the "man on horseback" is an accurate representation of the problem that many political systems in the world do face. In many of the states of Latin America, the Middle East, Africa and Asia, the military coup d'état is a common if not chronic problem. Thus, concern for civil control in the traditional sense of protection of governmental institutions and individual liberty from domination by the armed forces is a fundamental reality. Even in political systems not plagued by the threat or reality of military coup d'état, such as the Canadian, problems in the relationship of the military establishment of society are in many instances distinctively different from those found in the US"[7].

In the above context, the role and function of military public relations would be to alleviate such fears and to reassure the general public that the military does not constitute a threat to national governments and further reassure on their continued subjection to civilian control. Although this aspect may be more relevant in countries with institutionalized democracy, such public relations roles and functions are particularly relevant in countries that are frequently prone to coups. Military seizure of power in such countries is usually accompanied with pledges to return power to civilians soon enough, but in most cases these promises are not fulfilled. The role of military public relations in this regard would be to design programmes through which to re-establish the military's credibility in such situations by among others, informing the public of what are being done by the military to restore the democratic process. The Nigerian military since return to democracy in 1999 has been engaged in such a project with the community relations approach to civil military relations through strengthening of the bonds that binds civil military relationship. The programme which aims at engendering and sustaining a harmonious relationship with civilians was started by former Chief of Defence Staff, Air Vice Marshal Paul Dike. The former CDS speaking at the public presentation of a book "Winning Hearts and Minds: A Community Relation's Approach for the Nigerian Military", edited by scholars and retired military officers, noted that "with the Nigerian Military, which has the added challenges of professionalism as well as the need to gain citizens' confidence and support in the aftermath of prolonged military rule, the importance of the community-relations approach could not be over-emphasised"[8]. This was against the background of the scepticism of many Nigerians of the possibility of military incursion into Nigerian politics in spite of the transition to democracy in May 1999.

The book was published by the authors after interactive workshops at military locations aimed at underscoring core conceptual elements of the community relations approach[9]. As an analyst noted in this regard, the approach underscores the fundamentality of human rights, rule of law, transparency, accountability and effective communications and the importance of negotiation and conflict management skills for community relations in particular and civil-military relations in general[10]. The CDS at that forum further harped on the need to gain the confidence of the Nigerian populace and change their rigid mind-sets and perceptions, which have made it difficult for many in the civil populace to appreciate the noble roles of the military, especially, "its steady transformation into a pro-people, citizen-friendly and responsive institution". The book content among others highlights issues of human rights, effective communication, negotiation and conflict management skills, rule of law, transparency and accountability and how they underpin positive and effective community relations for the armed forces in Nigeria[11]. Approaches deriving from the collective philosophy of the book needs to be heightened as well as sustained in the Nigerian military. As Olukolade noted appropriately, Dike's position introduced the dimension of emphasis on the civil military relations and community relations. The latter is integral to the former and beneficial to both military and civilians alike. It is however, curious that subsequent effort in connection with Dike 2010 did not indicate any significant public relations input despite the vast structures for the practice in all the services[12].

Another aspect to the role and function of public relations derives from the sense of conflicting public perception of the military which is seen differently in various lights by members of the society. In times of war and crisis or other national emergency, when its prime role comes under public focus, the military is looked upon to come to the rescue of the society. It is hailed if it emerges victorious. During periods of prolonged peace, however, its role is rather seen as of marginal significance with the profession often looked upon as a burden on society. Such situations make for especially the youths of the country to become antagonistic to the military especially where national service (conscription) is in force. In the developing countries especially, youths treat the military with much discourtesy, insult and derision. This attitude often results in frequent clashes between sections of the military and the civil populace, and is accompanied with adverse anti-military media comments often championed by the media. Civil military relationships under situations of this nature can be improved through "deliberate, planned and sustained" public relations efforts aimed at establishing mutual understanding between the armed forces and the public. In the above context, the role of public relations would be to highlight the essential function of the military not only in war and crisis but also in peace time, emphasising that the security provided by the military is a prerequisite for the continued existence and stability of the society as a whole. Peace time roles of the military are quite as essential as war time roles especially in safeguarding national economic interests.

Within the overall framework of the national security system also lie the role and function of public relations towards promoting military interests as they relate to the performance of their specified legitimate functions. This aspect as elucidated by Martin Edmonds emphasizes that "the armed services, as part of the national security system, have an active interest in promoting their interests and projecting their professional assessment of world affairs, the threats they and the state face, and the most appropriate ways of securing the integrity of the country and protecting its interests... the national security system has a second output... one that endeavours to maintain good relations with the population at large and create an acceptable image of the national security system as a set of public institutions. This endeavour to project and persuade is a little more than a public relations exercise, but should not be underestimated or belittled for that. The success that it achieves not only brings the armed services dividends in terms of moral support, but also makes the resources requested by them easier to acquire"[13].

The role of public relations also comes into armed services' operations in internal security duties, especially in the advanced capitalist societies where sometimes, against existing norms of individual and group liberties, the governments of these societies have had cause to call in the armed forces to combat terrorism, "to break strikes" and use "the special branch to monitor militancy" and other radical actions. Call of the military to internal security duties are nowadays very common sights in many nations of the world especially developing nations of Africa, Asia and the Middle East. Countries such as Pakistan, Nigeria, Egypt and Kenya are notable in this regard. Carol Ackroyd, etal, offered a possible explanation for such actions, stating that "the reason why advanced capitalist states are confronted with the `need' to take such steps towards authoritarian rules is that they are all faced with the economic and political consequences of the end of the post-war boom"[14]. Although the use of the armed services in such duties falls within their obligation to be subject to civil political control, they inevitably face the moral dilemma as to public's perception of their role as protectors rather than serving as agents of repression. Thus by obeying legal orders, the military is placed in "an invidious position, knowing that they stand between disobeying legal orders on the one hand and potentially alienating large sections of the population on the other"[15]. While arguably, public relations role in this regard might prove difficult, it poses a challenge to military public relations to be able to explain the role of the armed services as it relates to the execution of such duties.

In addition to the broader aspects of the role and function of public relations in the interface of military and society, the more common traditional role and function of public relations have been to assist in providing information about military policies and operations; assure prompt and accurate response to inquiries from the public; facilitate public understanding of defence aims, activities and needs; and provide liaison and cooperation with information media representatives. These functions also include lending support to the military's drive for recruitment from time to time and the provision of advice to the military on the maintenance of good relationship between military installations and the surrounding communities. These features of public relations functions as Martin Edmonds asserts, are arguably more relevant to today's military than hitherto.

References

1. Haywood, R. (1990) **All About Public Relations** London, McGraw-Hill, p.3
2. Stanhope, H. (1979) **The Soldiers London** Hamish Hamilton p.295
3. Pockock, T, "Defence and Public Relations" in RUSSI Journal Sept 1969
4. Sotomi E.F, quoted in "Public Relations Hand Book", Directorate of Army Public Relations, October 1973
5. Adediji, T., "Improving the Image of the Armed Forces through Public Relations", Lecture delivered at Nigerian Army Public Relations Department Training Seminar, 29-30 Dec 1987
6. Gene, Kovarik "Informing the public on National Security" in Air Force Magazine (UK) June 1984 p.35
7. Lovel, P. in Cochran, L.C. (ed) (1974) **Civil Military Relations**, London, Collier Macmillan p.17
8. Air Vice Marshal Paul Dike, quoted by Chris Agbambu in Nigerian Tribune, Monday 29 March 2010
9. Chris Agbambu, "Strenthening the Cord that Binds Civil Military Relationship" in Nigerian Tribune, Monday 29 March 2010
10. Ibid
11. Ibid
12. Olukolade, A. C. Mobilization of Public Support for Nigerias Military Operations: A Framework for Public Information Management", Research Project submitted to the National Institute for Policy and Strategic Studies, Kuru, November 2011, P. 31
13. Edmonds, M. **Armed Services and Society**, Leicester, U.P. 1988 p.132.
14. Ackroyd, et al, **The Technology of Political Control,** p.73
15. Edmonds, M. **Armed Services and Society Leicester**, op cit

CHAPTER FIVE

'COMPETENCE' OF THE MILITARY TO CONDUCT PUBLIC RELATIONS

The question has often been put: Does the military have authority to conduct public relations? The issue of the military's 'competence' to conduct public relations is one which essentially questions the legality of such activity without prior political authorisation. It is an issue that obtains within countries under the liberal democratic model of civil military relations in the Western world especially United States of America. By its nature, political power within such a system is attained through competitive struggle in an open electoral democratic process. Structurally in such a system, channels of communication are adhered to and the implementation of policy is placed on bureaucratic and military elites who are subordinate to a central political authority. That same authority oversees the formation and implementation of the national defence policy. The military under this system operates in a manner that is similar to civil servants in obeisance to directives of the political masters. By such operation, the military is made wholly accountable to the political authority with "civil control" of all military affairs from the commitment of troops to battle in time of war to the conduct of military public relations and information programmes in peace and in war.

However, the tendency arising from observations has been for the military in western nations, especially the United States, to indulge in public relations outside the machinery of government seemingly, without necessary political authorisation. Should the military, be allowed to carry its views directly to the people without clearance from political superiors? Furthermore, whose views would they carry or be speaking for? The seeming persistence in such conduct by the American military impelled Morris Janowitz's observations that "despite Congressional opposition, the military establishment has been able to develop and maintain extensive public relations, or in official terminology, public information programmes"[1]. The extent of political concern about such conduct is reflected in Janowitz's observation that "the targets of (military) persuasion are no longer merely the leaders of opposing nations in war time. The targets have become total populations, not only of unfriendly states, but of allies, neutrals and of one's own nation as well"[2].

By charging the military of moulding public opinion through "community relations" and elaborate "public relations programmes" such as the 1971 CBS-TV primetime documentary, "The selling of the Pentagon", the US military was further accused not only of using the tax payers' money to fund such campaigns but that the possibility also existed that it could also carry to the public, "strategic views at variance from administration's policy,... or budgetary requests exceeding what the administration believes desirable"[3],.Secretary of State for Defence, Robert McNamara in the Kennedy administration also questioned the competence of the military to speak, especially as it touched on politics and foreign policy issues. As he put it, "it is inappropriate for any members of the defence department to speak on the subject of foreign policy; that's a field that should be reserved for the President, the Secretary of State and other officials of the state department. A military officer speaking on a matter of foreign policy is speaking about a field that lies outside his responsibility and yet as a representative of this government - an official representative - his words are taken as the policy of the government. That is inappropriate"[4]. Besides this, an international implication was added to the issue as the opinion was also expressed by calling "the talkativeness of American military men... an international scandal. Throughout the world it causes us trouble; it causes great loss of respect and confidence. No other military establishment on earth, except perhaps in small disorderly countries, thus permits a running commentary on critical affairs by its generals and admirals and the colonels down the line"[5].

However, it would seem from a critical analysis of the charges being levelled against the military on the issue of conducting public relations that these assessments are from a rather narrow angle of negative political connotation which seems to discount and totally ignore the wider benefits of public relations for the military. The military as an institution desires at all times to excel and to that extent takes initiatives that are to military and largely national interests. In spite however, of such views, the scope of conduct of public relations activities have widened much more even in the United States especially with its commitment of troops to many battle and operational scenarios around the world since the end of the cold war. Furthermore, public relations activities are being conducted nowadays by most militaries around the world as countries like the United Kingdom, Australia, Canada, Brazil, Indonesia, South Africa and Ghana do it in a very elaborate manner.

The relevance indeed of public relations for the military has even come to be better appreciated by international military missions such as the United Nations (UN), European Union (EU), African Union (AU), Economic Community of West African States, (ECOWAS), and even by standing intergovernmental military organizations such as the North Atlantic Treaty Organization – NATO. Admiral Giampaolo di Paola, Chairman of NATO's Military Committee on the importance of information to NATO's Military Public Affairs asserted that: we have seen rapid changes in the information environment, specifically in information technology, which enable a 24 hour flow of information of all kinds, some accurate, some less so. How do people differentiate between the two and who can they trust in seeking answers to their questions"[6]. The Admiral in posing these questions also tried to proffer answers saying that with the vast number of social networks now even reaching out to the most remote populations, there is "confusion of mass information"... our publics have the democratic right to know what the alliance is doing on their behalf and why. NATO therefore has the obligation to inform about its policies and activities, and especially about its operations... information is only credible if it is accurate and timely. Providing this information is the role of NATOs Military Public Affairs Officer[7]. Harping also on military public affairs personnel qualities, he said it requires high professionalism, an analytical mind and strong commitment. The Public Affairs Officer is a key advisor to the NATO Commander... the challenge of the NATO Public Affairs practitioners is to explain to a wide and diverse audience, including the media, the complexities of the issues the military deals with in response to the security challenges of the 21st Century, and how the military supports NATOs political decision makers. This is particularly critical during times of crisis, when NATO is urged to action[8]. Along same line of thought, Robert Reilly argued equally that "although some critics lament the use of tax dollars to promote viewpoint of the military, it seems clear that adequate public relations programme is a necessity for the military, as it is for business. There is a story to be told here, sometimes a controversial one, and in the interests of balance, public relations personnel should be allowed to develop a professional response"[9].

Notwithstanding the charge of its "consistent violation of the law" and the "persistence of its illegal propaganda", through public relations, the military, however, strongly believes in the rightness of its actions. John Swomley pointed this out in relation to the US Military by his expression that the military had "asserted its right to propagandize civilians against the expressed will of Congress. No President or Secretary of Defence has been able to stop it except temporarily and then only at a few specific points in the interests of coordinating military policy with the State Department's policy"[10]. While it is thus becomes difficult to stop the US military's conduct of public relations without due 'competence', it is arguably appropriate to look at the issue in the same light as the involvement of the military in politics, and, in government affairs against its presumed apolitical standing. Martin Edmonds view on the issue of the military's involvement in politics argues that "armed services involvement in the affairs of states should not, in the first instance, carry with it any sense of moral disapprobation... Any act, argument, opinion, or judgement made by representatives of the armed services, even in a sphere of competence for which they are alone responsible, is, in the strict sense political in that it is directed at changing the status quo, presumably in a manner advantageous to their own interests or their perceived interests of the state"[11]. Against this view, it may thus be argued that, most importantly, what else do military public relations stand for than as a tool of military political interests? For as it is well recognized, public relations through its strategies and tactics have for long not only served as useful tools for commercial, industrial and other corporate goals but have in addition always enhanced the success of political goals as well. It is relevant to point out this aspect even though the main question relates to who sets the agenda and defines what the public relations goals are.

The above argument can be taken further, and yet, still compatible with the position taken by Martin Edmonds in relation to politics. In respect of military public relations, it may equally be argued that it is of no value to question the 'competence' of the military to conduct public relations but rather to look at the factors that motivated its involvement and formed the basis of its action. Furthermore, given that the military has been involved in the politics of many states, how could its public relations programmes be made to be in harmony with government positions and policies, given that military public relations functions must necessarily conform with the demands of the political authority? The conduct of military public relations from the above premise, it may be argued, is meant first, to serve military interest. In support of such view of military self-interest, James Clotfelter stated that "like any interest group, the military tries to influence public opinion to support its programmes. Together with its civilian allies, it creates images and sells policies. The Pentagon is able to sponsor more elaborate publicity than other governmental agencies; the efforts represented by the films produced, flights arranged, letters answered, honour guards provided, press conferences held, and newspaper articles placed undoubtedly is matched only by soap or soft drinks companies"[12].

In conducting its public relations the military is better placed to speak effectively for itself on matters that affect its interests. This aspect is rather relevant given that a second or third party may not represent it adequately. As C. Wright Mills equally argues in relation to the US, "in all of pluralistic America... there is no possible combination of interests that has anywhere near the time, the money, the manpower to present a point of view that can effectively compete with the views presented by the war lords"[13]. Although this reference refers to more than just the military at the time, the argument was used all the same in view of the fact that the military were the main actors.

There is perhaps also a justification for the military's indulgence in public relations without legal authorisation considering the advantages offered by the West's democratic principles which, among others, recognizes individual and group liberties to carry out functions which does not interfere with, or constitute a legal breach of the law. One avenue through which this could be done is through public relations and, this perhaps, explains why, as James Clotfelter pointed out, "civilian attempts to merge service operations in 1947 and to control military leaders' public speeches in the early 1960's led to military charges of gagging"[14]. The public's "right to know" and the military's "right to tell" is well recognized by the US military which firmly insist on informing the American public of issues of military interest. Jack Raymond also in relation to the US recognized this when he affirmed that "military regulations acknowledge that the American people have a right to maximum information concerning the armed services. In the Army for example, regulations provide explicitly that the impetus for the release of information should come from the Army as part of a comprehensive effort to achieve information objectives"[15]. These objectives were to gain public understanding and support of the Army's role in a sound national military programme; inspire public confidence in the Army's ability to accomplish its mission now and in the future, and develop public esteem.

The climate of Press freedom which pervades in Western society may equally be another factor that motivates the military to seek and achieve publicity. Morris Janowitz illustrates this appropriately when pointing out the media acknowledgement of military sourced information by Alistair Cooke, a correspondent for the Manchester Guardian. Janowitz recognized Cooke as one of the few Journalists who accepted that public relations activities of the military establishment are not only "a product of the services themselves, but are also as a result of pressures from newspapers to produce news"[16].

While the argument may yet continue as to the issue of the military's competence to speak for itself, it is equally pertinent to point out that there is, perhaps, no cause for fear of undue military influence on public opinion contrary to that expressed by government. Samuel Finer's observation is relevant in reference to the United States, where he noted that it is the pressure of the American system which compels the military to shout for its objectives, a situation that "gives an impression of a vast military influence in government, whereas it is only a vast amount of necessitated noise"[17]. Morris Janowitz also lends credence to this position when asserting that: "the military profession is not a monolithic power group. A deep split pervades its ranks in respect to its doctrine and viewpoints on foreign affairs; a split which mirrors civilian disagreements"[18]. This view highlights the issue of service rivalry which, as indicated, is a sort of safety valve insofar as a combined military assault on American and indeed western public opinion and institutions might be concerned.

References

1. Janowitz, M. (1964) **The Professional Soldier**, London, Collier Macmillan p.395.
2. Janowitz, M. cited in Raymond, J's power at the Pentagon London, Heinemann, 1964 P.175
3. Clotfelter, J. (1973) **The military in American Politics** New York, Harper and Row, p. 134
4. Raymond, J. (1964) **Power at the Pentagon** London, Heinemann p. 176.
5. Cited in Swomley, J. (1967) **The Military Establishment**, Boston, Beacon press, p.113
6. Admiral Giampaolo di Paola, Foreword to NATO Military policy on public affairs @ http://www.nato.int/ims/docu/mil-publ-aff-policy.htm
7. Ibid
8. Ibid
9. Reilly, R.T. (1987) **Public Relations in Action** 2nd ed New Jersey, Prentice-Hall p.523
10. Swomley, J. **The Military Establishment,** Op cit p.127
11. Edmonds, M. (1988) **Armed Services and Society** Leicester U. P. p. 95
12. Clotfelter, J. (1973) **The Military in American Politics** New York Harper & Row p.134
13. C. Wright Mills, cited in Swomley, J., **The Military Establishment**, Op cit p.134
14. Quoted in Clotfelter, J. **The Military in American Politics**, Op cit p.135
15. Raymond, J. **Power at the Pentagon** London, Op cit p. 177
16. Janowitz, cited in Raymond, J, (Ibid) p. 187
17. Finer, S. (ibid)
18. Janowitz, M. cited (ibid)

CHAPTER SIX

THE PURPOSE OF MILITARY PUBLIC RELATIONS

The statement of General Omar Bradley, a respected American military figure during the Second World War underscores the relevance of military public relations. He quipped that "no organisation so directly concerned with public interest can hope to escape the effects of popular opinion, nor can personnel do their best work without adequate knowledge of where they fit in"[1]. Cutlip, Center and Broom corroborates this statement especially in relation to the American Military that in the above quote lies the key to the military public relations mission - to maintain public support and to maintain adequate internal communication over a large organisation as the American military.

Essentially, the purpose of military public relations lies in supporting the fulfilment of the legitimate roles of the military, namely to provide defence and security for a nation. It is apparent from historical experience that achieving this objective does not only entail going into battle but that other factors equally go into play. Military public relations falls among such factors and therefore, the focus of this chapter is to look at the general purpose of military public relations in peace and in war.

Cultivating People

Beginning with peace time operations, military public relations activities are very importantly aimed at cultivating the attitudes of people from various sections of society to hold a favourable disposition towards the military. This is very relevant for, as Henry Stanhope appropriately mentions, if the military does not bother to cultivate such attitudes, the tendency might be that it could be forgotten until the next war breaks out. The same line of argument could be seen in Martin Edmonds argument that "in sum, the pattern of public relations and 'keeping the armed services in the public eye'(a phrase used by the British army for just that purpose) is a necessary, non-operational element in the output of the national security system. All states engage in it, more or less, and they would be less than prudent not to"[2]. The corporate nature of the military is an important factor that counts in favour of military discipline, oneness and esprit de corps. It is on this premise that the military emphasizes its public relations goals with in-house mission to foster and maintain a climate of understanding. Through this, members are motivated to serve and perform their roles to the best of their ability both in the service interest and, more importantly, in the overall goals of national defence and security.

Internal Operations

General public relations practice recognizes the vital role of harmonious internal relations within and amongst members of every organisation. Cutlip, Center and Broom emphasised this aspect by their assertion that it is essential for any organisation to "identify, establish, and maintain relationships important to its survival and growth"[3]. They identify tasks of internal relations to include candid open communication in addition to other particular organisational internal relations programmes. Internal relations in the armed forces is given a top priority, for example, in the United States, it is placed at the top level of the Department of Defence and functions under the Assistant Secretary, Defence (Manpower, Personnel and Reserve). The information responsibility of the Office provides support to the internal relations programmes of all the services. Arthur Dreyer stresses the importance of information within the military by his assertion that "the object of troop information is recognized by the Army as keeping the individual Soldier so informed regarding his part in accomplishing his unit's mission that he is motivated to do his best. The Commander uses every means available to accomplish troop information objectives"[4].

Political

Another aspect of the purpose of military public relations is probably political, bearing in mind that the military are either directly or indirectly involved in politics, and that such involvement is essentially tailored towards military interests. David Easton's words in relation to military involvement in politics may after all not be out of place. As he stated, "if politics is concerned with the authoritative allocation of values and power within a society, the military as a vital institution in the polity, can hardly be wished out of participatory bounds, at least as an institutional interest group with a stake in the political decision making"[5].The role of the military through this dimension is to enhance government and public understanding of its role in national security. Public relations serve as a tool in this dimension as the military is keenly aware of its place, role and purpose. In many of today's nations, the armed services constitute a heavy drain on the national wealth, manpower and natural resources. These demand a lot of sacrifice from the masses: hence the people must be convinced to continue to pay their taxes and provide other forms of support towards adequate provision for national defence efforts. As further illustrated by Martin Edmonds, this is especially relevant: "given the relatively high proportion of public expenditure allocated to armed services today, and their being in receipt of a constant proportion of the state's GNP... especially when seen in the context of scarce national resources, and other pressing needs such as health, education, welfare and the environment... the challenge of those responsible for national security is to gauge public attitudes so that the need to acquire the necessary resources to fulfil the defence and security obligations does not itself generate internal opposition"[6].

Providing Information about Military Policies and Operations

A further purpose of military public relations is to provide information about military policies and operations. The armed forces must be concerned about keeping the public informed in such matters based on the strong democratic requirement to operate in conformity with the principle of public accountability. It has always been apparent that no organisation, civil or military, can afford to take public opinion for granted. The understanding of public opinion, and how it is formed, is very fundamental to public relations. As Dennis Wilcox etal emphasised, "such knowledge enables the practitioner to (1) effectively monitor shifts in public opinion, (2) pinpoint formal and informal opinion leaders who should be reached with specific messages, and (3) understand that the dissemination of information through the mass media can only create awareness, not tell people what to think"[7].

The function of information can therefore be seen as an essential outflow of public opinion; hence, the military places much emphasis on it. For example, in the United States, where "public affairs" is the military designation for public relations at the Department of Defence level, there are, under the direction of an Assistant Secretary of Defence, trained information officers from the Army, Navy, Marine Corps, and Air Force assigned to the office of the Public Affairs at the Pentagon in Washington. With civil service public relations specialists, they are responsible for providing and releasing all military news at the seat of government. The United States Army for its part emphasises that the function of its Public Information division is to contribute towards "...fulfilling the army's obligation to report on its activities to the American people and other publics as appropriate... As with other services, the activities of these branches at the seat of government with national news media are a part of the coordinated Department of Defence information programme"[8].

Manpower Recruitment

The issue of manpower recruitment into the armed forces constitutes yet another vital goal of military public relations. One sure means by which to ensure availability of manpower and to ensure service continuity in the armed forces is through regular recruitment into the forces. If military manpower needs are therefore to be met, especially now that compulsory national service through conscription has been abolished in many countries, the need for young people to be encouraged and persuaded to volunteer for military service indeed becomes very crucial. For example, the task of meeting military manpower needs in Britain, according to Henry Stanhope, is such that "the army has been battling to fill its ranks ever since national service ended. At no time have its recruiting officers been able to sit back and take it easy... Since the end of national service in 1962-63 the history of recruiting has been one of peaks and troughs"[9].

J.C.M. Baynes shares a similar view by his assertion that "there was much pessimistic speculation in 1957, both in the army and among civilians as to whether enough men could be recruited to keep the corps and regiments up to strength after national service ended in 1960"[10]. As he further stated, "each summer displays are organised all over Britain under the heading of `KAPE': `Keeping the Army in the Public Eye', corps and regiments provide caravans, display teams, and bodies of men to tour certain selected areas in strength..."[11], for the purpose of wooing youths into the army.

Community Relations

The achievement of community relations goals is also fundamental to military public relations practice and as such highly recommended for military formations to establish relationship with their community neighbourhoods. Through good community relations programmes, beneficial relationships could be established and fostered. Pat Bowman and Ellis emphasised the essence, motivation and technique of community relations for all organisations. As they put it, "there are three basic motivations for operating a community relations policy: a sense of corporate social responsibility; an acknowledgement of the attitude that nowadays all organisations are expected to participate in life beyond their own doors; and quite bluntly, because the understanding and appreciation of everyone around is of genuine practical value. Community relations may involve many of the techniques of communication that are used in other areas of a company's public relations. It needs the same disciplines of selectivity and control, but it differs in that it is almost difficult to lay down general rules. The reason for this is simply that no two communities are the same and that no two relationships between an organisation and the various communities in which it may find itself are the same either"[12].

From the above broad premise, an army defines its community relations programme as "the command function that appraises the attitudes of the civilian community toward the command as well as the attitude of the command toward the civilian community; and initiates programme of action to earn community respect and confidence"[13]. From this perspective, the community relations efforts of military commands, therefore, encompass all actions taken by the army that are related to the public, whether international, national, regional, state or local, whether it be an open day, a speaker's programme, an aerial demonstration, or a band to march in a parade. Towards achieving its community relations objectives, the United States Army usually encourages its units to form civilian advisory committees. In many communities where there is more than one Service, these become Joint Armed Forces Advisory Groups. These committees, composed of military personnel and civilians, assist in resolving common problems of military and community and also develop, in addition, mutual cooperation and understanding.

Community relations activities are equally taken seriously by international military organizations. In NATO for instance, Community Relations is one of the three basic functions of NATO Military Public Affairs as described in the NATO Military Public Affairs Policy. Community Relations programs are associated with the interaction between NATO military installations in NATO member states and their surrounding civilian communities. These programs can take the form of addressing issues of interest to and fostering relations with the general public business. One main Community Relations event is the annual Norfolk NATO Festival when – since 1953 – the City of Norfolk honours NATO and its member nations. Key programs include Model NATO

Challenge, Student Forum, Flag Raising Ceremony, International Tattoo, Parade of Nations and the NATO Festival[14].

Providing Information and Communication During Crisis

Another aspect to the purpose of military public relations lies in the delicate nature of military duties with regard to the handling of military hardware and materiel in the course of which huge accidents may occur and cause loss of lives not only of military personnel but also of people in the surrounding neighbourhoods. The role of public relations here will be to provide appropriate information on such unforeseen, given that the public is usually very sensitive about such issues. A further expansion of this aspect is the recognition by Cutlip, Center and Broom that "the military has a unique problem in the area of disasters or accidents. No matter how severe or how routine a mishap may be, it always involves tax payers' investment and often the lives of citizens serving in the armed forces. Either of these factors increases public attention when circumstance, mismanagement or misunderstanding create crisis: 265 marines die in a Beirut bombing, a congressional committee claims that a new army tank costing millions to develop catches fire too easily; an American destroyer collides with an Australian Aircraft carrier, costing nearly 100 lives; an Air force bomber carrying nuclear weapons crashes on foreign soil. These and countless other incidents create the necessity for immediate factual information to Congress, the press, and the people. The sensitivity of all segments of American society to such problems compels recognition of the role and responsibility of those directly responsible for moving information from the military establishment into the public domain"[15]. It is thus important to point out that the Nigerian public are very sceptical with information from the military especially during any accident or disaster that occurs in the military. A glaring case in point was the case of the Charlie 130 Aircraft which was involved in air crash in Lagos with over 200 officers mainly of the rank of Major on their way back to Jaji after a visit to military installations in Lagos. During such occurrences, the Nigerian military needs to be more forthcoming with information and on time too in order to assuage especially, public fears and anxieties.

Managing Conflict

A vital purpose for which the Nigerian Army set up its public relations branch is " to develop an effective two-way channel of communication between the army and the public, capitalising on opportunities for better relations and resolving potential and actual areas of conflict"[16]. This is relevant to all military institutions, but which is much more important in the developing countries of Africa, Asia, and the Middle East. In these countries, problems arising out of disagreements and conflicts between military personnel and civilians are usually frequent. Apart from the fact that military governments until recently, held sway in most of these countries, the tendency was that sight of military personnel in military uniforms are very common in public means of transport and places - buses, trains, markets, offices and many other public forums.

As a result, civilians hold much disdain for the military class which they perceive to have special privileges by virtue of their profession. Military-civilian tension and clashes occur frequently in African countries. An incident occurred in Zaire where "soldiers went on rampage in the locality of Kindu in the centre of Zaire... the incident followed an argument between a group of students and soldiers which developed into "undisciplined elements" of the army "running wild"[17]. Usually when such civil military conflicts occur in such countries, the military is usually blamed by the media, which tends to use the argument that the military has the advantage of force to intimidate civilians.

Such issues of civil military conflicts are hardly debated in the developed countries. As Henry Stanhope reports in relation to the United Kingdom, "so far Britain has managed to avoid having a military caste in the more sinister sense. Officers avoid strutting around the West End of London in gold braids and epaulettes, except when on special duty. As soon as they finish work for the day, they change into civilian clothes and staff officers of the MOD wear lounge suits for most of the time. An increasing number of families now live among the civilian community... their children go to civilian schools. Unlike soldiers in many countries, they are never looked upon as a privileged class"[18].

PR Role during Tension and War

A very crucial goal of military public relations lies in its utility in time of tension and war. One factor that contributed so much to the growth and expansion of the public relations profession during the period of its transition to its modern practice was the First World War as its much value was much recognized in terms of providing organised publicity. Between the First and the Second World War, there was a remarkable expansion of public relations activities, especially in the United States. The outbreak of the Second World War further accelerated the pace with the formation of the Office of War Information which also encouraged extensive expansion of public relations in the armed forces.

Initially, military public relations practice in time of war was a mixture of public relations, propaganda and some aspects of psychological warfare. Modern day aspects of public relations activities in time of war and tension, however, emphasise a lot of factual information and news management, even though elements of propaganda are not totally ruled out. Proper news and information management in time of war is very relevant, especially as it is a major determinant of the extent and degree of public support for the war effort. For example, the involvement of the United States forces in Indochina in the seventies apparently enjoyed public support initially but the situation later changed especially when the graphic pictures of war casualties were being shown on television and truthful positions of the war situation were not being conveyed to the American people. Public support was withdrawn by the public not only for the government but also for the military. This proved to be a situation which the numerous propaganda attempts by the Pentagon to reverse did not prove successful.

In contrast, the experience of Britain in the South Atlantic War-the Falklands war - in 1982 indicates the strength of favourable public opinion in support of a war.

Although the Falklands conflict generated its own share of public relations problems, it has been revealed, that the experience of the British in that conflict demonstrated the need "to enhance understanding and to ensure greater awareness within the MOD and the Armed Services of the importance of public relations and of the need of the media for accurate information in time of tension and war"[19]. As was stressed after the event, "the single most important element is to ensure that Ministers and their Service and civilian advisers have up-to-date, comprehensive public relations advice. This means that the MOD's Chief of Public Relations and his staff must not only be fully aware of the political, diplomatic and security issues during a period of tension and war but must be attuned to the needs of the media"[20].

The conducts of military public relations in war, especially in relation to satisfying media needs, are subject to numerous intricacies and technicalities especially from a security interest perspective. The point here is well made by Arthur Dreyer, especially in relation to the United States. As he implied, security considerations require that "...at all major command levels, there would be "field censorship" groups to provide security review and censorship of news release material, according to the Joint Service principles as outlined in the Department of Defence Field Censorship Manual"[21]. Although the issue of news censorship in war by the military normally raises disagreement between the military and the media, based on different interpretations of relevant war news, the military nevertheless always has its way in the "interest of security".

The issue of media censorship was highlighted during the first Gulf war in Iraq as a result of media complaints to which General Norman Schwarzkopf, the Supreme Commander of the coalition forces rose up in defence. In this regard, Philip M. Taylor had stated that although the General was aware of the importance of giving the correct information to the media, this could only be done in war within the bounds of operational security and military censorship. General Schwarzkopf defends his action in stating that: "why should I, as a military man, volunteer anything to the open press that would assist him (Saddam) in his analysis of what we are doing... It's not to preclude you having information. It is because when it gets in the open press, he watches CNN religiously, the Iraqi military Ambassador in Washington cuts articles from the (Washington) Post and sends them home every day, and I don't want to give him one damn thing that will help his military analysis if i can prevent it"[22]. Such issues of censorship have often been equally highlighted in several other military operation areas in the Middle East, Kosovo and Afghanistan.

It is pertinent to note that there has continued to be much stronger perception of the role of public relations in the conduct of war in modern times. H. Pyper, to this effect, observed that the British MOD continues to attach much value to the role and value of good public relations. Evidence to this effect was that the MOD had, in 1990, issued a directive which stated that: "public relations continues to be a vital aspect of our contribution to the multinational effort aimed at deterring further Iraqi aggression and ensuring that sanctions work... We must keep the support of the media and the public. The maintenance of constructive relationships with the media now is crucial to our PR effort in the event of hostilities. Good PR also contributes significantly to the moral of our deployed forces and their families"[23]. It is equally relevant as Hyper also added that "if there is one lesson which has been clearly demonstrated over the last 30 years it is that good PR is essential to the successful prosecution of wars. Perhaps time has come to add PR to the glorious list of the principles of war, for has it not been shown beyond reasonable doubt that it is at least as important as the other principles?"[24].

References

1. Omar Bradley, cited in Cutlip, S.M. et al, (1985) **Effective Public Relations** 6th ed, New Jersey, Prentice_Hall, p.582
2. Edmonds M. (1988) Armed Services and Society, Leicester University press, p.130
3. Cutlip, S.M. Center, A., and Broom, G.M. Op citp.3
4. Stephenson, H. (1960) **Handbook of Public Relations** New York, McGraw-Hill P. 775
5. David Easton, cited in Kurkeja, V. (1990) **Civil-Military Relations in South East Asia** New Delhi, Sage publications p.18
6. Edmonds, M. (1988) **Armed Services and Society** Leicester U.P. p.127
7. Wilcox, D. et al (1989) **Public Relations: Strategies and Tactics** 2nd ed New York, Harper and Row, p.233
8. Stephenson, H. (1960) **Handbook of Public Relations** New York McGraw-Hill p.777
9. Stanhope, H. (1979) **The Soldiers London**, Hamish Hamilton, p.44
10. Baynes, J.C.M. (1972) **The Soldier in Modern Society** London, Eyre-Methuen, p.182
11. ibid p.187
12. Bowman, P. and Nigel E. (1969) **Manual of Public Relations**, London, Heinemann, p.191
13. See serial 8, p.778
14. http://www.nato.int/ims/docu/mil-publ-aff-policy.htm
15. See serial 3, p.583
16. Report of Nigerian Army Public Relations training seminar, 1987, p.44
17. West Africa magazine, 10-16 August 1992, p.1365
18. See serial 9, p.294
19. MOD, London, Paper on "Working Arrangement with the Media in time of Tension and War"
20. Ibid
21. See serial 8. p.786
22. Taylor, P.M. (1992) (1992, Manchester University press,, p.41
23. Hyper, H, "The media in modern warfare: Friend or Foe?" in Hawk Bracknell RAF Staff College 1992, p. 53
24. Ibid, p. 60

CHAPTER SEVEN

TARGETS OF MILITARY PUBLIC RELATIONS

Most complex organisations in society maintain relationships with several outside groups for various reasons that may be associated with organisational objectives. At the same time, new groups, services or products are also being sought on an on-going basis. In the field of public relations, the term, `publics' is used to refer to various groups that may have dealings with an organisation or in whom the organisation may have interest for the purpose of pointing or `targeting' its public relations programmes. The aim at all times in most cases is to cultivate in such groups a favourable disposition towards the organisation.

There are, broadly speaking, two types of `publics' in public relations, the `internal' and the `external' publics. Internal publics are the employees or personnel of the organisation whether junior or senior, while the external publics comprise all other groups outside the organisation with whom it already has dealings or is interested in having dealings. They may either be individuals, shareholders in a company, corporate groups, the general public, the government or even members of Parliament.

The military is an organisation which has interest and dealings with several groups of publics, be they those within or outside the military circles. It is a necessary relationship in the interest of the military's corporate objectives. Morris Janowitz recognizes the essence of such interrelationship stressing that "the effectiveness of the military as a pressure group depends on the network of its civilian alliances and contacts. Since the politics of the military in the domestic arena are not the politics of a distinct social stratum, the more elaborate the linkage - formal and informal - of the military officer with civilian leadership groups and institutions, the greater is its potential influence"[1]. The focus of this chapter is, therefore, to identify the various interest or pressure groups in society in whom the military is primarily interested. They are the "targets of military public relations".

Internal Public

Targets of military public relations must essentially, begin with its internal public. This, arguably, may be its most vital public, given that it is the internal public that constitutes the military organisation. Without this group, the military as an institution may, after all, not be in existence. The internal public of the military are the regular active duty personnel namely: Soldiers of the Army, Ratings and Seamen and women of the Navy, as well as Air men and women of the Air Force. It includes also, the entire Officer cadre of all the military services. Civilians employed by the Services may also be considered as part of the internal public even though they are not strictly military professionals.

The essence of the internal publics to an organisation is well elucidated by Cutlip, Center, and Broom. As they noted, "every organisation is made up of task units with production or service responsibilities related to the overall mission. The nature of many tasks in increasingly computerised organisations and automated factories makes paying attention to personal satisfaction and social relationships a high priority. Each task unit is also a social unit that must meet the human needs of the individuals accomplishing work... The work groups themselves are part of a larger social unit, the organisation, comprised of a mix of relationships that range from face to face to distance and meditated, from simple to complex, from peer to peer, to subordinate to supervisor, and from supportive and friendly to hostile and competitive... As a result of this and other forces in the work place, internal public relations usually called "employee communication" has become the fastest growing area of practice"[2].

The military is highly conscious of its internal relations and, as such, endeavours to map out appropriate communication programmes. The aim of the internal relations programme of the military is very clear. Lowndes, F. Stephens, stresses that, it is "to maintain an internal information effort that fulfils the information wants and needs of the Total Army's internal audiences in order to sustain an effective motivated and loyal force"[3].

Reservists

Reserve component personnel (known in the Nigerian Military as ex-service men for soldiers, retired officers for officers) constitute a second target of military public relations. Reserve forces exist in the military of many nations and are liable for service call-ups especially in times of emergency to increase the number of available combat forces and provide necessary additional support. In the United States especially, reserve forces form a very large and influential group. According to Jack Raymond, "among the most powerful special interest groups with a military orientation are the reserve organisations, particularly the National Guard Association. Most of the Pentagon Chiefs regard the reserve organisations as more of a nuisance than an ally. The reserve organisations, many of whose members are also members of Congress, command strong support in Congress and in the state governments as well[4].

The strategic position of members of the Reserves and Reservists especially those in government and parliamentary positions, are of advantage to the military as they are in position to generate external support for issues of military interest. Samuel Huntington also acknowledges the value of the reserve organisations to the US military by stating that "the services also use the reserve structure to reach public opinion. The reserve organisations, and, to an even greater extent, the National Guard, are influential with Congress simply because they are organised for local political action"[5].

Veteran Organisations

Following the reserves closely, Veteran Organisations constitute another target of military public relations. Through its links with veteran associations, the military continues to promote esprit de corps with retired colleagues. Furthermore, Veterans in their own right, form a very important military oriented lobby group. Jack Raymond takes the view that although the primary objectives of veteran groups is to concentrate on programmes of direct benefit to their members in form of cash payments, tax benefits and the like, they, nevertheless tend actively to support national security programmes. John Swomley provides a relevant example in this regard. Using the campaign for Universal Military Training in the United States during the First and the Second World War, he identified groups that were in favour of securing the adoption of the measure through Congress to include "the United States Army, the American Legion and the Veterans of Foreign Wars..."[6].

Potential Recruits

The group which the military identify as "prior personnel" or "potential recruits" are also a very important target of military public relations. The complex nature of the modern military, and its technological advancement, has made it necessary for the military to compete with other industrial and commercial organisations in society for qualified technically oriented manpower which will be required to service and operate its many sophisticated weapons and other military hardware. It is, therefore, incumbent on the military to orient appropriate public relations programmes towards this group. This is an aspect that has often been combined with direct advertising through many media of advertising.

Civilian Employees

Civilian employees of the armed services also constitute another target of military public relations. These form a crucial group in the modern day concept of military organisation, within the defence environment. The nature of their roles bears on the overall success of military objectives as they not only provide essential support services, but also are involved in defence management functions through policy formulation and execution.

Defence Contractors

The group of supplier publics also referred to as defence contractors are also another target of military public relations, and are composed mainly of defence contractors and defence oriented industries. Apart from supplying military needs, the contractors and industries constitute, equally, a powerful conglomerate that has the ability to influence support for issues of military interest. Using the example of the United States military, Samuel Huntington pointed out that "in their search for support in civil society, the services could hardly overlook their contractors... In mobilising industry the Navy and the Air Force started with two advantages over the army. Both the Navy and the Air force furnished a substantial portion of the demand for the products of two distinct industries. The Ship building industry would always encourage a larger Navy, and the Aircraft industry, a substantial Air force"[7].

Backstop Associations

Another special interest group that constitutes a target of military public relations is the group which Huntington quotes as "backstop associations"; a group that is said "to best epitomise the Military industrial complex". It comprises the organisation of the military service supporters in the United States such as the Association of the US Army, the Air Force Association and the Navy League. Their programmes of activities are very relevant to the military as they are often said to define and articulate service interests. The scope of their membership and activities is adequately captured by Jack Raymond to the effect that, "the members are active, reserve and retired members of the armed forces, defence contractors, community leaders and other supporters. The organisations are financed by membership fees and sums from contractors who pay for exhibits at conventions, subscribe to various dinner meetings and rallies, and place advertisements in the official publications. These organisations of service supporters unabashedly fight the battles of the military. The Navy group calls itself the "civilian arm of the Navy"[8].

As Raymond elaborated further, organisation's activities on behalf of the services come in statements supporting the services' policies. "The Army Association has repeatedly advocated a large standing Army and supports army weapons projects and the expansion of the capability for fighting ground warfare. The Navy League was an early and consistent supporter of the Polaris submarine programme and is a constant champion of US reliance upon aircraft carriers. It also has fought bravely in support of the Navy's traditional resistance to service unification. The Air Force Association has backed investments in bombers as well as missiles and has championed Air force policies in favour of military unification and counterforce strategies"[9].

The Government

The government also constitutes a very vital and primary legitimate target of military public relations. This group includes inter alia the executive arm of government, legislature and government agencies. Military public relations activities towards the government are essential in the sense that the government does not only set the guidelines for the military, but also the legislature demands accountability from the armed services by exercising checks through the constitutional machinery of "civilian control". At all times, this group will need to be convinced and carried along the military view point if the armed services are to get their needs. To enable them perform their functions properly, the armed services usually press for their needs to be met from the political authorities on such issues as "the military budget, broad military policies, pay, promotion, retirement, housing, medical care, and many other matters"[10].

The Media

The media as an organisation and its group members are also an important target of military public relations. They constitute a focal group not only because they own, control or operate the media channels through which most public relations messages are conveyed, but most importantly are in a vantage position to shape public opinion for, or against, the military. The role of the media in public relations is indeed central and paramount to its activities. This probably, is why the media are often regarded as the most important channel through which to direct military public relations programmes. Tom Pockock, argued that public relations can act through many media and through many types of intermediary, "but probably the most important single link is the correspondent of the press, television or radio who specialises in defence and the reporting of warlike operations"[11].

Experience has shown that the media are a group that needs to be delicately cultivated and handled by the military, considering that some form of misunderstanding has always pervaded military media relationship. S.F. Crozier confirms the existence of such misunderstanding between the two groups by his statement that "there can be few professions more ready to misunderstand each other than Journalists and Soldiers"[12]. From the point of view of the media world, the impression has always been that the military have always harboured a long-standing tradition of hostility to the press. This is a situation for which Morris Janowitz offers a possible explanation that the "military dislike contradiction by the press. They saw Journalists as particularly obnoxious source of public criticism"[13].

It has always been obvious that most arguments between the military and the media have normally arisen from the issue of "the public's right to know" which the press has always championed, and the military's counter arguments that to disclose certain information was not possible for "security and operational reasons". Censorship of information by the military occurs more frequently in war situations. For example, during the Falklands war in 1982, some media observations on news censorship by the British military includes such comments as "their only contribution was to rigorously enforce increasingly erratic restrictions on outgoing news"[14], and that "there were times when information was messed about for reasons which had nothing to do with military information"[15]. The highpoint of such complaint after the war was, perhaps, the opinion of the BBC spelled out in a memorandum to the House of Commons Defence Committee. In it, the BBC alleged that "even within identifiable parameters of security, there have been attempts to `manage' or `manipulate' the news"[16]. Similar complaints of this nature by the media were also frequent during and after the Gulf war. Equally similar complaints have on occasions been raised in Nigeria in course of the many internal security operations carried out by Military Joint Task Forces, JTF, in operations in the Niger Delta, Plateau and the North East region of the country.

While such complaints may well continue in the future, the problem is certainly, a crucial one which the military really need to address. In a study of military media relationships, Allan Hooper, relevantly noted that "it follows that an understanding of the relationship between the military and the media is important not only in itself but also in the context of the rapport between the public and the Services. Both sides have much to learn about each other, and they are likely to suffer accordingly if they fail to do so. Furthermore during the last 35 years there has been no world war and yet the British Armed forces have been involved continuously in low level conflict including 13 years in Northern Ireland. The reporting of armed conflict by the media is now almost a constant requirement and therefore accurate and informed coverage is a matter of public importance"[17].

The general Public

Above all targets of military public relations, the most important group, outside the internal public, must be the general public. Public opinion is a strong element in all matters and affairs of any nation, including defence and security. The support which the general public may provide for the military come from many directions and the military requires at all times to have good relations with the general public. This is why they must always continue to be involved in promoting good public relations towards this most important target.

References

1. Janowitz, M. (1960) **The Professional Soldier**, New York, Collier Macmillan, P.372
2. Cutlip,S.M. et al (1985) **Effective Public Relations,** 6th ed, New Jersey, Prentice-Hall, pp. 314-315
3. Lowndes, F. Stephens, "The professional orientation of Military Public Affairs Officers" in Public Relations Quarterly, vol. 23, 1978, pp. 19- 23
4. Raymond, J. (1964) **Power at the Pentagon**, London, Heinemann, P. 194
5. Huntignton, S.P. (1961) **The Common Defence**, New York, Columbia University Press, p.293
6. Swomley, J. (1964) **The Military Establishment**, Boston Beacon Press, p.10
7. Huntigton S.P. Op cit P. 399
8. Raymond J. Op cit P. 192
9. Ibid, p.199
10. Ibid, p.202
11. Pockock, T. "Defence and Public Relations" in RUSSI Journal Sept 1969
12. Cited in Hooper Allan (1982) **The Military and the Media**, Aldershot,, p.3
13. Janowitz, M. (1960) **The Professional Soldier** Op Cit P. 395
14. Pyper, H Hawk, Bracknell RAF Staff College, 1982, p. 52
15. Ibid, p.52
16. Ibid, P 53
17. Hooper, A Op cit P. 4 and 8

CHAPTER EIGHT

STRATEGIES AND TACTICS OF MILITARY PUBLIC RELATIONS

'Strategies' and 'tactics' are two well-known terms in the military as the two terms indeed owe their historical origins to the military. While strategy encompass the crucial decisions of a war or campaign, such as the nature or mode of force to be utilised, be it through infantry assault, amphibious operations or aerial bombardment, tactics involve on-the-spot mini-decisions made in action to serve the ends of the overall strategic planning. Strategy is one word that has acquired general usage especially its application to different aspects of human endeavour namely, political strategy, economic strategy, social strategy, business strategy, sports strategy and military strategy. Momah identifies plan as one element that is common to all the forms of strategy[1]. Each of them involves a series of advanced and well-articulated decisions formulated in a more or less fixed coherent plan. So strategy is policy oriented. Once there is a policy, it follows logically that there is a goal. It is strategy which establishes the link between policy and goal desired[2]. Military strategy, it is posited, is the most exceptional of all forms of strategy in human endeavour. It is the only form of strategy which establishes the link between life and death, war and peace[3]. Tactics involve on-the-spot mini-decisions made in action to serve the ends of the overall strategic planning. On the other hand, it is a variant of military strategy. It is not strategy in itself but a means to achieve desired strategic objectives. While strategy expresses a master plan of principles and modalities of prosecuting war, tactics is more situational[4].

Public relations have its own peculiar strategies and tactics that are often used to prosecute its goals and thus, strategy and tactics that are suited to public relations needs are equally relevant to military public relations planning as they help towards the achievement of set goals. Public relations experts have often emphasized that an organization is only as strong as its reputation; the PR function is to manage that reputation and not simply of producing publicity material. Planning ensures needs assessment and helps an organization to manage its expectations and achieve real, measurable results. The purpose of public relations strategy is thus:

- To complement the overall business plan of an organization
- To identify ways in which PR can help achieve an organizations objectives
- To focus and manage all the communications of an organization

- To ensure maximum benefit from all PR activities and
- It can also help educate those within an organization about the value of PR[5].

Cutlip, Center and Broom, affirming the relevance of strategy to public relations, states that, "thinking in terms of strategy is at the heart of public relations planning. In the pure sense, a strategy is a plan to use selected means in predetermined ways to attain a desired result. Strategic thinking links the fact-finding phase to the planning and programming"[6]. Therefore in planning for military public relations, an overall strategic objective may be set to include among others, the goal of keeping the public informed on military affairs, to render service, and to lobby or propagandize depending on the target audience and the nature of goal to be attained. It is out of the broad strategic plans that tactical means and programmes are conceptualized for implementation to achieve the public relations mission.

The applications of certain tactics used to attain public relations objectives have proved to be very effective. However, modern day practices, coupled with new developments in the profession are increasingly encouraging the principle of creativity in deciding the nature of tactics or technique to adopt. This point is emphasised by Roger Haywood in stating that "the programme of activity to achieve the agreed public relations objectives will be constructed using a number of techniques. Some of these will be well established, others more innovative. Creative public relations are introducing new ideas all the time. The fact that a particular method is well proven does not mean that it should be rejected for something more novel. Equally, just because an idea is new, does not mean that it is better"[7]. In relation to the military, the same approach on a particular well used technique by the military was emphasised by John Swomley. As he puts it, "public relations techniques are used also for more general purposes. Various programmes are utilised, as befits the need. One such programme is intended to keep the industrial allies of the military informed so that public opinion may be properly moulded..."[8].

Although strategies and tactics applied to public relations in overall terms may serve a common purpose, there are those that are particularly peculiar to some professions, including the military. In the military also, the target very much determines the mode of tactics for a public relations programme. For example in the United States Air Force, the Internal Information Division has a twofold strategic objective: "(1) to support the Air Force wide internal information objectives; and (2) to provide for general support of the information function at all levels of command"[9]. To achieve such objectives the military employ means such as formal instructions, informal briefings and talks, military newspapers and magazines, bulletin boards and displays, films and motion pictures, Armed Forces radio and Television programmes, and informal military avenues of communication such as `Durbars' and `Commanders Call".

News or Press Conference

For external publics, public relations tactics are also applied, following from an overall established strategic objective. In this regard, the first tactics that may be considered is the News Conference. This is an aspect of media relations that is often regarded as the most important part of public relations. Sam Black describes press or media relations as being essentially a two-way operation. "It is the link between an organisation and a press, radio and television news and newsreels. On the one hand, the organisation supplies information and provides facilities to the press on request, and on the other it takes steps to initiate comment and news. Confidence and respect between an organisation and the press are the necessary basis for good press relations"[10]. A news conference, therefore, provides a good opportunity through which to convey some vital information to the media. Judicious use of news conference may be made by the military as it will not only offer opportunities to media representatives to ask questions and clarify issues about the military, but equally serve as a useful forum for providing some necessary background to some military activities for the media.

Media Reception

Following the above aspect closely is the Media Reception programme. Occasional forums of this nature are essential to bring the media into the military environment for socializing and, entertainment. The aim here is to promote and enhance good relations. Such receptions could be arranged deliberately for the media, or they could be any of occasional social events such as a Military Cocktail reception or dinner to which they may be invited. The basis of all these may not necessarily be that there is some news information to be obtained, but rather that opportunities may be available for the media representatives to engage senior military officers in informal discussion. This could help to achieve better military media relationship. The Media Reception is therefore an aspect of public relations hospitality and is highly recommended for the purpose of promoting goodwill. It is a programme that should be organised very naturally as, according to Sam Black, "the art of hospitality in business should be exactly the same as it is in private life. True hospitality does not seek to buy friendship; it is the background to the establishment of a cordial and lasting relationship. Critics of public relations insinuate that it consist mainly of wining and dining and of entertaining lavishly to curry favour or to place other people under an obligation. This type of behaviour does occur at times in the world of business but it is definitely not a part of public relations practice."[11].

Lectures and Seminars

Lectures and seminars organized occasionally also constitute another tactics behind military public relations. This may be done to involve not only top military officers and senior executives of the Defence Ministry, but also involves experts from the civilian public to take part. The focus is usually on military issues and arrangements made for adequate media coverage. This aspect is very common in the United States where the Industrial College of the Armed Forces has a system of travelling national security seminars on board Air Force Jets, and on naval sea cruises. These are accompanied equally with generous entertainment of some sort. In these programmes, leaders and senior officers of the military reserve, who are themselves largely drawn from the business and professional community, are the frequent and important participants.

Conferences

A further technique that is related to the above is that of organising of conferences. In the United States, it is called the `Orientation Conference', the purpose of which is to sell the national military establishment and its programme to the important opinion forming leaders invited to attend. It is a very popular and effective strategy which John Swomley comments upon: "The officer who developed this technique must have known his psychology, for it is extremely difficult for a person not to be friendly to anything military after several days as a guest of the military, with Colonels opening and shutting doors for him, and various demonstrations, boat rides, plane rides, etc being put on just for his benefit... even if a person attending one of these orientation conferences disagreed with military policy, having once accepted the invitation ... he could not denounce the military convincingly. It is an effective technique"[12].

Facility Visits

Media Facility visits organized for the media to military establishments equally constitute another dimension. The advantage of such visits is based on the tendency that people get more easily impressed by what they see and feel than from what they hear, or are told of in relation to problems of the armed forces. It is organised to comprise representatives from various groups of the media,- press and electronic medium reporters, photographers and others. This certainly may be a good means by which to secure the interest and cooperation of the media, which is then well placed to inform and educate the government and the general public on military problems.

Speeches and Interviews

The media may also be made use of by the military in several other ways. This includes publishing inspiring news stories which may serve the vested interests of one or more branches of the armed services. Speeches and interviews by top military officers to selected group of reporters could also be arranged, thereby generating for reputable magazines, feature articles conveying the military view point which are written by people outside the military, or by retired officers who are less accountable than those on active duty. Furthermore, private briefing of writers and editors by some civilian consultant to the military may be undertaken in addition to building goodwill among columnists and reporters as well as publishers.

Advertising

Direct advertising and promotion is another technique that is used in military public relations. These may be done in relation to the specific military objectives of building support and prestige, in addition to advertising for recruiting purposes. Recruiting advertisements in modern times tend to rely much more in playing up aspects of the military such as career opportunities, educational training, foreign adventure, and the glamorous aspects of military life. This is in contrast to previous styles which had always tended to invoke the patriotic spirits in youths through the injunction, "your nation needs you".

A lot of money is usually expended by the military on advertising and promotional programmes especially in Britain and the United States where the Pentagon and the military services are counted among the heaviest annual spenders on advertising. Given such enormous expenditures by the armed services and, often, their industrial allies on advertising, John Swomley reiterates that "it is not surprising that the newspapers and magazines of the nation tend to cooperate with rather than oppose military policies that kept the cold war going"[13]. This, however, does not discount the value of advertisements placed by the military in those periods.

Special Events

The military equally uses Special Events as another of its tactics. They include military ceremonies such as parades on Army, Navy, or Air Force Days, or during other occasions such as presentation of Regimental Colours to Regiments, Military Tattoos, and such as, in France, the transfer of command from one officer to another which is conducted in public view. There is also the aspect of memorial services to the fallen in war which have "a spiritual dimension, whilst also serving a more practical purpose to keep armed services and the need for security in the public eye"[14].

For special events, every avenue that can be used is identified and exploited; for example, arrangements may be made to liaise with national organisations to arrange military exhibits at national, regional or local fairs. Another such aspect that is effectively employed by the Nigerian Army is to invite top civil personalities and the general public to events such as *wasa cultural activities* where varieties of Nigerian dances are featured annually. There are also the Army Inter-Formational Sports Meets as well as Small Arms Target Shooting Competitions - an event in which civilians participate and to whom such shooting practices are something of a novelty.

A very effective technique of military public relations work is done by using military bands to perform at various functions. This is not confined to military activities alone but also for civil functions at national, regional and community levels. Sometimes the band is even called to perform at international engagements, such as the Commonwealth Games, Olympic Games and African Nations Soccer Competitions. In addition, sports also provide another public relation opportunity as it is an area where members of the military and civilians can meet to compete on equal terms. In Nigeria, members of the armed forces compete in the biennial National Sports Festivals. Military personnel of many nations also represent their countries in big sports meetings such as the Olympic Games, and when military athletes do achieve victory, deliberate effort is made by the military to play up their contributions.

Historical Relics and Monuments

The military have a good reputation in many nations in terms of having a good and keen sense of history, especially military history. They are known all over the world to respect the past through the remembrance and propping up of fallen heroes. Military Museums the world over, attest to the collection of many past military relics and war artefacts. Their value in the military, apart from enhancing *esprit de corps*, very importantly preserves the links between military communities, Museums in their locations and the local population. These Museums are sources of attraction both for local, national and international tourists that visit them. Their importance also bears on good relationships in drawing civilians and military personnel closer. As Henry Stanhope points out in relation to the British National Army Museum, "...it is very much a shop window for the Army - an antique shop perhaps but one which plays a part in maintaining good civil military relations"[15].

Military Aid to Civil Authority (MACA)

Perhaps a more visible impressionistic and seemingly most important and realistic public relations strategy in the military relates to operations in which the military provides assistance to the public during disasters. Such occasions may involve providing air and sea rescues, hostage rescues, rescues from earth quake crumbles, and the like, at various times. An aspect closely related to this is that of providing Civil Aid. This is expanded upon by Henry Stanhope in noting that that "the army also has a peace time role which entails giving Military Aid to Civil Authorities (MACA). This means backing up the government, central or local, in anything from internal security to building a children's playground. In many third world countries where the army is the only available kind of loyal, skilled manpower this is the only contribution it can make. In Britain, civil aid is divided into three main sections. One is Military Aid to Civil Power (MACP), another is Civil Aid to the Civil Ministry (MACM), and the third is Military Aid to the Civil Community (MACC). Not all, however, provide the kind of publicity that the MOD likes to make use of"[16].

Community Relations

Community relations programmes or community affairs programmes as also referred to are other aspects to public relations strategies. Militaries all over the world are very conscious of this. As identified by Robert Reilly, one aspect of community affairs programmes is the outreach into local problems. Military personnel- particularly reserve units-have been in evidence at disaster sites, such as floods or tornadoes: they have furnished trucks and supplies, picked up stranded persons via helicopter, helped move library books, provided toys for orphans, supervised summer camps, and built playgrounds. Not only do these acts constitute good public relations, they also put into practice some of the tools the military employs best-manpower and organization. Every plan for a field exercise, disaster, emergency or actual war situation includes the PR function - everything from setting up of reception centres for media to fill-in-the-blanks advance release forms[17].

References

1. Momah Sam, "Global Strategy: From its Genesis to the Post-Cold War Era, quoted in AjaAkpuru – Aja, (1999) **Policy & Strategic Studies**, Abakaliki, Willy Rose, P. 1
2. Carl von Clausewitz, On War vols 1&11 cited in AjaAkpuru-Aja (Ibid)
3. AjaAkpuru-Aja, "Issues in Contemporary Defence and Strategic Studies" Un Published Manuscript (quoted) Ibid
4. Jonathan Green, The A – Z of Nuclear Jargon (quoted) Ibid
5. www.terena.org/activities/tf-pr/
6. Cutlip, S.M. et al (1985) **Effective Public Relations** 6th ed New Jersey, Prentice Hall Inc., p.235
7. Haywood, R. (1991) **All About Public Relations,** 2nd ed, new York, McGraw-Hill, p.193
8. Smomley, J.M. (1964) **The Military Establishment**, Boston, Beacon press, P. 117
9. Stephenson, H. (1960) **Handbook of Public Relations**, New York, McGraw-Hill,, p.795
10. Black, Sam, (1966) **Practical Public Relations**, London, Sir Isaac Pitman, p.31
11. Ibid, P. 133
12. Haywood, R, Op cit P.119 and 121
13. Ibid, P. 121
14. Edmonds, M. (1988) **Armed Services and Society**, Leicester U.P., p. 130
15. Stanhope, H. (1979) **The Soldiers**, London, Hamish Hamilton, p. 308
16. Ibid, p. 298
17. Robert Reilly, (1987) **Public Relations in Action**, Prentice-Hall, Englewood Cliffs, New Jersey, P. 527

Part Three

Public Perception and Nigerian Military, Public Relations Practice and Training

CHAPTER NINE

PUBLIC PERCEPTION AND ITS MANAGEMENT BY THE NIGERIAN MILITARY

Introduction

It is perhaps apposite to premise the discussion of this chapter on the assertion that in a democracy, the level of trust that the people have in their armed forces is a measure of the quality of the civil-military relationship. The armed forces in fact have the responsibility of ensuring that they gain public confidence and respect as distrust by the civil population will lead to illegitimacy and question public expenses on forces[1]. Public perception on an issue relating to an individual or group aggregates usually out of public opinion which by itself constitutes cumulative individual attitudes or beliefs that people generally hold. It can be defined as collection of beliefs and/or opinions held by people of diverse backgrounds. Public perception is therefore, an issue that cannot and should not be taken for granted. While individual organisations may strive to do the right things for the right reasons, public perception of the establishment as a whole can make those things much more challenging to put into motion. Public perception can affect how people think about you, your product or establishment[2].

The correction or mitigation of negative public perception or any effort to talk about improving the image of the military or of any complex organization must be premised on the fact that the image of a person or an establishment is not only the way they appear to the people but most importantly, the manner by which such image is projected out. This could be done through cultivation of friendship, establishment of goodwill and through promotion of self or organization. The image factor to a person or institution constitutes its whole being or essence. This explains why some persons or organizations when the need arises will take or seek measures that may include legal to correct or restore anything that will tend to distort or suggest a negative imputation to an existing image status[3]. Outside of seeking to maintain an image status quo, organizations continually seek to improve on their image, and correct extant negative perceptions with their clientele publics. Roger Haywood, an image expert noted the importance of image building and improvement with the assertion that an organization which succeeds without a good image is as likely as say, a sales man, a politician, a lawyer or any other professional persuader succeeding without personality. The importance of personality or good image is such that there are a few organizations that have such a revolutionary product or unassailable monopoly or privileged role in society that they can afford not to bother about making friends and influencing people[4].

The military is a unique institution of society that is well recognized to be performing a legitimate and privileged role in society. Yet the Armed forces of many nations have over time, come to recognize as well as appreciate not only the immense potential of image making by its ordinary meaning, but also of recognizing the need to continue to sway perceptions as well as improve on their image. The military to that extent especially in the developed nations have developed elaborate mechanisms by which to keep themselves in the "public eye". Stanhope, in relation to the British, asserted that the British Army needed to strengthen its links with the outside society, because it must do so or civilians would know nothing of the Army outside those glossy recruitment advertisements which few people seriously believe. If it did not bother to cultivate these contacts, it will be forgotten until the next war broke out[5]. Negative public perception for an elaborate organization as the military could have unfathomable consequences and therefore the constant need to continue to monitor and gauge it. Dennis Wilcox elaborates further on this aspect by his postulation that the primary area of corporate public relations work rest essentially on reputation protection and enhancement. It involves pressing and building goodwill for a company by demonstrating to the public that the firm is efficient, honest, fair and equitable... and a responsible corporate citizen[6]. Monitoring and gauging of public opinion and indeed of public perception is therefore very crucial to all institutions so as to facilitate the adoption of counter measure processes of corrections for proper perception management.

Organizations use perception management in daily internal and external interactions as well as prior to major product/strategy introductions and following events of crisis. Life cycle models of organizational development suggest that the growth and ultimate survival of a firm is dependent on how effectively business leaders navigate crisis, or crisis-like events through their life cycles[7]. As some studies have suggested, organizational perception management involves actions that are designed and carried out by organizational spokespersons to influence audiences' perceptions of the organization. This definition is based on the understanding of four unique components of organizational perception management: perception of the organization; actions or tactics; organizational spokespersons; and organizational audiences[8].

Key Words and their Meanings

Perception

The meaning of perception as provided in the Hyper Dictionary is to become aware of something via the senses, the process of perceiving, knowledge gained by perceiving, a way of conceiving something, the representation of what is perceived[9]. Wikipedia sees it as the process of attaining awareness or understanding of the environment by organizing and interpreting sensory information. All perception involves signal in the nervous system, which in turn result from physical stimulation of the nervous organs...

perception can be shaped by learning, memory or expectation... it involves top-down effects as well as the bottom-up process of processing sensory input[10].

Public Perception

The social phenomenon known as *public perception* can be seen as the difference between an absolute truth based on facts and a virtual truth shaped by popular opinion, media coverage and/or reputation. Celebrities, politicians and corporations all face the same scrutiny by the public they serve, and it can be very difficult to overcome a negative public perception[11]. During the 2008 US presidential election campaign, for example, the two contending candidates from the Republican and Democratic parties both faced difficult public perception issues. The Republican candidate, John McCain, was often portrayed by media outlets as being too old for the position or too moderate politically to represent his entire political party. Democratic candidate Barack Obama also had difficulties with public perception, often portrayed as an Ivy League elitist or ineffectual Commander in Chief. Both men used public speeches and media interviews to overcome much of the negative public perception[12]. The public perception of say the police in most African societies is largely negative. Such perception may be based on accurate assessment of the police, presumptions or may be based on biased media reports and/or prejudice. The bottom line is that a negative public perception would make it more difficult for organisations to improve their image or make substantial changes[13]. The same also applies to political figures, military figures or celebrities.

Perception Management

This is a term originated by the US military. The Department of Defence (DOD) defines it as actions to convey and/or deny selected information and indicators to foreign audiences to influence their emotions, motives, and objective reasoning as well as to intelligence systems and leaders at all levels to influence official estimates, ultimately resulting in foreign behaviours and official actions favourable to the originator's objectives. In various ways, perception management combines truth projection, operations security, covert operation, deception, and psychological operations. Perception management was also known as public diplomacy in the Ronald Reagan era; however, some people also argue that perception management is now an accepted part of international strategic influence. There are different levels and aspects to a perception management process that includes those of individuals, groups or organizations[14].

Organizations use perception management in daily internal and external interactions as well as prior to major product/strategy introductions and following events of crisis. Life cycle models of organizational development suggest that the growth and ultimate survival of a firm is dependent on how effectively business leaders navigate crisis, or crisis-like events through their life cycles. As deduced from studies, organizational perception management involves actions that are designed and carried out by organizational spokespersons to influence audiences' perceptions of the organization[15].

Perception Management Events

Perception management is often used by an organization in dealing with perception-threatening situations such as scandals, accidents, product failures, controversial identity changes, upcoming performance reviews, and introduction of new identity or vision. It also relates to dealing with perception enhancing events such as positive/negative ranking or rating by industry groups, overcoming hardships, and achievement of desired goals. An example of perception management in relation to the US Department of Defence includes its use of sleight and deception as a means to achieving security goals. Deception and sleight of hand are important in gaining advantages in war, both to gain domestic support of the operations and for the military against the enemy. Although perception management is specifically defined as being limited to foreign audiences, critics of the DoD charge that it also engages in domestic perception management. An example cited is the prohibition of viewing or photographing the flag draped caskets of dead military as they are unloaded in bulk upon arrival in the US for further distribution, a policy only recently implemented[16].

The DoD also describes perception management as intent to provoke the behaviour you want out of a given individual. During the Cold War, the Pentagon sent undercover US journalists to Russia and Eastern Europe to write pro-American articles for local media outlets. A similar situation occurred in Iraq in 2005 when the US military covertly paid Iraqi newspapers to print stories written by US soldiers; these stories were geared towards enhancing the appearance of the US mission in Iraq. Domestically, during the Vietnam War, the Pentagon exaggerated communist threats to the United States in order to gain more public support for an increasingly bloody war. This was similarly seen in 2003 with the government's embellishment of the threat and existence of weapons of mass destruction in Iraq. More recently, the US government has used perception management techniques to promote the belief that weapons of mass destruction were indeed being manufactured in Iraq, and that Iraq had aided and assisted the Al-Quaeda terrorists responsible for the September11, 2001 attacks upon the World Trade Centre. These "facts" were, in part, the government's justification for invading Iraq and beginning the war[17].

Public perception of the Nigerian Military

It may not be out of place to state categorically that public perception of the military in Nigeria from the period of colonial rule through independence to the present day has not been very much on a friendly and respectable note. This cannot be divorced from the manner of evolvement of the military which as well known, was formed to serve the interest of the British colonial masters for the protection essentially of her economic interests. During the colonial era, it is on record that indigenous soldiers were used to conquer and subjugate their own people for the establishment of imperial rule and in the process many of the natives were brutalized. This generated hatred and bitterness for the soldiers with consequent distrust between the military and the populace. This was a characteristic of the nature of civil-military relationship in northern Nigeria. Giving assertion to this position, Sir Ahmadu Bello, late Premier of

Northern Nigeria was once quoted to have said that "we do not like the soldiers, they were our own people, and had conquered us for strangers and defeated our people on the plains just before us. Such feelings were common all over the North"[18].

In the southern parts of Nigeria especially the eastern parts, the army was perceived as a vocation for illiterates with brusque behaviour. They were equally not liked by the civil populace in those areas. Public perception thus of the military from this period up till independence in 1960 did not fare any better especially given the pattern of civil military relations. From 1960-1999, Nigeria had experience of direct military ruler ship spanning six regimes with a cumulative total ruling period of 29 years. This meant that by 1999 when Nigeria was 39 years of age, the military had ruled for a total of 29 out of 39 years and thus with only 10 years' experience of civilian rule: a situation which till date is a sore point of bitterness with the military by the civilian populace[19].

As Zabadi asserted in this regard, since the NA made the mistake of invading the Nigerian political space to govern, it has ended up sacrificing its uniqueness as an institution founded on the high ideals of nationalism, patriotism and political neutrality, among others. The coup d'etat of January 15 1966 opened the floodgates to the divisive factors of ethnicity, regionalism and now sectarianism to enter the barracks and make their homes. Successive military administrations only seemed to erode the espirit de corps which existed among them[20]. Adebajo along the same line also noted that, it would seem that the only distinguishing feature between the barracks and the larger society is the uniform. For the most part, people on both sides of the divide think alike and probably act alike. Therefore, the failure of the military to rid society of the ills for which they sacked the civilians who were elected to rule while keeping monopoly over the political space, only turned the public against them. As we have indicated above, the pro-democracy struggle resulting from the annulment of the June 12 presidential elections was the highpoint of not only the rejection of military rule, but also of the military. One area in which this was also demonstrated was the lack of public support for Nigeria's involvement in the wars in Liberia and later Sierra Leone, through the ECOWAS Monitoring Group (ECOMOG). Even with the many lives that were being lost as a result of NA operations in this area, the public seemed unconcerned[21].

Thus with Nigeria's return to democratic rule in 1999, the extent of the low perception of the NA became very visible. When the new government immediately retired all officers who had held political offices, this move was hailed. Some of the new civilian political leaders even attempted to throw their new-found power in the face of the military. For instance, a motion was moved in the House of Representatives by a member who was himself ex-army, to the effect that the presence of military barracks within Abuja Central area was dangerous for democracy: they should be relocated outside of the place to border areas.

The attempt to deny former military Heads of State recognition as deserving to enjoy the privileges accorded former Presidents by the 1999 Constitution was part of this low image of the military[22]. The 'travails' of the military continued with the speech of President Obasanjo delivered at the graduation of Participants of the National War College in August 1999 in which the 'riot act' was read and indicating that the military would be down-sized. The issue of down-sizing caused a lot of apprehension in the military, including the use of the American Military Professional Resources Incorporated (MPRI) and the Operation Focus Relief to start off a transformation process. Furthermore, the new political masters did not immediately seem favourably disposed to funding the military which had also suffered under military rule as an institution[23].

The return to civil rule in Nigeria witnessed security challenges in virtually all parts of the country of which paradoxically, the NA became the main instrument which the government used in addressing the internal security challenges ...The period since 1999 has witnessed the rise of militia and terrorist groups from the Niger Delta to the North East corner of Nigeria. Apart from terrorism, there were many cases of communal, ethnic, religious and ethno-religions violent conflicts which still persist today. The NA has been permanently engaged in internal security operations in all these areas and in the process, has lost officers and men. Some of these losses have come by way of brazen attacks by some of the militia and terrorist groups, on the NA troops deployed on these operations[24].

In all these situations, the NA received more condemnation for the actions taken than the expected gratitude from the public. In some of the cases, the NA was seen by one side or the other in the conflict as part of the problem rather than a welcome help out of the situation. The low point of this was the sight of citizens of Dogo Nahawa "chasing" NA soldiers out of their village who were there on duty. This indifference, at best to the NA is also demonstrated in the lack of public support for troops who go on peacekeeping especially when they die in action. We do not see the kind of support which the British public gives to their own troops who they see as having gone out there to represent them. Therefore, it is clear that public perception of the NA remains poor and something has to be done to change it. The NA needs to take action like other service-providers mentioned above, to win the public to its side[25].

The above reference even if made in relation to the Nigerian Army indeed covers the entire Nigerian Military as a corporate entity. It is in realization of such negative perception for the Nigerian Military that Air Vice Marshal Paul Dike, as Chief of Defence Staff made some cogent remarks. He noted that for the Nigerian military, which has added the challenges of professionalization to gain citizen confidence and support in the aftermath of prolonged military rule and to optimize operational efficiency, community relations approach towards winning the hearts and minds of the people was necessary. This was necessary because, rigid and fixed mind-sets and perceptions have made it difficult for many civilians and civilian groups to appreciate the noble roles of the military and its steady transformation into a pro-people, citizen-friendly and responsive institution since the return to democratic rule in 1999. The costs of the attendant civil-military dissonance are all too obvious[26]. Following similar line, Air Marshal Oluseyi Petinrin, who succeeded Air Vice Marshal Dike as Chief of Defence Staff has continued to harp on the need for the military to get properly subordinated to civil authority in order to regain public trust and confidence. It is to that extent that issues bothering on civil military relations are now being taken very seriously by the Nigerian Military with the defence Headquarters pioneering the establishment of a Department of Civil Military Relations headed by Major general D.M. Chong. The Department in living up to its mandate has organized series of workshops and seminars for members of the Armed Forces to which other stakeholders in the civil sector including the press were invited. The seminar among others are to foster better and closer cooperation between the Armed Forces and their civilian counterparts as well as engender better understanding of the democratic process for the military including the essence of the military being subject to civil control.

The Nigerian Army has similarly opened a Department of Civil Military Affairs at the instance of the Chief of Army Staff, Lt General O.A. Ihejirika. The Department is headed by Major General B.V.T. Kwaji as Chief of Civil Military Affairs. The Department has been sensitizing troops and the general public on thematic issues relating to civil military relations and organized a very successful and well acclaimed seminar on public perception of the Nigerian Army with a view to charting a way forward. The Chief of Naval Staff, Vice-Admiral O. S. Ibrahim and the Chief of Air Staff, Air Vice Marshal Mohammed Umar have both equally established Departments of Civil Military Relations in the Nigerian Navy and Nigerian Air Force respectively, with the mission of reorienting personnel along appropriate civil military relations tenets.

Nigerian Military Management of Public Perception

The management of negative public perception towards it especially arising out of its many years of political governance during military regime was handled by the Nigerian Army Public Relations Department. This was carried out under four levels of objectives. The objectives as outlined were set to Fulfil its own Nigerian Army objectives

- To fulfil the objectives of the military government in power
- To fulfil Armed Forces objectives and,
- To fulfil International Military objectives especially in relation to peacekeeping[27].

The Nigerian Army Public Relations Directorate as the foremost branch of military public relations vigorously took on this challenge by reaching the civil populace through formal and informal channels of communication to relate with and to explain the military's point of view on all issues that tended to paint the military in bad light and which also engendered negative public perception of the military. Although public relations or image building during military regime is very tasking and complex, General Fred Chijuka, a prominent military spokesman during those trying periods to a large extent, acquitted himself well in doing a yeo man's job of that difficult assignment. Public perception for the military since return to civil rule since May 1999 even if with the military's involvement in many internal security duties across the country with some unpleasant experiences by civilians, has no doubt seen a great deal of improvement resulting in some measure of positive public perception rating for the Nigerian military.

Engendering More Positive Perception for the Military

While the US Department of Defence as part of its strategy uses sleight and deception as a means of achieving its security goals including boosting its advantages in war, and of gaining domestic support for its military operations, the Nigerian military should be able to fathom its own modes, means and approaches especially in this era of democracy when the military has set for itself, appreciable agenda of military transformation and of restoring professionalism to the forces. Zabadi attests to the fact that in a democracy, the people are the sovereign and their will rules. The people can make government; they can also unmake it through the use of their votes. They also have other instruments by which to apply pressure on government through their representatives to cause change in policy or action of government or any of its departments. Therefore, it is important to have the people on one's side in the political terrain of 'who gets what, when and how'. The Nigerian Army, indeed the military, being an instrument of policy in the hand of the state, must actively cultivate the friendship of the people. With the people behind it, they always get the support they need as is common in most advanced democracies[28].

As to what needs to be done, he enjoins that the Nigerian military must be seen to be subordinated to civil and civilian control. This is important considering Nigeria's history of long military rule[29]. This subordination "must be broad, to the entire governmental structure, not simply to the president or prime minister who exercises command... Accountability to the Parliament or to the legislature implies accountability to the populace"[30]. As Zabadi equally posited, this should strengthen national defence by reinforcing military identification with the people and popular identification with the military. A related issue is the need for the military to remain neutral for it is necessary to demonstrate practically that soldiers can be trusted to be neutral servants of the state and guardians of society, in the way they carry out internal security operations. It will remain involved in internal security management for the foreseeable future; therefore, it must refrain and condition its troops to be very professional in their actions. It... equally needs to take drastic action to stamp out any signs or expression of ethnic or sectarian sentiments... be a cohesive national institution in the service of Nigeria and not a section thereof. This attitudinal change must be relentlessly pursued in the context of the current transformation programme[31]. It is thus quite clear from the foregoing that the Nigerian Military needs in overall terms to attach a high level of importance to public perception of its institutional image at all times. The military therefore needs to plan and implement programmes on a sustainable basis in order to engender favourable public disposition for the military.

References

1. Adamolekun, W. "Sustainable Public Relations Strategies to enhance the Operations of the Nigerian Air Force", A lead Paper presented at Nigerian Air Force Seminar on Proactive Public Relations in the NAF in July 2010.

2. Zabadi, I.S. "Public Perception of the Nigerian Army in a Democracy: The Way Forward" A paper presented at the Nigerian Army Workshop on "Enhancing Civil-Military Relations to meet Contemporary Challenges of the Nigerian Army in a Democratic Environment", held at the Headquarters of 2 Division, Nigerian Army, Ibadan, 11 - 13 June 2011

3. Adache John, "Improving the Image of the Army in a Democratic Dispensation: Significance", Presentation at Capacity Building Workshop for Defence Correspondents at Yenagoa, Bayelsa State, 16-18 May, 2007.

4. Haywood Roger, (1990) **All About Public Relations,** London: McGraw-Hill, P. 3

5. Henry Stanhope, (1979) **The Soldiers**, London: Hamish Hamilton, P. 295

6. Wilcox, Dennis, et al, (1989) **Public Relations: Strategies and Tactics,** New York, Harper& Row P. 319

7. http://en.wikipedia.org/wiki/perception_management

8. Ibid

9. http://www.hyperdictionary.com/dictionary/perception

10. http:/en.wikipedia.org/wiki/perception

11. http://www.wisegeek.com/what-is-public-perception.htm

12. Ibid

13. Wisegeek, "Public Perception", http://www.wisegeek.com/what-is-public-perception.htm

14. http://en.wikipedia.org/wiki/perception_management

15. Ibid

16. Ibid

17. Ibid

18. Nwolise, O.B.C., "Democratic Control of the Military: The Nigerian Experience in Nigerian Forum, NIIA vol 23, Nos 11-12, Nov-Dec, Lagos, NIIA, P. 138

19. Ibid

20. Zabadi, I.S. "Public Perception of the Nigerian Army in a Democracy: The Way Forward"

21. Adekeye Adebajo, "Mad Dogs and Glory: Nigeria's Interventions in Liberia and Sierra Leone", quoted in I.S. Zabadi, (Ibid)

22. Zabadi, I.S. Op cit

23. Ibid

24. ibid
25. Ibid
26. Air Vice Marshal Paul Dike in Onwudiwe E. & Osaghae (eds) (2010) **Winning Hearts and Minds: A Community Relations Approach for the Nigerian Military,** (Ibadan, John Archer Pub) P. V
27. Nwolise, O.B.C. "Public Relations Tools for Maximising Objectives in the Nigerian Army", lecture delivered at Directorate of Army Public Relations Training Period, Ibadan, 22-27 December, 1991.
28. I.S. Zabadi, Op cit
29. Istifanus S. Zabadi, "Civil-Military Relations in a Democracy, in Sani L. Mohammed (eds) (2006) Civil and Security Agencies relationship: Role of the Military in Consolidating Democracy in Nigeria. Abuja: Friedrich Ebert Stiftung,
30. Richard H. Kohn, "An Essay in Civilian Control of the Military" in I.S. Zabadi, "Public Perception of the Nigerian Army in a Democracy: The Way Forward" Op cit
31. I.S. Zabadi (Ibid)

CHAPTER TEN

PUBLIC RELATIONS PRACTICE IN THE NIGERIAN MILITARY

Introduction

The Nigerian Military comprises of the Nigerian Army, Nigerian Navy and the Nigerian Air Force. The three Services are under the Ministry of Defence (MOD) which has institutional as well as constitutional responsibility for their administration. The Ministry also has under its ambit, the Defence Headquarters (DHQ) which was created in 1980. The creation of the DHQ was predicated on the need to have a central purely military organ of Higher Defence Management in the Nigerian Armed Forces whose primary role would among others, revolve around coordinating and harmonizing the activities of the three services. Nigeria's National Defence Policy (NNDP) indeed provides that the chain of command for the planning and conduct of military operations flows from the National Defence Council (NDC) to the Honourable Minister of Defence (HMOD), and to the Chief of Defence Staff (CDS). The chain of command proceeds further down from the CDS to either the Service Chiefs or the Commander of a Joint Task Force (Comd. JTF). The NNDP specifically states that control of the Armed Forces, their joint operations and training shall rest with the CDS, who shall also coordinate the three Services[1]. Under the DHQ also are the tri-service training institutions namely, Nigerian Defence Academy (NDA), the Armed Forces Command and Staff College (AFCSC), and the National Defence College (NDC). The DHQ, the three Services and the tri-Service institutions all have functional Public Relations/Information offices embedded within them at various levels and hierarchies of command.

Public relations are a profession with universal message and appeal, nature and practice. It is therefore suitable for application to every segment of the human society and to both simple and complex organizations. There are however, differences between military public relations and civil public relations. As earlier pointed out in chapter 2, whereas, commercial, corporate and institutional public relations are based on the free market enterprise concepts of marketing a product or service for a private organization, military public relations programmes exist to provide information and to maintain awareness and concern for public opinion regarding an organization that is owned and operated by and for the citizenry[2].While civil public relations practitioners are answerable to the management of their company, the consumers and to some

77

extent the shareholders, the military PR officers are answerable to their commands, services, the defence ministry, the president and through the government, to the citizenry[2]. Although military PR officers fully recognize and appreciate the public's right and need to know often championed by the mass media, military PR officers have to operate in the interest of the same public by keeping the public informed only within the limitations of security, accuracy, propriety and policy[3].

The story of public relations evolvement and practice in the Services including DHQ is not far-fetched and therefore not divorced from the individual history and development of the Services themselves. Similar to what obtains in the armed forces of other nations especially those of the Western world whose military values, hierarchy and tradition the Armed Forces of Nigeria had imbibed over the years, public relations/ Information branches in the armed forces of these nations did not evolve at the same time. With regards to the British Army, Allan Hooper noted that as the impact of the media is gradually being acknowledged by the armed forces, so the importance of the public relations organizations is being recognized as well. However, the speed of recognition and the acknowledgement of the importance vary within the three Services and there is a variation of attitude within each service[4]. Similar experience of the historical evolution of public relations/information departments is applicable equally to the Pentagon – the defence department of the United States under which falls the US Army, Navy, Air Force and the Marine Corps respectively.

The Nigerian Armed Forces have come to appreciate and to accord recognition to the importance, role and relevance of public relations in their operations as specified in the Nigerian constitution. Deriving from this, the National Defence Policy indeed appreciate the essence of media relations, a critical instrumentality of public relations practice which the policy suggests could be used by the armed forces for orderly reporting of events to the Nigerian public[5]. Subsequent parts of this chapter thus focus on the nature, scope and form of public relations practice by the three Services and the Defence Headquarters in the Nigerian Military.

The Nigerian Army:

The Nigerian Army's history dates back to 1863, when Lt Glover of the Royal Navy selected 18 indigenes from the Northern part of the country and organized them into a local force, known as the "Glover Hausas". The small force was used by Glover as governor of Lagos to mount punitive expeditions in the Lagos hinterland and to protect trade routes around Lagos. In 1865, the "Glover Hausas" became a regular force with the name "Hausa Constabulary." It performed both police and military duties for the Lagos colonial government. It later became "Lagos constabulary. On incorporation into the West African Frontier Force (WAFF) in 1901, it became the "Lagos Battalion". In addition to this force, the British Government included the Royal Niger Company (RNC), Constabulary Force in Northern Nigeria in 1886 and oil Rivers Irregular in 1891[6].

In 1889, Lord Fredrick Lugard had formed incipient body of what was to be known in 1890, as the West African Frontier Force, (WAFF), in Jebba, Northern Nigeria. The new unit expanded by absorbing the Northern Nigeria – based element of the Royal Niger Company (RNC) Constabulary. By the end of 1901, it had incorporated all para-military units in the other British dependencies into its command, thus fully meriting its designation "WAFF". The establishment of West African Frontier Force (WAFF) led to the merger of all units into a regiment in each of the dependencies. The merger in Nigeria produced the Northern Nigerian Regiment and Southern Nigerian Regiments. With the amalgamation of Nigeria in 1914, by Lord Lugard, the unification of the Northern and Southern Regiments came into being and this witnessed the birth of Nigerian Regiments.

The Northern Nigerian Regiment became the 1st and 2nd Battalions of the Nigerian Regiment, while the Southern Nigerian Regiment became the 3rd and 4th Battalions of the Nigerian Regiment (NR). The Mounted infantry of the Northern Regiment became an ordinary Infantry Battalion after the Second World War. A field artillery also existed within the Nigerian Regiment. With the visit of Queen Elizabeth of Britain between 28th January and 15th February, 1956, the Nigerian Regiment was renamed the Queens own Nigerian Regiment (QONR). Also in the same year, the regionalization of the WAFF came into existence and each Military force became independent of the other. As a result, the QONR became the Nigerian Military force (NMF). By 1st June, 1958, the British Army Council in London relinquished control of the NMF to the Nigerian Government. In 1960, when Nigeria became independent, the NMF became known as the Royal Nigerian Army (RNA). When Nigeria became a republic, the RNA changed to the Nigerian Army. In the same year, the Army Uniform, rank structure and instruments from those of RWAFF to new ones including green khaki uniform[7].

Directorate of Army Public Relations

The evolution of the Directorate of Army Public Relations (DAPR) and indeed of public relations practice in the Nigerian Army dating back to 1962 was highlighted in chapter one alongside the development of public relations in the United Kingdom and the United States Armed Forces. The Nigerian Army pioneered the establishment of public relations into the Nigerian Military. The rationale for its establishment stems amongst others from the realization that army public relations is a craft for the projection of the Nigerian Army; for the organization of a two-way communication between the Army and all the target publics to create understanding and support for the Army corporate objectives, policies and programmes. The practice of public relations demands a fair and inventive mind in the ever changing world of communication. The rationale further lies in the sophistication and awareness of the average Nigerian which has become so high that there is a demand to know all about government programmes of which they contribute to maintain. There is therefore the absolute need for a strong and virile public relations outfit to provide adequate awareness of Army programmes for the Nigerian Public. And also in realization that sustained effort by adequately trained public relations staff is imperative to achieve the Nigerian Army aim to produce a favourable image as well as support its programmes and ensure a feedback system[8].

In consonance with the above rationale, the pioneers and former Directors of Army Public relations, past Chiefs of Army Staff and top hierarchy personalities of the Army have always given serious attention and impetus to public relations. Brigadier E.F. Sotomi, pioneer Director of Military public Relations in the early 70s saw its establishment as recognition of the need to bring the army closer to the public so as to enable civilians have a clearer understanding of what the Army does for the nation. Besides, it also underscores the Army awareness of the influence of public opinion on human endeavour and behaviour[9]. Brigadier Fred Chijuka, a long standing former Director of Army Public Relations and also of Defence Information when it was established in later years remarked that Army public relations is quite critical for all global armies... public relations roles through command information, public information and even community relations amongst others, are all veritable channels of its practice, they are used to advance the interests and image of not just the Army but of the nation as well[10]. On the same note, Major General David Ejoor, a former Chief of Staff, Army in his assertion noted that the extent to which the Army's contribution to national development is appreciated by the public depends largely on the esteem in which the soldiers are held, and this esteem is influenced by the level of understanding which the public or civilians have of our policy[11].

In his assertion, Vice Admiral J.E.A. Wey, a former Chief of Staff Supreme headquarters said that the army is often criticized by members of the public for one thing or the other. These criticisms are caused by lack of understanding resulting from the gap existing between the Army and the community. To bridge this gap, there is urgent need for dynamic public relations in the Nigerian army. It is indeed a desirable and welcome innovation[12]. Also in his view, General Ibrahim Babangida, a former Chief of Army Staff and former Head of State, Commander-in-Chief, reiterated the critical role of public relations in fostering and sustaining a lasting understanding in the relationship between nations and peoples. We have witnessed political ideas and systems, long held as indubitable, give way to new and more liberal ideas and systems which allows for the free interaction of individuals and groups, soldiers and non-soldiers. These processes are enhanced through public relations[13]. These statements clearly highlights and underscore the essence, relevance and importance of public relations not just for the army or military but for all complex organizations in society.

Deriving therefore from the rationale for the institution of public relations and of its importance thereof, the Nigerian Army thus set out the following objectives /mission. It is among others to:

- To foster and maintain within the Army, a climate of understanding in which each member will be motivated to perform to the best of his ability.
- To increase public understanding of the Army's role in national security, social and economic development.
- Conducting a periodic reappraisal of the community relations situation and public attitude towards the Army to determine the best way of improving Army/ Civilian relationship.
- To develop an effective two-way channel of communication between the Army and the public, capitalizing on opportunities for better relations and resolving potential and actual areas of conflict.
- To serve as an instrument of psychological warfare during combat or emergency operations[14].

The Directorate of Army Public Relations in order to fulfil its objectives equally meet the ever increasing demand for information by Nigerians, has since its inception continued to undergo structural changes in consonance with Nigerian Army's Order of Battle (ORBAT), along with other branches of the Army. The DAPR has an elaborate organizational structure, patterned along its national institutional spread in the country. This approach, translated in practical terms, has seen public relations embedded inevitably at command level structures beginning from the apex at the Army Headquarters, Divisional formations, Brigades, Operational Task Forces and in Peace Keeping (PK) as well as Peace Support Operations (PSOs). It is interesting to note and remarkable that Military Public Relations indeed derived its very first roots from Nigeria's participation in its very first peace keeping operation in the Congo in 1963. Thereafter, through many other peace keeping missions including the United Nations Interim Force in Lebanon (UNIFIL), in 1978, to peace keeping missions in Chad, Yugoslavia, Somalia, Liberia, Sierra Leone and Darfur among others, public relations has always been part of Nigeria's mission. The contributions of army public relation activities to Nigeria's peace keeping missions abroad have been quite enormous as they have over time been able to relay back home, the performances and progress of Nigerian troops in mission areas through reports conveyed through print, photographs and through other graphic images.

Areas of Public Relations Practice

The NA Handbook on Public Relations practice categorized its areas of practice to include:

- Day to day or peace time PR
- Operation or war time PR.
- PR in adverse or emergency situation[15].

Specific functions of public relations are further highlighted as follows:

Day to Day Public Relations

The functions in peace time as stipulated include the following:

- Advising the Chief of Army Staff /General Officers Commanding GOsC/ Commanders on matter relating to socio – political and public affairs.
- Providing advice on matters of political/military affairs.
- Control and administration of civilians in occupied territory in conjunction with Military Police and Army Intelligence during war and emergency situations
- Providing advice on media and general matters.
- Liaising with media organizations for press release concerning the NA
- Designing and executing a 2 – way communication process to assist Commanders at durbar and other official matters[16].

Operational Public Relations

The functions as stipulated include:

- Planning and dissemination of war propaganda materials to gain public support as well as to gain support of international organizations.
- Provision of PR situation analysis as a good framework for disseminating effective information to the public.
- Preparing and coordinating PR situation reports which would assist the NA in psychological operations and planning
- Dissemination of information to the media about the battle situation on the need – to – know basis.
- Dissemination of news about war from other sectors to all formations and units using radio and television programmes of reputable media organizations.
- Collection, collating and dissemination of vital information and news as far as security permits. Such news could be in form of news sheet or newsletters.
- Establishing, manning and operating information centres at the Divisional and Brigade Headquarters or at an acceptable strategic spot in the field
- Assist in the manning of operation rooms.
- Preparing operational records and reports which may later form part of research materials for the Nigerian Army.
- Audio visual records and the photographs obtained during the war will also serve not only as research materials but also as training documents.
- Assist in the control and administration of the refugees and internally displaced persons (IDP) during emergencies and natural disasters.
- Establishment of PR centres in conjunction with Nigerian Navy (NN) and the Nigerian Air Force (NAF) information and PR departments for effective joint operation exercises.
- Building and maintenance of morale and confidence among civil populace (the tax payers) in time of emergencies and natural disasters.
- Operational PR is also the responsibility of the commanders at all levels and the DAPR officers of the formation/units. But the practice of PR is entirely the prerogative of the DAPR officer(s) of the particular formation/unit because they are experts in communication and PR strategy. The DAPR officer by his experience and training should always strive for professionalism and excellence in presenting the unit through the media to the general public. Therefore, direct contact with the public through the media remains, as it has always been the sole responsibility of the DAPR officer[17].

Aspects of the Practice

Aspects of PR practice in peace or war time, in adverse or emergency situations are conducted through Command Information channels, Public Information and Community Relations programmes. These are further elaborated upon:

Command Information

In this phase, instructions or orders come from the top hierarchy down the line... a link is established between the office of the Chief of Army Staff and the most junior rank in the army. Such orders that are not classified as secret are made to get to the soldiers and officers through Army Public relations publications especially the SOJA Newsletter.... It is through this process among others that gossips, rumour mongering and spread of fear and uncertainty are easily dispelled... free flow of information ensure constant relationship, promotes stability and guarantees stability and support for the leadership[18]..

Public Information

This aspect in relation to the role of public relations according to Chijuka comes to mind especially during military administrations as happened in the past because when the military was in government, the public became naturally more inquisitive about all aspects of the inside working of the military. This situation was inevitable as it was the responsibility of the military administration to be in constant touch with the different publics, so as to have control over all forms of rumour peddling and the unwholesome speculations that arose from time to time.[19]

Nwolise expands further on this aspect by his assertion that Army Public relations department through its activities was well placed to fully maximize the achievement of its objectives for the Nigerian Army. Such objectives he identifies as image polishing, goodwill promotion as well as advertising. He categorizes from this plank, four different categories of objectives to be pursued by the APRD on behalf of the Nigerian Army. The first of such objectives he classified as APRD Objectives which is to foster and maintain within the army, a climate of understanding in which each member was motivated to understand the army's role in national security, social and economic development. It also includes conducting periodic reappraisal of the community relations situation and public attitude towards the Army to determine the best way of improving Army-civilian relations. It further includes developing effective two way channel of communication between the army and the public, and resolving potential and actual areas of conflict, monitoring relations with foreign armies and serving as instrument of psychological warfare during combat or emergency operations[20].

The second level objective as also classified by Nwolise was military government objectives. Whenever as he put it, Nigeria came under military rule, the Army Public Relations Directorate took on additional responsibilities as it had to intermittently explain, promote, and defend the policies and programmes of the military government. The third level objectives are the armed forces objectives of which the APRD also was in the fore front. The armed forces objectives are those provided in the Nigerian constitution which the APRD was also better placed to explain. He further lists at the fourth level, the international military objectives. As he also explained, the APRD has four major publics to relate to: the army, the armed forces, the Nigerian citizens and the external environment (military and civil). Within the external environment, the specific public of significance to the APRD is made up of the armed forces of other nations. This is because; the APRD has to forge improved relations with the foreign forces[21]. Nwolise concludes by saying that APRD when applying public relations tools requires to bear in mind, the four levels of objectives in relation to the target audiences.

Community Relations

Community relations in the army as Chijuka viewed it was something near to the police community relations which involves the participation of the police personnel and local personalities in regulated dialogues to enable the police to do better than subsisting public judgments of its performance. This he recommends for the military too and should involve the Army, Police and selected members of the public to discuss problems that may come up from time to time among them. This will be most useful to civilians in particular, in that they can easily have a hearing whenever they feel molested... the military for its part has done very well in trying to remove fears from civilians by promoting common places of worship, interactions through cinema houses, mammy markets, provision of recreational facilities, and publications for both the military and the civilians to enjoy[22]. The Nigerian Army has however, gone beyond this primary level of community relations activities and is actively involved in so many aspects of community relations work deriving from the recognition that the Army across all sections is obligated to carry out community relations projects within its neighbourhoods all over the country.

Army Public Relations and Nigeria's 'New Democracy'

Nigeria's 51 years as an independent nation in political terms had been dominated by intermittent rule by the military for nearly a decade before her return to democratic governance in May 1999. With about 13 years of uninterrupted period of civil rule; a period dubbed by some analysts as Nigeria's new democracy, army personnel no doubt, have been able to embrace this new democratic dawn and its ideals and precepts. The Nigerian Army since 1999 has deliberately embarked on the reorientation of its manpower to ensure that prejudiced and negative public perception about the Army and its personnel are properly corrected. This is being achieved through deliberate training and retraining of its officers and men. The army through this avenue is seeking to restore discipline in the ranks and file and work to improve relations between soldiers and civilians in a country which over time had endured about three decades of military rule. According to General Danbazau, a former Chief of Army Staff, there is a manifest decline of discipline, regimentation, commitment, welfare, command and control ... throughout the Nigerian army, ... several forms of attitudinal problems have manifested in units and elsewhere throughout the Nigerian army. He stressed the need for officers and men of the Nigerian Army to cultivate a more robust relationship with the civilians in their local environments[23]. Recognizing Public Relations in the Army as vehicle to achievement of excellent civil military relations, he pioneered the establishment of Nigerian Army School of Public Relations and Information (NASPRI) to cater for all training needs in contemporary military public relations and information.

This contribution among others earned him the Nigerian Institute of Public Relations (NIPR) Honorary Fellowship of the Institute[24].

Status of Public Relations in the Nigerian Army

Public Relations is a management function. This is an aspect which over time its practitioners and experts have always harped upon. It is a generally established aspect of its benchmark by which the PR Manager is considered part of top or decision level making management. The hierarchy at which organizations place recognition on their PR establishments and indeed their PR managers goes a long way to reveal the esteem to which they place public relations. The Public relations profession thus places great premium on status rating of its practitioners in view of the important role of the PR manager to every organization. He should usually be a very visible personality within the organization and outside of it with unhindered access to the chief executive and other top level personalities. Many organizations fail to accord PR this recognition and would rather see PR by its "gin and tonic" image. According to Coulson – Thomas: While some public relations officials are accepted as an indispensible part of the boardroom team others still man the press and do little else. The gap between best and worst practice is wide[25].

The practice of public relations in the Nigerian Army has come a long way, so also is the status accorded its practice within the force including recognizing it as a management function. It is to that extent that the Nigerian Army has come to take its practice very seriously especially since the institution of democracy bearing in mind its potential and utility as a vehicle to advance the cause of civil military relations in Nigeria. The Director of Army Public Relations is the manager of PR in the Nigerian Army; so also are the Assistant Directors of Army Public Relations, ADAPR in the respective Divisions. The DAPR has access to the COAS. Administratively, however, he is answerable to the AHQ Department of Policy and Plans. The Assistant Directors and other PROs are responsible to General Officers Commanding and their various Commanders respectively for all PR matters. The Brigades and Training Institutions have equally Public Relations Officers. Many officers and soldiers of DAPR are members of the Nigerian Institute of Public Relations NIPR[26].

SOJA Magazine as Tool of Information Dissemination

Since its establishment, the DAPR has made giant stride in educating and keeping the Army and the civil populace informed about the activities of the NA. This remarkable achievement is recorded through well-organized aggressive information gathering and dissemination across all formations of the Nigerian Army. Quarterly publication like the new SOJA Magazine, an authoritative news bulletin of the NA, pamphlet and other information periodicals as well as media releases are printed and distributed to personnel and members of the public with a view to informing and/or enlightening them on the current NA activities and thereby mustering their support for the realization of NA set goals and COAS vision.

The SOJA Magazine whose publication dates back to the early seventies is however, preceded by other magazines. After the Second World War, the *Journal of the Nigeria Regiment* was prominent. In the forties and fifties, the Nigeria Public Relations Department published magazines like *Spearheads of Victory, Our Regiment*, and *Our Military Forces*. All of these evolved into the *Nigerian Military Forces Magazine*, then the *Royal Nigerian Army Magazine* and finally, the *Nigerian Army Magazine*[27]. The SOJA magazine which evolved into the New SOJA is aimed at both military and civilian audiences. Printed on glossy art paper, the magazine in the last few years has improved tremendously by both content and quality of print. Nowa Omoigui attests to this in saying that the contents of the magazine are well researched, broad and exciting. The front and back covers as well as the inside pages are of better gloss and thickness than even the *Time* and *Newsweek* magazines can boast of. For the *New* SOJA magazine one hopes it will continue to showcase the best traditions and personnel of the Nigerian Army and grow from strength to strength[28]. Just as the Directorate of Army Public Relations publishes the quarterly SOJA Magazine, the Divisions, Brigades, and Corps equally all publish their own unique journals or newsletters for information dissemination as well. The DAPR has an internet website and each edition of New SOJA Magazine can now be accessed on the internet, thus availing information about Nigerian Army activities to the outside world.

Nigerian Navy:

The Nigerian Navy by pecking order is the second most senior service after the Nigerian Army. The Navy came into existence in 1956 after approval for its establishment was granted by the House of Representatives on the 26th March of that year. Initially labelled the Nigerian Naval Force, it was created out of a former quasi-military force under the Ministry of Transport for Maritime policing duties. The authorization of the Nigerian Navy as a branch of the Armed Forces in 1958 came as part of the pre-independence Nigerian Nationalism which demanded that Nigeria ought to be an independent nation state and have correspondingly independent Armed Forces to defend its sovereignty and to protect its economic resources. That year, the name Nigerian Naval Force was changed to Royal Nigerian Navy (RNN)[29]. The 1964 Navy Act specified five broad roles for the Navy. Such roles however, with time and the pace of socio-economic and political development of Nigeria been further broadened by outlining its military roles, policing roles as well as diplomatic roles.

Directorate of Naval Information

The demands of modern navies the world over compels attention to the basic tenets of navy public information, conscious of the fact that personnel and public information is a prime area of responsibility in view of the necessity for developing and sustaining public understanding and support for the force. The growth, development and incremental expansion of the Navy as a critical arm of Nigeria's military force was to in later years require the establishment of a naval information arm. Naval public relations and information in relation to the other services became especially imperative in view if the of the "invisibility" of the Nigerian Navy in comparison with other arms of the services, given the inaccessibility of its area of operations with the resultant inadequate knowledge about the Navy, maritime affairs and the needs of the Service[30].

It was in that regard that the Navy became the second Service to establish a public relations outfit in the Nigerian Armed Forces. As Oladimeji revealed, the process which started in 1968 as an Officers 'Mess function assigned to the Director of Music, eventually got duly established as a professional public relations department, with the commissioning of two journalists and a graduate of Mass Communications as Public Relations Officers in August 1972. The three professional PR officers initially commissioned had a tough time setting out a professional outfit for the Service. They had the herculean task of communicating the best practices in public relations. Thus with formal establishment of naval public relations, expectations were high within the naval community that the Navy will be better known, misconceptions in the mass media corrected, bad press eliminated to put the Navy in good light, irrespective of what it does. In addition, public relations people should be able to get all that the Navy wants from civilian organisations including those things that make partying groovy![31]. Under leadership of Commodore Oladimeji as pioneer Director, the Directorate remained focussed to give the Navy the best PR service possible with the available human and financial resources.

The established outfit was attached to support the Naval Headquarters as well as the Eastern and Western Naval Commands in Calabar and Apapa, respectively. The outfit reportedly continued to face the problem of ambivalence and lack of full integration into the Navy's structure for a long time just as was the case with its Army counterpart. It remained an integral arm of the Navy's Seaman Branch. The Post of Director of Naval Information was eventually created in 1981, fortifying the practice of Public Information Support to the Navy's operations. The Directorate gained full autonomy under the reforms of the then Chief of the Naval Staff. It was transformed as the Naval Information Management Corps with direct access to the Chief of the Naval Staff. Its responsibility was expanded to cover operations support (including psychological warfare), training support, publicity, printing, archives, information technology, and public relations. It lost this autonomy and expanded vision following the abolition of the corps system[32].

The Directorate was later brought under the Personnel Branch. Following some structural reforms that were carried out, it was then moved to the newly created Administration Branch. In 2001, it was felt that for maximum efficiency, the Directorate should be part of the Policy and plans Branch. The Directorate has since then remained under the Policy and Plans Branch. At the various units are Command Information Officers, who are responsible to the flag Officers Commanding. Altogether, there are 38 Officers and 215 Ratings serving in the Directorate. They are deployed at the Naval Headquarters, the Commands and Bases as well as in tri–service establishments performing Public Relations duties[33].

Naval Information Responsibilities

The Directorate of Naval Information is among others shouldered with the following responsibilities:

- Formulation of information management policy and programmes of NN.
- Development of Naval Management Information Systems for its operational, financial, and technical needs and data analysis
- Preparation, publication and distribution of policy guidelines.
- Establishing harmonious relationship with the public, press and information media so as to ensure good image for NN[34].

Core Missions

From the onset, five core missions were conceptualised for the Directorate of Naval Information. The missions include:

- To ensure public enlightenment about the Nigerian Navy and its activities in spite of its remoteness from the public.
- To maintain engender public interest and public support for the Nigerian Navy.
- To maintain cordial relationship between members of the naval units and the communities in which naval bases and naval ships are located.
- To contribute to the maintenance of effective internal communications to ensure an informed fighting force.
- To ensure mutual understanding between the mass media and the Navy, given the mass media role and influence in putting the naval messages across to the public[35].

The Nigerian Navy conducts its public relations and information programmes through media relations events and activities, newsletters and news releases, community relations, special events especially during the annual Navy Week, facility visits, and internal information programmes and through publication of the monthly Sailor Magazine which was launched in 1985.

Naval Public Relations – Strategies and Tactics

The Directorate of Naval Information recognises the essence and immense benefits of public relations and thus has striven over the years to apply a number of them to prosecute the mission. Some of these strategies and tactics outlined by Commodore Oladimeji include[36]:

(1) Publications and Manuals:
Myriad of articles were contributed over the years to national mass media and foreign defence and naval magazines such as the African Defence Review and

the well-known *US Naval Institute Proceedings* on sea power as window through which Navy and naval operations would be better known and appreciated.

(2) Electronic Media and Documentaries:
The directorate coordinated inputs into radio and television programmes as well as Nigerian Television Authority, NTA documentaries.

(3) Public and Media Relations Lectures:
Many lectures on public and media relations were delivered in universities, Command and Staff College Jaji and at the National Defence College, Abuja. One of such lectures on "Military Public Relations" was organized by Commander OA Oladimeji at the All-Nigeria Seminar on Public Relations at the University of Lagos from 22 to 24 October 1986.

(4) Public Enlightenment Forum:
The Nigerian Navy initiated a public enlightenment forum where experts come to deliver papers on to increase knowledge content of officers and men. Two of such lectures worthy of mention are the one by Mr AO Banjo, Director of Library and Documentation of the Nigerian Institute of International Affairs on "Library: Storehouse of Knowledge." The Directorate also hosted an eminent scholar, Professor Robert Linsay, an ex-marine officer and Professor of Communication and International Relations, who gave a lecture on Public Relations and the Military on 12 July 1985. Some other major strategic initiatives include the following:

- In 1987, the Nigerian Navy commenced the Chief of the Naval Staff Annual Conference. This is a huge PR programme that takes the bulk of senior naval officers to choice resorts in difference geopolitical zones – Oguta in Imo State, Sokoto, Yola, Ilorin, Abuja, Akure and several other places.

- In 1988, the Directorate of Information coordinated the staging of a "Citizens' Dialogue" about the NN. It was a big success and resulted in the publication of *Sea Power: Agenda for National Survival,* edited by Captain Olutunde Oladimeji.

- In 1986, the Navy organised a huge float during national day parade [with scintillating commentary] on low-loaders in Abuja to showcase the ships and weapon fit of the NN, since ships cannot be brought to Abuja like Army tanks and NAF aircraft.

- The Directorate of Naval Information spearheaded the formation of Defence Writers Association mainly for defence correspondents and people who are involved in carrying out defence reporting and research.

- The Navy cooperates with the Nigerian Institute of International Affairs in sponsoring Seminars and Conferences relating to maritime affairs. One of such seminars was the Law of Sea Conference in Port Harcourt in 1982 and the Seminar on Smuggling and Coastal Piracy in Nigeria in February 1983.

- Naval Public Relations Guide Publications: Two such guides are worthy of mention. In attempt to train the naval officers and men in news and feature writing, *Creative News & Feature Writing* was published and launched at NIIA in 1985. In 1988, a somewhat comprehensive "Public Relations Guide" was also written to guide naval public relations people and others.

Nigerian Air Force:

The idea of establishing an Air Force for Nigeria was first mooted in 1961 following the nation's participation in peace – keeping operations in Congo and Tanganyika (now Tanzania). During these peace keeping operations, foreign air forces were employed to airlift Nigerian Army regiments to and from the theatres of operation. The Nigerian Government at the time, no doubt, recognized the urgent need to establish an air force actively supported by modern facilities to provide a full complement of forces to enhance the nation's military posture. Early in 1962, the Government agreed in principle that Nigerian Air Force be established. Parliament, therefore, approved the establishment of the force and recruitment of cadets commenced in June 1962. Consequently, the Nigerian Air Force was officially established by a statutory Act of Parliament in April 1964 for the purpose of being a complement to Nigeria's military defence system, ensure versatile mobility of the Armed forces, provide close support for ground based and sea-borne forces in all phases of operations to ensure the territorial integrity of a United Nigeria, and to give the country deserved prestige in international affairs[37].

Public relations and information activities are taken very seriously by Air Forces across the world. In the United States, the Director of the Office of Information (which is within the Office of the Secretary of the Air Force) advises and assists the Secretary of the Air Force and all other principal civilian and military officials of the Department of the Air Force concerning information matters. He is responsible for conducting the operations of the United States Air Force information programme; planning, directing and supervising internal and external information activities; and developing and monitoring programmes designed to maintain Air Force Community Relations. While directly under the Secretary of the Air Force, he maintains close daily contact with the Chief and Vice Chief of Staff, Headquarters, United States Air Force[38].

Nigerian Air Force Directorate of Public Relations and Information (DOPRI)

The establishment of public relations and information branch in the Nigerian Air Force did not quite happen in the conscious manner as it did earlier on in the Nigerian Army and Nigerian Navies respectively. As a result of the subsisting attitude and belief among senior Air Force Officers who felt that public relations was a job to which anybody could be assigned to carry out and not necessarily a professional, the Nigerian Air Force over time, did not consider it necessary to establish a public relations outfit until about 1970. Constrained therefore to draw from the developments in the Army, Navy, and the Police with establishment of public relations outfits, however, the Nigerian Air Force eventually decided to experiment the idea and commissioned 2 Officers for the purpose. By 1979, it went further to commission three Mass Communications Graduates for Public Relations duties. The specialty gained a new impetus and its practice began to secure more acceptance and popularity in the Air Force in due course. More hands were recruited or posted in to support its establishment[39]. By 13 July, 1984, the outfit was upgraded and designated Directorate of Public Relations and Information (DOPRI). The outfit has grown tremendously and is manned by about 18 officers and 70 airmen supported by civilians and its deployment extend to commands, Groups and Wings which are the main categories of formations in the forces. With the primary mission of building trust and relationship with varied audience through the provision of forthright, truthful, and timely information either as it becomes available or on demand.

Objectives of NAF Information Directorate

The objectives of the directorate are anchored on its effort to assist Nigerians to understand:

- Threats to Nigeria and the world, and the need for Air Force to be alert against potential aggressions.
- The relationship of the Air Force to other Armed Forces
- The day to day activities of the Air Force and an instrument of National Policy.
- The need for continual research, development and modernization of NAF
- The need to attract and retain qualified Air Force personnel and
- The essential role of Nigeria Air Force in International relations
- To present the NAF story as favourable as possible[40].

The Directorate is also responsible for cultivating, creating and maintaining favourable public opinion, goodwill, understanding, support and cooperation through deliberate and planned public relations programmes. It monitors public opinion about the NAF and uses communication to influence public opinion or respond to criticisms or adverse reports and comments. Headed by the Director (DOPRI) who is responsible to the Chief of Air Staff operationally and administratively to the Air Force Officer Administration (AOA), the Directorate is charged with the conduct of all Public Relations related activities by ensuring the sustenance of effective information flow between the NAF and the Public through the print and electronic media. At the command level, there are information departments headed by CPROs, who provide similar services though at a lower scale. In addition, there are information offices at some key NAF units such as: Air Mobility Group AMG, 97 Special Operations Group SOG, 99 Advanced Weapons School AWS, 303 Flying Training School FTS, and 330 NAF stations. The Directorate also deploys tri – service institutions like Nigerian Defence Academy, Armed Forces Command and Staff College, Nigerian Armed Forces Rehabilitation Centre, Military Pensions Board and Defence Headquarters[41].

The Nigerian Air Force conducts its public relations and information programmes through media relations events and activities, community relations, special events, facility visits, and internal information programmes and through publication of the monthly Air Man Journal among others.

Defence Headquarters

As with other military organisations the world over, the creation of Defence Headquarters (DHQ) was predicated on the need to have an organ within the Nigerian Armed Forces whose primary role would be to harmonize and coordinate the activities of the 3 services. This aspect of the Armed Forces hierarchy came into existence with the creation of the office of the Chief of Defence Staff (CDS) by the 1979 Constitution of the Federal Republic of Nigeria. The CDS formally took office in April 1980. The Defence Headquarters was however abolished with the change of Government in 1983. In 1985, it was re – established as Joint Chiefs of Staff Headquarters and headed by the Chairman. When the military embarked on restructuring and preparation for civil rule, the Defence Headquarters along with the Office of the CDS, recognised in the Constitution was re – introduced with effect from September 1990. In its basic concept therefore, the DHQ is tasked with the duty of removing operational bottlenecks in inter - service combat functions by giving firm policy guidelines on command, control, communication and intelligence. Other tasks of the DHQ include general administration and information which are co–ordinated by five Departments namely Department of Training, Operation and Plans (DTOP), Department of Logistics (DLOG), Department of Administration[42].

Directorate of Defence Information

With recognition and appreciation of the growing need for public relations and information functions in the Armed Forces, the Directorate of Defence Information was established in 1993. It is one of the 4 staff branches of the Directorate of Training and Operations, headed by a Director and 2 Assistant Directors with tri-service staff complement. The Directorate is thus one of the youngest and most recent outfits for public relations and information activities in the Nigerian Armed Forces. Although, it retains its place as the foremost in the hierarchy of public relations/information especially by virtue of its position at the Defence Headquarters, the directorate still depends almost entirely on the Services for specialist manpower and operations. The functions of the Directorate remains focused mainly on information management and dissemination on the military generally. It is the best equipped and funded among the Directorates established for public information management in the armed forces[43].

Objectives of the Directorate of Defence Information

It has the following objectives:

- To coordinate information for the Defence Headquarters for dissemination to all the other services on issues that can promote understanding and cooperation among the three services: Army, Navy, and Air Force.

- To advise the information and public relations outfits of the three services whenever it is found necessary.
- To ensure adequate information is made available to the Armed Forces and the Nigerian public about the activities of members to the Armed Forces on foreign missions and operations.
- To assist all the other information outfits in the country to enhance the proper and correct situation of events as they affect military personnel in particular and country in general.
- To organise seminars and conferences involving information and public relations practitioners in order to improve knowledge of military activities and attain workable arrangement at improving press and military relations.
- To publish a newsletter and other relevant information materials that can assist to sustain the sound image of the military[44].

The Directorate carries out its public relations and information activities through media relations activities especially press conferences and interviews that are held most often. It also carries out community relations programmes, coordinates special events of the armed forces especially during national events, advertisements, seminars and workshops. The Directorate publishes the Defence Newsletter, a quarterly magazine with circulation in the armed forces, within the country and which are also circulated abroad including operational areas for the purpose of informing and educating troops about developments in the country.

References

1. National Defence Policy of Nigeria, 2006
2. Adediji, Tola, "Improving the Image of the Armed Forces through Public Relations", Lecture delivered at Nigerian Army Public Relations Training Seminar, Lagos, 29-30 Dec 1987
3. Ibid
4. Allan Hooper, (1982) The Military and the Media (Aldershot, Gower Pub Co) P. 215
5. National Defence Policy of Nigeria, 2006
6. Nigerian Army Diary 2002 – Brief History of Nigerian Army
7. Ibid
8. Manual of the Directorate of Army Public Relations 1991, P. 3
9. Sotomi, E.F. in Army Public Relations Officers Handbook, HQ APRD, Lagos, 1973
10. Chijuka Fred, Opening Address at Nigerian Army Public Relations Training Seminar, Lagos, 29-30 Dec 1987
11. Ejoor David, in Army Public Relations Officers Handbook, HQ APRD, Lagos, 1973
12. Wey J.E.A. in Army Public Relations Officers Handbook, HQ APRD, Lagos, 1973
13. Babangida Ibrahim in Army Public Relations Officers Handbook, HQ APRD, Lagos, 1973
14. Army Public Relations Officers Handbook, HQ APRD, Lagos, 1973
15. Ibid
16. Ibid
17. Ibid
18. Chijukka Fred, Opening Address at Nigerian Army Public Relations Training Seminar Op cit
19. Ibid
20. Nwolise O.B.C. "Public Relations Tools for Maximising Objectives in the Nigerian Army", Lecture delivered at Directorate of Army Public Relations Training Period Ibadan, 25 – 27 September 1991
21. Ibid
22. Chijuka Fred, Op cit
23. Reuben Buhari, "Danmbazau Harps on Civil Military Relations" @ http://www.nigerianbestforum.com/blog
24. "Nigeria: The Army Under Danbazau", Thisday 16 September 2010
25. Collin Coulson – Thomas, Public Relations: A Practical Guide (New York: Bath Macdonald and Evans, 1979) P. 6

26. Tokoya OO, Public Relations Practice in the Nigerian Army: Challenges and Prospects", National Defence College Project, August 2009, P. 34
27. Nowa A. Omoigui @ http;//www.dawodu.com/soja.htm
28. Ibid
29. Ministry of Defence Diary 1999
30. Oladimeji, O.A. Naval Public Relations Notes
31. Ibid
32. Oladimeji, O.A. quoted in Olukolade, A.C. "Mobilisation of Public Support for Nigerias Military Operations: A Framework For Public Information Management", Research Project submitted to the National Institute for Policy and Strategic Studies Kuru, November 2011, P. 42
33. Ibid
34. Ibid
35. OA Oladimeji, Naval Public Relations Notes
36. Ibid
37. Ministry of Defence Diary 1999
38. Arthur Dreyer, "Functions and Responsibilities in the Department of Defence, Army, Navy, Marine Corps, and Air Force Information Services in Military Public Affairs" in Hand Book of Public Relations, P. 775
39. Olukolade A.C. Op cit
40. Ibid
41. Ibid
42. Ministry of Defence Diary 1999
43. Olukolade, A.C. "Mobilisation of Public Support for Nigeria's Military Operations: A Framework For Public Information Management", Research Project submitted to the National Institute for Policy and Strategic Studies Kuru, November 2011, P. 43
44. Ibid

CHAPTER ELEVEN

THE IMPERATIVE OF PROFESSIONAL PUBLIC RELATIONS TRAINING IN THE MILITARY

Training is a means of learning which involves the acquisition of knowledge, skills and competencies, rules and concepts through the process of teaching. It is aimed essentially at improving or enhancing the performance of the trainee or employee of an organization. The concept is also defined as organized activity aimed at imparting information and/or instructions to improve the recipient's performance or to help him or her attain a required level of knowledge or skill[1]. For every trade, occupation or even profession, best practices tenet advocate continuous training for the purpose of upgrading knowledge beyond the initial training or qualifications towards occupational or professional development in specific areas. Such modes of training are usually undertaken "on-the-job" at normal work place settings or done "off-the-job" outside of normal work settings. Training is a key part of an organizations strategy towards effective and efficient performance. The need for training may arise due to advancement in technology, improved performance or of professional development. Benefits of training are intangible and its benefits accrue to both the organization and the trainee. In addition to enhancing the skills of trainees, it provides a sense of satisfaction and is equally a source of motivation.

Although debates have often arisen as to whether public relations is a profession or not, in the mould of the well-known traditionally established professions such as medicine, law and engineering, public relations education and training nevertheless has always been given a lot of attention at national and international levels by its practitioners. In the United States, the Public Relations Society of America plays a critical role especially in having to accredit public relations specialists who have at least 5 years' experience in the field and have passed a comprehensive examination in the written and oral aspects. A good number of colleges and universities offer degree programmes in especially journalism or communications departments. Such colleges or universities even go further to help students gain part time internships in public relations to enable them gain experience. The US Armed Forces has been cited as an excellent place to gain good training and experience in public relations as there is intern as well as civilian career opportunities in the US Army Public Affairs Department.

The beginnings of Public relations education and training as highlighted in chapter one could be traced to the United States with Scott M. Cutlip, a central figure to it. As Major in the US Army, he made outstanding contribution in the improvement of military public affairs with the establishment of the Defence Information School (DINFOS). Prior to the establishment of the School, the Services had their organic information schools. The Army Information School was founded at Carlisle Barracks, Pennsylvania, in 1946. The Navy established a Journalist School at Great Lakes Naval Station, Illinois, in 1948. The Army Information School was renamed the Armed Forces Information School in 1948. The Army and Navy Schools were merged in 1964 by then Secretary of Defence, Robert S. McNamara when he directed that one Information School be established with a joint staff and faculty to conduct all information training for the Department of Defence.

The Defence Information School, (DINFOS) moved to Fort Benjamin Harrison, Indiana, in 1965[2]. The School has a long-standing tradition of producing outstanding Public Affairs and Visual Information personnel for the US Department of Defence. Its mission is to grow and sustain a corps of professional organizational communicators who fulfil the communication needs of the military and government leaders and audiences while its vision centres on being a recognized national asset for organizational communication success. Its goals include to: Deliver total professional development support to organizational communicators throughout their careers; Sustain DINFOS as a premier accredited military/government training centre and sought-after assignment for faculty and staff and to grow the DINFOS infrastructure to support the expanding training mission. Its organizational communication encompasses the entire professional community supported by DINFOS, including public affairs, visual information and related fields[3]. DINFOS provides public affairs training for officers, enlisted and civilian personnel from all branches of service and from more than 39 allied nations. The eight-week information officer course covers DoD policies and procedures; available mass communications resources; the principles of management applicable to public officers in the areas of public information, internal information, community relations; and policies unique to individual military departments. Students also learn basic writing and photo-journalism skills. The six weeks Broadcast Officer Course prepares officers to manage American Forces Radio[4].

In the United Kingdom, the London School of Public Relations and Branding (LSPR), established in 1992 is one of the leading educational bodies offering training in public relations, branding, sponsorship and event management, corporate identity, risk and issues analysis, media relations, leadership and reputation management... the key mission and purpose of LSPR is to provide the most up-to-date course and training of its kind on PR and reputation management[5].

The awareness of, and development of public relations in the African continent is accompanied equally by the serious impetus which has been given to PR education and training. As a course, public relations in Africa is taught as part of Bachelor's Degree in Communication, Journalism and Mass Communication in South Africa, Kenya, Egypt, Ghana and Nigerian Universities among others. The University of Nigeria, Nsukka, which for instance, pioneered the introduction of Mass Communication as a degree programme following from same tradition in the US has public relations as one of the integral courses of the programme. The public relations land scape in Nigeria today in the private and the public sector has many personalities who are alumni of Jackson Building - the Department of Mass Communication of the University of Nigeria,

Nsukka (UNN). Following the footsteps of the University of Nigeria, the University of Lagos (UNILAG) and the Institute of Management and Technology, (IMT) Enugu, later followed with introduction of Mass Communication courses. Bayero University Kano, and many other new generation Universities and Polytechnics today have departments of Mass Communication which have public relations as embedded taught courses that provide grounding for public relations education and training. The University of Nigeria has even gone further with introduction of Master's Degree Programme in Public Relations.

Training in the Military

In the military, training is considered to be its most important life wire. Militaries all over the world take training very seriously whether in peace or in war. The Army as Baynes rightly observed, achieves results partly because, it continues the educational process throughout a man's service, and has a highly developed way of training him and following up each stage of his career[6]. Training in the military begins at the point of recruitment with attempts to impart information and training bothering on techniques that would enhance effective membership of the force. After initial training, personnel are then posted to different specialty areas where they equally undergo training in those specialty areas. Public relations are a specialty area in the military. The job of the public relations branch within the military, as noted in chapter one is quite crucial to the armed forces as a result not only of changes in the nature and conduct of war but also as a result of increased societal awareness and other evolving dimensions that play on the interrelationship between the military and society.

There are several aspects to the interrelationship between the military and society and it requires an enlightened military to be able to continuously cope with such interplay and therefore the need for training and re-training. Such training as obtains in the British Army's training at Sand Hurst Military Academy seeks among others to develop the qualities of leadership and to provide the basic knowledge required by all young officers of any arm or service so that, after the necessary special to arm training given by the appropriate arm or service, they will be fit to be a junior officer[7]. The curriculum at Sand Hurst also includes a lecture by the Director of Public relations for the Army (DPR (A)) which is usually followed by a seminar on Public relations. The Seminar also includes the use of closed circuit television to improve an officer's competence and powers of expression[8]. As also attested to by Hooper, the next relevant stage in an officer's career is attendance at one of the staff colleges. The syllabi at Greenwich, Camberley and Bracknell are similar in that they include a 'press Day', visits to national newspapers and to television. The Press Day at Camberley is designed to provide the opportunity for exchange of ideas between the military students and representatives of the Press. To this end, a number of journalists representing television, radio, national and provincial press are invited to attend. The morning is normally devoted to series of lectures given by DPR (A) and representatives of the media, followed by a central discussion[9].

Public Relations Training and Orientation in Nigerian Military

The Nigerian Military experience is similar to that of the British as elements of media experience are part of the curriculum of the Nigerian Armed Forces at the Command and Staff College. This is further enhanced at the strategic level where the National Defence College has as integral to its curriculum, an annual seminar on the Media and the Military. To this annual seminar are invited all Directors of Public Relations and Information of the Services and DHQ or their representatives. Equally invited are managerial level executives of the media, both from the public and the private sector. A lead paper would normally be given by any of the designated participants with interventions and discussions by others after which there is an interactive session by all including the course participants. The session is usually a very lively and interesting spectacle which gets the military and members of the media to get to better understand themselves. Television interview techniques are also taught to the participants of the courses. This is the extent of what could be regarded as media and or public relations orientation for especially combatant officers in the Nigerian Military.

However, for professional preparation and development of career specialist public relations officers in the Nigerian Military, professional orientation had over the years been left to the whims of the individual services. The Army particularly from the onset had tried to enlist graduate professionals in Mass Communications and the Social Sciences who got commissioned as Direct Regular Officers into the force and on entry were given two weeks specialist military PR orientation. The officers were then posted to units and formations as Army Public Relations Officers and in the process learning on the job most of the times. Those of them who on commission did not have Mass Communication or journalism background were in course of service sent to the Daily Times Training School, Times Institute of Journalism and the Nigerian Institute of Public Information. While the Navy equally tried to follow in the footsteps of the Army, the Nigerian Air Force seemingly was not particular about recruiting professional communications specialists as information officers. Any commissioned officer, regardless of background, who was considered fit was appointed. The practice however, changed in later years as the Air Force equally started to recruit into service, people with professional background in communications and public relations.

Generally now, the Nigerian Military indeed has well trained and competent public relations and information officers in its fold that have the professional background, competency and capacity that matches their counterparts and contemporaries civil or military, around the world. However, as Oladimeji, a retired Navy Commodore and a foremost long standing Director of Naval Public Relations and Information lamented, in spite of their training, the Nigerian Armed Forces did not take full advantage of public relations techniques to solve problems of public opinion and attitude towards the military. This was because, the top hierarchy of the military don't accord it priority; it is misunderstood at heavy cost to the image of the armed forces[10]. He avers further that the specialist public relations officers in the military were always swimming against the heavy tide of prejudice. Rank ceilings for them were low; the best and brightest professional could not be attracted; funding was ridiculously low for the job at hand. This was why the public relations departments in the Armed Forces had to cope with ups and downs in their fortunes[11]. Similar experience for public relations obtains in Britain. According to Hooper, the speed of recognition and the acknowledgement of the importance of public relations vary between the three Services and there is even a variation of attitude within each service... the promotion prospects for those serving in PR appointments are not thought to be good[12]. Lack of appreciation of the place of public relations in the Nigerian military could be attributed to ignorance or misunderstanding of its potential. There is therefore the need for change of attitude as the job in fact, provides an exciting and stimulating challenge for an officer who has the imagination to seize upon its importance and its opportunities. It will open up a new dimension in his understanding of what really matters most in modern conflict[13].

The Nigerian Army has however, taken the lead in recognizing the importance of public relations education and training for its PR personnel with establishment of the Nigerian Army School of Public Relations and Information (NASPRI) which formally took off in 2010. The objectives of the School includes among others to cater for all training needs in contemporary military public relations and information for officers and soldiers of the Nigerian Army and other sister services[14].The school also hopes with time to extend such training services to the police and other para military services. NASPRI has so far trained over 300 course participants[15]. The School on annual basis organizes a 3- Months Military Public Relations Course – its own Young Officers Course (YOC) in Public Relations Management. The School is staffed essentially with qualified instructors sourced from the Directorate most of who hold Bachelors and Master's Degree in Mass Communication or Journalism. The staffs are often complemented with external resource persons from the academia and from among media executives and communication experts who come to deliver lectures. The soldiers undertake basic, intermediate and advanced level courses in basic reporting skills, photography and video camera handling.

The officer's course focuses on communication, military public relations, media operations and journalism. The officers have in addition the opportunity on nomination to equally attend media operations course often organized by the Kofi Annan Peacekeeping Training Centre, (KAPTC). The course content, depth and scope however, needs to be broadened and attuned to meet up with standards requirements of military PR courses as for example, obtains at the Defence Information School, in the United States.

With establishment of NASPRI by the Nigerian Army and its utility by the Services, the future of public relations education and training in the Nigerian military looks bright. It hopefully should be a matter of time for the Nigerian Defence establishment to adequately realize the need for public relations education and training by converting NASPRI to a Defence Information School that will be able to serve the Nigerian Armed Forces, the police, para military and other security services. Indeed for the Nigerian military, the establishment of a Defence Information School for professional public relations education and training has indeed become an imperative.

References

1. http://www.businessdictionary.com/definition/organized.html
2. Lowndes F. Stephens, "The Professional Orientation of Military Public Affairs Officers" in Public Relations Quarterly, Vol 23, 1978, PP 19-23
3. See http://www.dinfos.osd.mil/DinfosWeb/About_main.aspx
4. Ibid
5. Welcome to LSPR – PR and Beyond @ http://www.pr-school-london.com/
6. Baynes, J.C.M. (1972) **The Soldier and Modern Society**, London: Eyre Methuen PP 4-5
7. Alan Hooper, (1982) **The Military and the Media**, Aldershot: Gower, P. 185
8. Ibid
9. Ibid
10. Oladimeji, O.A. (2001) **Military Image and Media Message**, Lagos: Miral Press P. ix
11. Ibid
12. Alan Hooper, **The Military and the Media**, Op cit
13. Ibid
14. Interview with Lt Col ED Idimah, Chief Instructor, Nigerian Army School of Information and Public Relations
15. Ibid

Part Four

Issues, Challenges and Conclusion

CHAPTER TWELVE

TECHNOLOGY, THE MILITARY AND PUBLIC RELATIONS

The view has often been expressed that today in the modern world; there is an evolving relationship between security challenges, the nature of war and new technologies. It has been further posited that the impact of technology on warfare and security indeed continue to unfold endlessly in the same manner as the nature and practice of international relations. Another view avers that with new evolving information and communication technologies, the developed nations of the West especially, have been able to take advantage of them to a great extent. Such technologies have immensely enhanced their capabilities and the ability to prosecute new kinds of war with superior fire power, mobility, flexibility, communication, intelligence, reconnaissance and surveillance. These factors according to Ron Mathews are relevant in military operational planning[1].

By the same token, an analysis of the relationship between public relations and technology, as would equally rub off on military public relations cannot by any means ignore the role which advances in technology especially information and communication technology have contributed and are contributing to enhancing public relations practice. Such aspects may equally be taken as 'revolutions' in those domains even if their benefits are not exclusive to the military. As Andrew Marshal views it:

> "A Revolution in Military Affairs (RMA) is a major change in the nature of warfare brought about by the innovative application of new technologies which, combined with dramatic changes in military doctrine and operational and organizational concepts, fundamentally alters the character and conduct of military operations[2]."

Such revolutions it has been pointed out have occurred many times in history for a variety of reasons. The most obvious cause is technological "push". The invention of gunpowder, the steam engine, the submarine, the internal combustion engine, the aero plane, the aircraft carrier, and the atom bomb are some of the most obvious innovations which led to fundamental changes in the conduct of warfare. Some of these technological changes had origins in the civilian world while other revolutions in military affairs were brought about by "social-military revolutions" such as the development of railways, which enabled military forces to be moved and supplied over great distances[3]. While there is a debate about what exactly constitutes a "revolution in military affairs", some analysts maintain that there have been only three and that these have been linked to the nature of the societies: agrarian, industrial, and information[4].

There is no doubt that today's modern society arising from so many factors including globalization especially belong to the information era. Public relations as a profession that is essentially communication driven, is by every calculation, strategically placed at the very vortex and heart of the information age. While public relations from its very beginnings had developed its unique tools of practice that includes among others the use of press releases and photographs that are put to the public through the news media, technology has with time, been able to provide advances that are being utilized by experts and practitioners of public relations with tremendous ease and advantage. Such developments often referred to as public relations technology improved and brought about tremendous changes in the mechanics as well as the processes of communication. No doubt, the proponents of the concept of revolution in military affairs may not have had in mind or thought about what non-technical revolutions in for instance, areas such as public relations could do to complement the technical aspects of military operations. But they probably today may not be of the same view given the enormous impact which advances arising from PR technology have engendered for the practice of public relations and communications generally including their application to the military. One product of technology that has emerged to the benefit of public relations among other disciplines is the computer. A computer is a programmable machine designed to automatically carry out a sequence of arithmetic or logical operations... the personal computers in their various forms are icons of the information age[5]. Computers could be put to multiple uses with numerous utility for public relations including word processing, Desktop Publishing, Mailing Lists, List of Contacts creation, On-Line Conferences, Data Bases, and Graphics[6]. There are in addition other more recent developments through the computer such as evolvement of the social media which constitutes a chapter of its own in this work.

THE COMPUTER AND ITS MANY USES

A computer accepts and processes information and supplies the results in a desired form. The digital computer processes information with figures, using binary or decimal notation to solve mathematical problems at high speed. Development of the microcomputer has added flexibility and convenience for users. Since a computer can store, codify, analyse and search out information at speeds far beyond human capability, its applications are enormous. With its ability to transmit such information over long distances at fantastically high speeds, its potential becomes even greater[6]. The computer is thus very useful and handy equipment for media and public relations practitioners as its effective use can make their jobs easier. The many uses to which the computer could be put to use by public relations practitioners and firms as highlighted by Wilcox et al[7], are as follows:

Word Processing

As a tool for writer, the computer has two striking advantages over the typewriter: (1) the capacity to store created material in its memory system for instant recall and (2) the ability to make corrections, insert fresh material, and move material from one portion of a document to another. Typewritten copy must be retyped to incorporate changes; in word processing, alterations are made by the push of keys and movement of the little cursor light to the indicated position. Material written on a computer can be transferred electrically to another person's computer for review, correction, and approval. By using a printer attachment, the writer can obtain a "hard copy" version printed on paper. Examples of how computer word processing can be used in public relations practice include Word processing in preparation of news releases which is very valuable. Like letters, releases can be reworded by computer for different types of publication, such as trade magazines, daily newspapers, and the business press. The draft of a news release can be placed in computer storage while the client makes revisions on a printout copy. These changes can then be made without the time-consuming process of retyping the entire release. Also, the draft news release can be entered in storage by its writer and later called up on another screen by the supervisor who must review and approve it.

Correction of Spelling and Grammar:

Special software programs-sets of construction telling the computer what to do – can improve the public relations writer's work by correction spelling and grammatical mistakes.

Electronic Mail:

A piece of writing delivered from the originator's computer into the recipient's computer, instead of being sent by mail or messenger service, often is called *electronic mail*. When a writer is creating copy for a brochure, the edited text can be recorded on a disk for delivery to the printing company. Or, if the printing company has suitable computer connections, the brochure copy can be transmitted electronically from the writer's computer into the printing company's computer. No paper is used. That computer in turn can feed the copy into a phototypesetting system, from which it will emerge as type on paper ready to be reproduced, with headlines included.

Desktop Publishing

Recent advances in computer techniques make possible the creation of professional-looking newsletters and graphically illustrated material on a personal computer right in the office. ... Desktop publishing allows the public relations writer and editor to design and layout reports, newsletters, brochures, and presentations by manipulating copy and graphics right on a computer screen instead of on a drawing board. It produces camera-ready pages for offset printing.

Mailing Lists

Up-to-date mailing lists are vital in public relations work. The old method was to have a separate metal plate for each person, with relevant information punched onto the plate. These plates were kept in rays and fed through a machine to stamp the addresses onto mailing pieces. Today, lists of names are typed into a computer and stored in its memory. Changes of address or other alternations can be made by calling up a name and using a few keystrokes. When a mailing is to be made, the desired names on the master list can be activated and printed on adhesive labels or on the individual envelopes. The capability to select groups of names from the master list assists the practitioner in reaching target audiences.

Lists of Contacts

In a related application, public relations offices use the storage and call-up facilities of computers to maintain ready-reference lists of individuals with their telephone numbers and addresses, job titles and other personal data, which can be listed by category. By keeping names and addresses on a computerized list, the public relations practitioner can easily add new names and make corrections-and the computer keeps everything in alphabetical order. This eliminates the traditional address card file.

With certain software programs, a person can summon a desired telephone number onto the screen and, with a single command, have the computer automatically dial the number.

On-line Conferences

When two or more persons tie their computers together by telephone line, they can hold discussions by exchanging a series of typed messages. In order to do so, their computers must be equipped with a modern (short for modulator/demodulator), an attachment that converts the computer's electric signals into signals that can move along the telephone line. On-line conferences are increasingly valuable in public relations work. Practitioners "converse" with clients and suppliers, or they participate in forums on professional matters with groups of their peers. The text of what has been said can be retained for the record in computer storage or typed out by a hard-copy printer.

Data Bases

With fact-finding and research essential in sophisticated practice today, the computer is becoming as important as a dictionary in a public relations office. Through it, personnel can extract information from an estimated 1500 data base that have in storage an enormous amount of current and historical information.

Public relations departments and firms use computer data bases in the following ways:

- Researching facts and figures to support a proposed project that requires top management approval.
- Keeping up-to-date with news about clients and their competitors and markets.
- Tracking the media campaigns of a company and the press announcements of its competitors.
- Finding a special quotation or impressive statistic for a speech or report.
- Tracking the press and business reaction to a company's latest actions.
- Finding an expert for advice on a new promotional campaign.
- Promoting more effectively and efficiently the products and services of a company.
- Keeping top management apprised of current business trends and issues.
- Learning the demographics and attitudes of target audiences[8].

Graphics

Use of computers to design eye-catching coloured graphics – drawings, graphs, charts and text – for publications is emerging as a new technology in public relations practice. Recent developments in computer software make such graphics possible although they remain expensive. Attractive graphics give visual impact to annual reports and employee publications, as well as video programmes and slide presentations. The techniques of computer graphics are still evolving and somewhat complicated, but the imaginative visual effects that experts can obtain are astonishing.

Satellite Transmission

Text messages and pictures can be flashed around the world in seconds by using satellite transmission, a fact of enormous significance to public relations communicators... So valuable is satellite transmission that a constantly growing number of satellites are being parked above the equator in what scientists call the geostationary belt. When information is dispatched by a computer through a ground "uplink" station to a transponder pad on a satellite, then bounced back to a receiving dish on the ground, and into a receiving computer, enormous amounts of material can be transported over great distances at breath-taking speeds. One computer can "talk" to another via satellite about 160 times faster than can be done over land lines, and at much lower costs.

The military no doubt has greatly benefited from the wonders of modern technology. While this may have been more in the technical areas where Revolutions in Military Affairs may have been more manifestly visible, it should not lose sight of developments associated with the non-technical areas such as public relations which the military could equally buy into. The two sides – technical and non-technical areas complement each other. They mutually stand to benefit military operations and objectives.

References

1. Ron Mathews, cited in "Security and Technology", lecture delivered by John Adache at Defence and Security Management Course 4, National Defence College, Abuja, October 2011
2. Andrew Marshal, cited at http://www.iwar.org.uk/rma/resources/nato/ar299stc-e.html
3. http://www.iwar.org.uk/rma/resources/nato/ar299stc-e.html
4. Ibid
5. http://en.wikipedia.org/wiki/Computer
6. Dennis L. Wilcox et al (1989) Public Relations – Strategies and Tactics, (New York, Harper & Row Pub) P 530
7. Ibid pp 530 – 538
8. Ibid

CHAPTER THIRTEEN

SOCIAL MEDIA, PUBLIC RELATIONS, AND THE MILITARY

Introduction

The world as widely acknowledged today belongs to the era of globalization. The concept of globalization is one lexicon which arguably, has gained much wider prominence and usage across the world than any other since the nineteen-nineties with end of the cold war and the eventual break-up of the former Soviet Union. The present era is associated with the age of globalization, a term that has come to encompass varying perspectives. It refers to the global outlook of different nations of the world coming closer and joining hands in the area of the economy, education, society and politics. Globalization empowers a view for the entire world as a whole irrespective of national identity and thus globalization has narrowed the world by bringing people of all nations closer[1]. Enabling people of one nation to communicate with those of the other nation(s) is the biggest achievement in terms of globalization and development. The culture, trade, business, ethics and conduct of one group in one part of the world can influence others who may or may not be of the same nation, origin or identity. The process of globalization is therefore, an amalgamation of interaction and integration among different groups of people, various organizations and governments of different nations. It is further an interactive communication process that is supported by information and communication technology[2]. Globalization thus has engendered innumerable outcomes that among others include what has come to be known as the social media.

And what is social media? It is perhaps expedient to begin by properly delineating the meaning of the concept for better understanding as most people have often taken it for granted, misunderstood and/or misapplied it. Daniel Nation throws up this angle by his assertion that social media is a phrase being tossed around a lot these days, but that it can sometimes be difficult to answer the question of what is social media... the best way to define social media is to break it down. Media is an instrument of communication, like a newspaper or radio, so social media would be a social instrument of communication[3]. Newspapers which provide daily news reports and analysis on hard copies, radios which offer news and entertainment through audio means and televisions that equally provide the same service combining audio and visual means all belong to what traditionally are known as the "regular one-way street media". Social media on the other hand is a "two-way street media". The difference is that while a one-way street media such as newspaper, radio or television offers the reader or listener limited ability to provide feedback or give thoughts on an issue, social media on the other hand, gives you the ability to chat or communicate instantaneously through the web sites[4]. Although radio and television often use support communication facilities such as during phone-in programmes to achieve the same purpose and equally generate some level of reaction and feedback, they nevertheless couldn't be said to be on the same status with the social media.

Social media by another definition includes web-based and mobile technologies used to turn communication into interactive dialogue. Andreas Kaplan and Michael Haenlein define social media as "a group of Internet-based applications that build on the ideological and technological foundations of Web 2.0 and that allow the creation and exchange of user-generated content[5]. Highlighting the advantages of Web 2.0 over Web 1.0, Amir Milson states that applications of the internet, distinctively the 'World-Wide Web' over the past two decades has evolved dramatically. The shift from Web 1.0 to the present Web 2.0, from stagnant to highly interactive web pages recognizes the cogent turning point in the use of rational internet. Web 2.0 allows individuals personal input or 'user generated content' to a public cyber arena allowing the ability to engage with others beyond geographic confinements[6]. Web 2.0 allows images and videos to be viewed throughout the world simultaneously and this cogently brings people closer together. It allows people with disabilities the ability to overcome restrictive barriers giving them access to view the world and connect with those who share similar disadvantages. Therefore, Web 2.0 amplifies human potential and creates new forms of life, more productivity and breaks down cultural barriers.

Everyone is an individual and Web 2.0 allows the expression of individualism and this is one of social media's strongest criterions in breaking down cultural barriers. By having the ability to express oneself to the world, prejudices and stereotypes are diminishing. Social media gives people the ability to represent oneself with personal interests rather than stereotypes of the area they are from. Therefore, the world is connecting more towards a common sense of interests rather than cultural stereotypes, breaking down the cultural barriers the world traditionally operated in[7]. Examples of social media networking sites include Facebook, MySpace, Twitter, Friendster, You Tube, Flickr and other sites aimed at photo and video sharing. There are also news aggregation and online reference sources such as Digg and Wikipedia which also are counted in the social media bucket. Social media takes on many different forms including magazines, internet forums, social blogs, wikis, and social bookmarking. Many of the social media services can be integrated via social networking aggregation platforms.

How Social Media benefits Public Relations

Advances in technology with creation of web sites have greatly improved the practice of public relations. Therefore by building a well-designed Web site, a company, individual or organization can share information that polishes its image and furthers its agenda.

Web sites increasingly have become good and effective means of getting information to several clientele publics including journalists. Many complex organizations, firms and businesses establish media rooms on their official Web site. The media room site on regular basis among other services post press releases, company history, executive biographies or profiles, high-resolution digital photos and even downloadable, digital press kits. Rather than seeking out media attention through mass-e-mailed press releases, a good Web site will draw in journalists by itself. Dave Roos, a public relations specialist acknowledges that sending press releases has become much easier with e-mail. With a few simple mouse clicks, a public relations specialist can send tens or thousands of press releases to a targeted group of journalists[8]. They should however, be wary of press release spams. Thus with explosion of the social media and its growth across the world, public relations firms and practitioners have found the utilization of social media platforms very useful. Adamolekun affirms that social media is an idea whose time has come[9]. Emphasizing the tremendous impact which social media have made within a short period, Adamolekun by comparative analysis said that while it took the radio 38 years to capture 50 million users, television, 13 years, the internet, 4 years and iPod, 3 years, Facebook astonishingly took just 9 months to add 100 million people to its existing users adding that Facebook, were it to be a country would be the fourth largest[10].

All over the world, the popularity, growth, impact and utilization of social media has become quite enormous for example, internet, social networking and elaborate media coverage are known to have played great role during the crisis in the Arab world with the series of protests against national governments and their regimes, organized largely by activists. By enabling people to broadcast and share their thoughts, opinions, sentiments and emotions on a reach and scale never before imagined, social media has engendered many complexities in terms of social and political relationships as well as interaction. More fundamentally, it has endowed people with the power to influence and shape perceptions and attitudes, and it is forcing many public relations professionals to recognize and include social media tools in their communication strategies. In Singapore social media is fast becoming a new "democratic" front for the country's fledgling political discourse as well as businesses. In the realm of business, social media has been able to transform the roles and relationships between businesses and customers by facilitating conversation amongst users.

Social media represents a shift from "traditional" media rooted in a broadcast mechanism to a dynamic, multi-faceted "many-to-many" conversational model that would enable as well as require businesses to engage more directly with customers. With social media, the traditional approach of "marketing at" people is changed into an "engaging in conversation" with people[11]. Public relations in social media participate in this conversation by contributing expert advice, information and content; it seeks to build portfolios of knowledge and develop online reputation that boost brands and raise profile of the businesses which the public relations professional and/or company represents. In this conversation, it is critical to engage with people on a one-on-one basis through an appropriate form and style of communication that actually speaks to people. People or customers want to hear stories that they can identify with; they also want to share these stories and build relationships with other people through these stories. People interact and build relationships with people, not faceless entities. And in the social media-scape, effective public relations is not about spamming media with generic messages and news releases, it is an art of personalized mass marketing built on a foundation of market research and analysis to understand peoples' needs and how to reach them at "street level"[12].

It has been established that social media sites - Facebook & Twitter are getting popularity day by day and the most important tool of PR, because of their interactive nature and user friendliness; having much customized options; a wide reach (huge amount of traffic daily); an online place where you do what you want and of providing so many facilities, writing, sharing, uploading, linking, networking and commenting, provide lot of fun and entertainment, and provides option of developing a unique page for business or personal interest[13]. It thus could be inferred from these experiences that social media must be an integral part of a successful public relations campaign. This is further supported by a report on a three-year-long international survey of public relations practitioners examining the impact which blogs and other social media are having on public relations practice.

Findings from that report show these new media to be dramatically changing public relations. Results indicate that blogs and social media have enhanced what happens in public relations and that social media and traditional mainstream media complement each other. The study also finds that the emergences of blogs and social media have changed the way organizations communicate, especially to external audiences. Findings suggest social media complement traditional news media, and that blogs and social media influence coverage in traditional news media. The study reports blogs and social media have made communications more instantaneous by encouraging organizations to respond more quickly to criticism[14].

Social Media as Tool of Military Public Relations

In the same manner as civilian corporate and business organizations have come to find social media as a useful tool in the promotion of their objectives, so equally could the military. The militaries in the advanced nations of the west have come to recognize this and have started to utilize them across military command levels and even at individual levels. These are done however, with security considerations in mind. It is in that regard that the US Department of Defence, (DoD), issued a new policy that, on the surface, seems likely to expand access to popular social networking sites like YouTube, Facebook and Twitter by troops using military computers. The new policy says that the default policy of the department will be to allow access to social networking sites from the military's non-classified computer network, known by its acronym, NIPRNET (for Non-classified Internet Protocol Router Network.)[15]. The development is considered a step forward by advocates of social networking in the military. Those advocates have complained for years that local commanders, sometimes for vague or arbitrary reasons, have shut down personal blogs or restricted access to social networking sites that an increasing number of troops use to maintain contact with friends and families.

A growing number of deployed units have also begun using Facebook, Twitter, Flickr and other networking sites to share photographs, release official information and disseminate newsletters. The new policy has its caveats. It says for instance that commanders shall "continue to defend against malicious activity," namely to stop cyber-attacks, safeguard missions and maintain adequate bandwidth. And it requires that access be denied to sites containing "prohibited content," such as pornography, gambling and hate-crime related activities[16]. "This directive recognizes the importance of balancing appropriate security measures while maximizing the capabilities afforded by 21st Century Internet tools." While few troops would disagree with those caveats, the wording is broad enough to leave much discretion with local commanders to shut down access to Internet sites. And that means that commanders who are uncomfortable with social networking — and military bloggers say there are many of them — will be able to find ways to restrict Internet access by their troops[17].

Lindy Kyzer, who advices the US Army Chief of Public Affairs on social media issues, said that while the new policy does leave much discretion in the hands of local commanders, it also opens up access to social networking in several significant ways. First, she said, all military units will be required to open access to social networking sites at least initially. And when they restrict access, she added, those restrictions are supposed to be temporary. Reacting to this development, Don Faul, Director, Online Operations at Facebook, who served six years active duty as a Marine Corps Infantry Officer before joining the company, issued this statement about the new policy: "Facebook is heartened by today's decision to begin to allow our nation's men and women in uniform and civilian employees across the Department of Defence responsible access to social media, which plays an important role in people's daily lives. Facebook is an efficient way for people with real-world connections to share information and communicate and can be a particularly beneficial link between those stationed around the world and their families at home[18]." DoD has already embraced Facebook by setting up a number of pages with hundreds of thousands of fans as follows:

> US Army, http://www.facebook.com/USarmy;
> US Navy, http://www.facebook.com/USnavy;
> US Marine Corps, http://www.facebook.com/marinecorps;
> US Air Force, http://www.facebook.com/USairforce;
> US National Guard, http://www.facebook.com/TheNationalGuard;

ChairmanJointChiefs, http://www.facebook.com/admiralmikemullen[19].

It was in consonance with such liberty that on assumption of duty as NATO's supreme allied commander for Europe in July 2009, Navy Adm. James Stavridis reached out in a way that none of the previous 15 NATO Commanders since Army Gen. Dwight D. Eisenhower had. He posted a blog in the bid to get word out about his goals for Supreme Headquarters Allied Powers Europe SHAPE, and European Command, EUCOM. Admiral Stavridis named his blog, 'from the Bridge', a reference to the two Commands focus on bridging the Atlantic to link the United States and Europe. With headquarters in Mons, Belgium, and Stuttgart, Germany, he acknowledged in his inaugural blog the importance of being able to Communicate EUCOM's and NATO's message intelligently, and his own leadership principles effectively." The Professional characteristics that matters to me are simple: civility, quiet confidence, creativity, teamwork and collaboration, determination, and above all, honesty and integrity, '' he wrote. '' I will write a future post about these characteristics and why I think they are essential[20]."

It was noted that apart from the Admiral, a growing number of senior military and defence leaders are turning to blogs, Facebook pages, twitter entries and other social networking venues to share information and seek feedbacks. They use these new tools to communicate their goals and activities, seek broader input they can apply to their decision making to engage with groups that simply can't be reached through traditional communication channels. Defence personalities like Robert M. Gates maintains a Facebook page while joint Chiefs Chairman Navy Admiral Mike Mullen's Twitter entries are to blogs that are regularly updated by everyone from combatant commanders to troops deployed to Iraq and Afghanistan.

Social media is a new phenomenon, with the first recognisable social network site tracing its roots to just 1997. But it's taken the world by storm. By some estimate, more than 60 million people maintain a blog. Meanwhile, MySpace and Facebook social networking sites have quickly risen to become the most – visited U.S we sites. The military has taken notice as Marine Gen. James E. Cartwright, Vice Chairman of the Joint Chiefs of Staff, was among the first military leaders to embrace social media. His goal was to cut through the traditional top –down military structure and information stovepipes to improve communication. When U.S Africa Command was standing up as the Newest geographic command, Army Gen. William E. "Kip" Ward made the first entry on its online blog, ÄFRICOM Dialogue" to describe the command's goals to his own staff and public at large. Since then, General Ward and his staff regularly post updates about the command's activities in the region, providing a feedback box that invites readers to respond[21].

Social Media Consciousness in Africa

Many African leaders are also beginning to appreciate the importance of social media. Brigadier (Ret.) Julius Maada Bio, of the Sierra Leonian Army who also was a former military ruler of his country, views social media as a potent weapon in the hands of people and, rulers around the world must respect their wishes. "In today's age information spreads much faster through Internet and people are more aware of happenings around the world. Bio said that the Arab Spring that brought changes in Tunisia, Egypt and Libya would not have been possible without the power of social media and Internet. "Who would have thought such an end to Gaddafi's reign," he said. The Presidential candidate for 2012 elections in Sierra Leone said that the world today is without borders and no attempts to suppress information would succeed[22].

Social media consciousness is becoming prevalent in Africa with many youths and people of the continent. Its impact no doubt came out clearly during the "Arab Spring" revolt as it no doubt helped to influence and shape the revolt in the countries that were experiencing them. For Nigeria, social media consciousness has surfaced tremendously given that, for the first time in Nigeria's political history ... the social media has equally provided a platform for youths to debate[23]. New Media especially social media, have given citizens more voice. The internet (Twitter, Facebook, and You Tube) and mobile phone text messaging were used extensively during the 2011 elections to share information and opinions about the polls with comparatively less fear than in the past elections.

Radio stations are also beginning to popularize call-in programmes, which give members of the public the opportunity to air their views[24]. Nigeria's President Goodluck Jonathan before the April 2011 elections in Nigeria opened a social media web site. Social media is known also to have greatly inspired the fuel subsidy protests in Nigeria in January 2012. Across the country, a series of "Occupy Nigeria" protests took place in response to President Goodluck Jonathan's January 1 announcement of the removal of fuel subsidy, which led to a price hike in fuel prices. Protests of varying levels took place in more than a dozen Nigerian cities. Social media played an impressive role in terms of documenting and for coordinating activities[25].

Nigerian Military and Social Media

For the Nigerian military however, there is of yet no seeming understanding or appreciation of what social media stands for or could do for the practice of public relations in the Nigerian military. Olukolade tended to offer explanations in this regard by his assertion that military operations often place priority on minimal delays with so much emphasis on secrecy and achievement of the surprise element. Nevertheless, the information age and technological revolution have tended to introduce a challenge with social demand for real time information[26]. Oyekola also corroborates this position by his assertion that there is always the tendency to attempt to beat the military to its game of security and surprise with the use of GSM pictures and placement on the internet, Facebook, U-Tube, Twitter, and other social media channels which the Nigerian military is yet to incorporate into its plans for information dissemination. Some of the unwholesome things about the military are propagated through the entertainment media of home video and films... the military needs to pay attention to the use of drama and social media approaches in managing this[27]. Generally however, for most African Armed Forces, there has been no serious evidence to show that social media as tool of communication has any root as of yet. In this era of globalization, African militaries including the Nigerian military cannot afford to be left behind.

References

1. http://education.ezine9.com/impact-of-globalization-146d7d24cc.html
2. Ibid
3. Daniel Nation @ http://webtrends.about.com/OD/web20/a/social-media.htm
4. Ibid
5. http://en.wikipedia.org/wiki/social_media
6. http://networkconference.netstudies.org/2010/04/social-media-and-globalisation/
7. ibid
8. Dave Roos @ http://communication.howstuffworks.com/how-public-relations-works5.htm
9. AdamolekunWole, "Sustainable Public Relations Strategies to Enhance the Operations of the Nigerian Air Force", Lecture delivered at Nigerian Air Force Training Seminar, Abuja, July 2010
10. ibid
11. http://sbr.com.sg/media-marketing/commentary/public-relations-in-era-social-media
12. ibid
13. http://www.virtualsocialmedia.com/social-media-the-best-public-relations-tool/
14. http://www.prsa.org/SearchResults/view/6D-020203/0/How Blogs and social Media are Changing Public Relations
15. James Dao @ http://atwar.blogs.nytimes.com/2010/02/26/military-announces new-social-media-policy/http://atwar.blogs.nytimes.com/2010/02/26/military-announces-new-social-media-policy/
16. ibid
17. ibid
18. ibid
19. ibid
20. http://www.military.com/news/article/air-force-news/military-leaders-embrace-social-media
21. ibid
22. http://gulfnews.com/news/gulf/oman/listen-to-people-s-voice-says-former-african-military-ruler-1.963086
23. http://www.bbc.co.uk/news/
24. Friedrich-Ebert Stiftung (2012) **African Media Barometer: Nigeria 2011**, P. 9

25. http://africanurbanism.blogspot.com/2012/01/protests-ignite-across-nigeria-against.html
26. Olukolade, A.C. "Mobilisation of Public Support for Nigerias Military Operations: A Framework For Public Information Management", Research Project submitted to the National Institute for Policy and Strategic SstudiesKuru, November 2011, P. 43
27. Oyekola, quoted in Olukolade A.C. (Ibid)

CHAPTER FOURTEEN

PUBLIC RELATIONS AND NEGATIVE CONOTATION: THE NIGERIAN DIMENSION

Introduction

The broad discipline of public relations has from time been always plagued by especially controversies of definitional problematic. Such definitional controversy as Jacques noted, could only compare to the definitional challenges that have been facing issue management and crisis management as a result of on-going definitional ambiguity. He contends that defining the term "public relations" has itself generated extensive scholarship, going back to the famous study by Harlow (1976), who reportedly identified 472 different definitions of public relations. Such analysis he noted, has over time proved over all to be less than helpful. Citing a study conducted by Cropp and Pincus (2001), it was for instance, observed that 25 years after Harlow's seminal work, definitions of public relations continue to proliferate with little common perspective, and that this decades-long confusion over the nature and applications of public relations has in fact seen a deteriorating clarity of its transcending purpose. They further concluded that "the confusion has been exacerbated by the myriad definitions and terminology applied to the various specialties, activities and literature falling under the rubric of public relations"[1].

Arising confusions from the above perspectives consequently, have led to myriads of definitions that are associated with public relations. While some definitions view public relations as promotion, propaganda, communication, lobbying and marketing, others see it as a marketing communications-mix, a means of cultivating the media and celebrities, reputation, value and relationship building. Yet others see it as a management function, a means of influencing public opinion as well as means of shaping and managing perception. Regardless of which definition of public relations is chosen as Cohen puts it, several factors are consistent. He holds PR to be part of an organization's overall marketing and communications function. PR is critical in helping to engage an organization's diverse publics across media platforms including third party and social media. Public relations must protect the organization's reputation and provide crisis management where necessary. Further, PR must accomplish this with an understanding of the search optimization opportunities[2].

Diverse perceptions on the notion of public relations have continued to exist along with its continuing evolvement. In this regard as a PR expert reflected: if Stauber, Rampton, and Bernays, three of its renowned experts were all put in one room to discuss public relations and propaganda, conflict would arise. All of them have opposing opinions. It is easy to compare and contrast all of their views because of their distinctive beliefs. Bernays, he stated, believes that public relations are necessary in a democratic society, while Stauber and Rampton have a negative outlook on propaganda and public relations. To them, public relations are "designed to alter perception, reshape reality, and manufacture consent". They are of the view also that public relations professionals add their own "spin" to a story, and further that PR firms do not put enough research into their stories... they carry out activities that are often considerably more secretive and sinister... they see public relations as conniving[3]. John Brissenden equally has similar notions about public relations. He sees the two initials of PR to be seemingly harmless but however says that the very use of the prefix PR seems to diminish whatever follows, by rendering it faintly ridiculous. PR person, PR stunt. Two decades later, the popular image of public relations still bears traces of the 1990s sitcom Absolutely Fabulous: all cocaine, champagne and shagging. In relation to Britain, he alludes to Miller and Dinnan's assertion that the role of PR has been to facilitate 'institutional corruption' in British governance, the effect of which will be with us for many years to come... A key role of the PR industry in the late 20th century Britain and a condition of its spectacular growth was to make profits from, and facilitate, the marked distribution of wealth from the poor to the rich[4].

The Nigerian Dimension

Definitions and perceptions of public relations globally, vary from one country to another. However, a disturbing dimension to its evolving meaning in Nigeria is that which equates public relations to a sort of bribery, a notion which public relations practitioners and even the Nigerian Institute of public relations have not done much to correct or discourage. This author, at a public lecture, once harped on the need for Nigerians to be educated on what public relations are and what they are not rather than the subsisting negative but generally believed notion of public relations or "PR" as known by its popularly abused acronym. He said that in Nigeria, what people generally refer to as PR is a form of gratification especially in cash or kind which people offer to show or express appreciation for a "good turn" as so called. This is a pervasive belief and practice that runs through the entire spectrum of Nigerian society. Public relations are not money, about money or material offer or, of other form or forms of gratuitous gratification that are used by people to register appreciation and goodwill[5]. The sad aspect of this subsisting notion is that even very educated and enlightened elites in government, the private sector and business share in this negative notion. Some analysts are of the view that such notion among others is what impelled the many reforms started by the Nigerian government especially the image rebranding project which they recommended should be better left to public relations experts.

Reform as Panacea

Reform by its basic meaning denotes a change that is made to a social system for correctional, improvement or re-structuring objective, all aimed at positive benefits. While experts are of the view that reforms in any instance are to bring about positive changes, which should either result in improvement or some form of correction, there are areas in which Nigeria is faulty in terms of reforms and therefore the need to get it right. They are of the view that the Nigerian government is not ignorant of the immense contributory solution which Public Relations proffers to the successful implementation of reforms in the polity, but that it is a misunderstanding of the concept of Public Relations, which makes most leaderships apply advertising, propaganda, publicity, assassination, bribery and others that are not Public Relations as instruments of reforms[6].

A very telling and glaringly cited example for instance, was the "case of a renowned professor and former minister of education, who ignorantly misconstrued public relations for bribery, yet he admitted it overlooking the ignominy such absurdity has on his person and the perception of the international society... about Nigeria; when the scandal became public knowledge, critics would have asked, how possible that a Minister of education in Nigeria does not know what public relations is[7]. The analyst is of the view that the same scandal has linkage with a similar one which once equally saw a serving senate president during Obasanjo regime in the fourth republic bow out in shame. He asserts that from studying the trend of such happenings in Nigeria, the conclusion may be drawn that for Nigeria's reform processes, government prefers making use of quacks and willing puppets in place of institutions responsible for reforms for mischievous and for selfish reasons[8].

He avers further that in looking at the relevance of Public Relations in reforms, it is necessary to see the import of the application of every concept as derived from the definition of that concept. It is thus not possible to understand the place of public relations in reforms without giving meaning to the concept. The most acceptable and generalized definition of public relations was propounded at an international conference in the city of Mexico in the year 1978 when about 30 national and international bodies of public relations met and came up with the view that: 'Public relations is the art and the social science of analyzing trends, predicting their consequences, counseling organization leaders, and implementing planned programmes of action which will serve both the organization's and the publics' interest'[9].

The involvement of professional public relations practitioners in the formulation of reform policies makes it possible for the policy to possess inherent proactive factors, which will make the policy fit into future arrangements... The programme of giving Nigeria a new brand or image is solely the responsibility of public relations, and until this is effected, there can be no truly branding of a new Nigeria. The involvement of Public relations in Nigerian reform programmes has all the advantages and potential for success as public interest would be put foremost in the formulation, expression and implementation of the reforms. Public policies such as the educational reform policy issue, fuel subsidy removal, and other socio economic policies all require public relations inputs for added value, better understanding and interpretation[10]. The potential of public relations in the fight against corruption by the government of Nigeria was highlighted in Abuja in 2008 at a summit organized by Timex Communications, Nigerian Institute of Public Relations, NIPR and Federation of African Public Relations Association, (FAPRA). The summit in noting the poor and uncoordinated publicity on progress made in the fight against corruption and that public relations practitioners and communications specialists generally have major roles to play in the war against corruption felt the need to marshal effective anti-corruption communication campaign strategies to support positive and pro-active stance of relevant agencies against corruption. It was recommended for collaboration amongst integrated marketing communications specialists involving public relations, advertising and marketing for synergy[11].

Public relations as the fundamental art and science of establishing relationships between an organization and its key audiences plays a key role in helping business and industry create strong relationships with clients and customers. Public relations involve supervising and assessing public attitudes, and maintaining mutual relations and understanding between an organization and its public. The function of public relations is to improve channels of communication and to institute new ways of setting up a two-way flow of information and understanding. It is effective in helping corporations convey information about their products or services to potential customers, reach local government and legislators, help politicians attract votes and raise money, and craft their public image and legacy, helps non-profit organizations, including schools, hospitals, social service agencies boost support of their programs such as awareness programmes, fund-raising programs, and to increase patronage of their services. As public image is important to all organizations and prominent personalities, the role of public relations specialist becomes pertinent in crisis situations. Public relations agencies provide important and timely transmission of information that helps save the face of an organization. Overall, public relations help an organization and its public adapt mutually to one another[12].

It should therefore not be a matter of debate that with such key roles in society, it is important for people to get to understand the proper place of public relations rather than harbour the many negative notions about the discipline. Public relations are certainly not about doing favours or about money and of giving out money in form of bribe. Public relations behaviour are conditioned and governed by a body of ethics which as Frank Jenkins asserts, apply particularly to the way the PR practitioner behaves. The personal integrity becomes an integral part of his professionalism, as with a doctor, lawyer or architect. A PRO has to do PR for himself in that he will be judged by the way he acts. He gives expert advice; he does not bribe and corrupt; he publishes stories on their merit, not because he entertains journalists: he is a professional[13].

Indeed public relations practitioners need to restore the image of public relations through their attitudes, actions and behaviour. They should equally be able to as well correct and dispel the many negative notions about the profession as ultimately such negative connotation derives from prejudice, ignorance or the lack of understanding of what public relations represents. The military especially its PR officers should not identify with this negativism and gradually creeping cultural misnomer. They should rather see PR for what it is as a genuine and honest design for bridging and enhancement of relations between an organization and its publics.

References

1. Tony Jaques, "Issue and Crisis Management: Quicksand in the Definitional Landscape" in "Public Relations Review, 2009, 35(3) 280-286" cited @ http://www.issueoutcomes.com.au/Websites/issueoutcomes/Images/Definitional-quicksand-PRR.pdf

2. Heidi Cohen, "31 public relations definition" @ http://heidicohen.com/public-relations-definition/

3. Propaganda and Public Relations: Stauber and RamptonvsBernays refer

4. John Brissenden, " Britain's PR Culture Breeds Corruption, Just Look at Hacgate" @http://www.opendemocracy.net/ourkingdom/john-brissenden.britains-pr-culture-breeds-corruption-just-look-at-hackgate

5. John Adache, "Public Relations: Its Role in Political and Legislative Matters", Lecture delivered to Legislative Aides of National Assembly, Abuja, 16 & 17 November, 2009.

6. Nelson O. Michael, "Reforms in Nigeria: the Place of Public Relations" http://www.articlesbase.com/organizational-articles/reforms-in-nigeria-the-place-of-public-relations-145498.html

7. ibid

8. ibid

9. ibid

10. Ibid

11. Communique issued at the end of Timex Communications, NIPR and FAPRA on sensitizing African citizens towards building a corruption free society at Abuja, 24-26 February 2008. ibid

12. Susan Jan "The Important Role of Public Relations" http://ezinearticles.com/?The-Important-Role-Of-Public-Relations&id=198392

13. Frank Jefkins, Public Relations (Plymouth, M&E Pub) P. 12

CHAPTER FIFTEEN

FOSTERING CORDIAL CIVILIAN-MILITARY RELATIONSHIP: OBLIGATIONS FOR THE MILITARY AND THE MEDIA

Introduction

The fundamental role which the media play in society at the national and international levels, developed and developing nations is generally widely acknowledged. Their importance are quite paramount to the extent that Boutros Ghali, a former UN Secretary General once described a media outfit, - the Cable News Network, CNN as the 16th Member of the United Nations Security Council[1].The role of the media therefore, as very well-known are basically to inform, educate and entertain, play the watchdog function, unfold and document history as well as perpetuate diverse cultures and heritages.

By especially playing the watchdog function, the media is able to assert its role in disseminating plural information and equally of creating awareness for the people. The media cover all and every form of societal events ranging from issues of general interest to news about conflict, security, the military and the entire spectrum of the defence establishment. The news media are thus able to provide vital linkages between the public, and the government bearing on all aspects of military operations in the field. The instant and increasing flow of television news does go a long way in initiating and setting the national agenda with the increasing political sensitivity towards public opinion polls and media coverage of military operations[2].

It is therefore crucial and prudent for military leaders to recognize that public opinion constitute a critical centre of gravity for all military operations because of its importance to the political well-being of any administration. The media do this realising that the people have the right and need to know more about the extent and implications of especially military operations in times of conflict. In peace and in war, reportage of events that relate to the military needs to be done with care and a high sense of responsibility and such reports must not only be those of operational matters but inclusive of reports that have bearing on the equipment, materiel, personnel and top personalities of the military hierarchy - their actions and inactions and so on. Such reports if not carefully handled have the propensity and great potential to impinging one way or the other on national security.

This therefore brings to the fore, the critical roles that could be played by the media in the process of reporting by way of balancing truth and accuracy as against sensationally peddling half-truths and falsehood. The coverage of military affairs and indeed, of the defence and security environment has most often always presented some very complex challenges for the Journalists that cover those Beats and equally for the military establishment that are reported upon. However, between reporting which is the function of the journalists and being reported upon of which the military are the beneficiary, there arises a lacuna going by the military belief that the essence of successful warfare is secrecy, while the media conversely believe that the essence of successful journalism is publicity[3]. In spite of such existing lacuna, the media does always have a substantial role to play in the same manner as the military has the responsibility to cooperate in providing necessary information all in the national interest. This chapter addresses this topic accordingly:

Military, Media and the lingering perception

There can be few professions more ready to misunderstand each other than journalists and soldiers[4]. SF Crozier made this statement many years ago in relation to the so called turbulent relationship which purportedly always exist between soldiers and journalists. It has been an age long lingering perception. No doubt, as Alan Hooper, a British Royal Marines Officer once noted, the shape of peoples life all over the world is constantly redirected by the results of armed conflicts and that despite man's increasing knowledge, he is apparently unable to solve many of his problems by peaceful means[5]. With numerous areas of conflict dotting all corners of the globe from the middle to the Far East, parts of Europe and North America, and of course not leaving out Africa, Crozier further observed that for good or ill, events such as these are pursued by newsmen, investigative reporters and television cameras[6]. There is no denying these facts as daily random glance at newspaper headlines or Television news items in any period of a month testifies to job outputs of Journalists in military settings. There is of course little doubt also about the public interest which these news stories arouse and continue to arouse. This probably explains why a lot of the news spotlight continues to be on the military as never before. The Nigerian military within Nigeria's setting provides a typical example.

Media interest in the Army and indeed the military is very necessary and healthy given as posited that a free press is fundamental to the survival of every democracy. Against this background therefore, it certainly follows that a good and robust relationship between the military and the media is very critical and vital. Both sides have much to learn about each other, and are both likely to suffer consequences if they fail to do so. In alluding again to the statement earlier credited to SF Crozier about the military and the media misunderstanding each other, he singled mutual ignorance as a primary reason for this misunderstanding. He averred that even in battle, where the soldier and the reporter share discomfort together, that very closeness divides them because the soldier is there as a participant, compelled to remain through discipline, whereas the reporter is there as an observer, free to leave when he wants, but compelled to remain only through self discipline[7]. The soldier, he rightly observes, owes his loyalty to superiors, the officer to his subordinates; the reporter owes his loyalty to his editor, the editor to his public. As noted in relation to the United Kingdom, in peacetime, the media become the watchdog of the tax payer and keep an eye on the military. He adds that they also keep an eye on the government on behalf of the apolitical armed forces; the media have one other vital role to play in peace time and that is to provide the link between the services and the public by keeping them in touch with each other, ensuring that the British people have a realistic view of defence[8].

The above context in all its ramifications is applicable to Nigeria as the link between the military and the public is becoming more important than ever before. Agim attributes the misunderstanding between the military and the media in Nigeria to stereotyping. He avers that there is so much stereotypes in the minds of both the press and the military. The military constantly look at the press as liars and those who enjoy misquoting and misrepresenting facts. Some senior officers do not accept to talk to the press or even read from a script for fear of being misquoted. The press paints the picture of illiterate military for the world but as soon as they retire and go into private lives, they are accepted as being civilized. Stereotypes bring about defensive behaviour, which may negate mutual interaction[9]. An understanding of the relationship between the military and the media is important not only in itself but equally in the context of the rapport between the public and the services. This is the task before the Nigerian Military and indeed militaries all over the world.

Balanced Reporting versus Sensationalism

The debate has been on-going as to whether or not to classify as friend or foe, mass media which report warfare and other security operations without due consideration for security and national interest. It is to that extent that Hyper, a Wing Commander in the Royal Air Force once remarked that over the last thirty years, media coverage of armed conflict around the world has become more graphic thus having an increasing effect on public opinion in the United Kingdom[10]. He then posed a question saying "has the point been reached where reasonable media coverage can inhibit the prosecution of a just war and if so, whether anything can or should be done to suppress that coverage?[11].This question is quite relevant given that with the many conflict hotspots in the world today, the Mass Media especially the Press and the Television are usually dominated with bogus and sensational headlines, and "Breaking News" at all times even when they border on issues that are sensitive and could be harmful to national security. With media reports having significant effect on public opinion as in the U.K for example, many Members of Parliament are inundated with letters from constituents demanding an end to the fighting, while mothers of troops serving abroad regularly demonstrate outside Downing Street[12].

The same scenario plays out equally in the United States and other countries whose troops are abroad fighting especially in Afghanistan where frequent casualties of Western troops arising from Taliban fighters are sensationally reported. Sensational reporting no doubt demoralizes the moral of fighting troops, strengthens the enemy and brings about negative public opinion against the war effort. In Nigeria, the nature of media reporting of conflicts or other hazards during internal security operations tends towards sensationalism as for example, with the many bogus media reports in relation to especially the Niger Delta crisis and even more recently of the Boko Haram crisis. When for example, clashes occur between militants and security forces, the reports are often blown out of proportion even when correct facts are not obtained. Essentially, given the potential effect of such reporting, what can or should be done to prevent such reports? It is thus necessary to examine the Media roles and of the military responsibility in that regard. In respect of the media and as practiced worldwide, Standing Operational Procedures (SOPs) in battle does recognize the role of the media to inform the public on progress of events during conflict so long as this does not compromise the security of the forces. While this is granted, Journalists should equally, on basis of journalistic ethics and dictum of social responsibility be required to discern and use proper judgement when reporting events that have security bearing. However, given the belief in some quarters within the military that journalists cannot be trusted, it is necessary to from time to time, to organize meetings at established forums where greater understanding of the issues could be better bridged. The mutual suspicion or rather, mistrust between the two parties is however, not confined to the Nigerian military and journalists as the trend abound all over the world. For example, in Britain as Alan Hooper noted, there is considerable misunderstanding and mutual ignorance between military officers and journalists, and yet, the characteristics of the military and the media are surprisingly similar[13].

On the military aspect, it must be realised that they are usually very rigid and sensitive to issues that border on security without much compromise. For example, if the military were to engage in an operation, it will be sensitive to any media report of casualty levels, loss of capability, or a percentage of it, as these will be valuable intelligence to an enemy. The media will therefore be required to exercise restraint in their reporting or at least, delay the information until it could be of no operational value to the enemy. The military by its ethic objects to the naming of any casualty before the Next of Kin (NOK) is informed but, the press by its own usually defined interest would rather want to publish most times without clearance; such situation fosters friction between the two organisations. This is why in order to go around this problem the military would often want to resort to various forms of censorship through exclusion, delay, through editing, and sometimes by total prohibition to the distaste of journalists.

Balanced Reporting Principles

A report is a written or spoken account of something that has happened, for example in a newspaper, or magazine, radio or television. Reporting therefore denotes the rendering of account or presenting of news or information about what had happened through any of the media of Mass communication. When you talk about balanced reporting, you are introducing the element of a scaling system that would or should ensure some form of equilibrium. Balanced reporting in this context would mean that apart from bringing truth and accuracy to any report through proper verification, you must also bring into it, the elements of fairness, justice and equity of the two sides to the story. Balanced reporting is a report that is quite considerate of the values of justice, fairness and equity. These values derive their basis from a theoretical framework; namely the Libertarian theory of the press, the philosophy of which belongs to people like John Milton, John Stuart Mills, and Thomas Jefferson among others. These philosophers belonged to the age of enlightenment. They had consistently questioned the old order of absolutism and other untenable values that existed at the time and are regarded as the forerunners of modern freedom and liberty.

The Media are regarded as the greatest beneficiaries as the most important effect of Libertarianism on the press was the ability to own private press outside of government. This engendered a lot more freedom as the press was no longer an instrument of Government or spokesman of the ruling elite. Therefore with private ownership and as democracy grew, the value of freedom of expression became much more emphasized. The Free Press now had a duty to report news, research, comment, editorialize, cartoon as long as the editors are ready to be responsible for their actions, and to also be ready to present the two sides of a story. These are the trends that are most often found in especially the western democracies that are very well known. How about the scenario in Nigeria as a country? No doubt, there have been a lot of complaints about the Nigerian press who have been accused of always tending to carry one sided stories and, of even sometimes carrying stories that have no foundations or substance. These are done without due diligence to cross checking of facts. The complaints come from all segments of the society including the military who often accuse the press of being too sensational with stories. It is further necessary to dwell on the concept of sensationalism in relation to this subject.

Sensationalism denotes the representation of facts in a way intended to produce strong feelings of shock, anger, or excitement. People usually feel affronted by newspapers or other publications that often resort to sensationalism and scandal. Newspaper sensationalism is usually associated with the tabloids, soft sell and general interest magazines that have such editorial tendencies. Vulgar tabloid sensationalism is a term that has come to be associated with those media that particularly thrive and without apologies, have made such tendencies, their trade mark. Media sensationalism is a dysfunction of mass communication and a negative value which its protagonists unfortunately benefit from.

But why do some media resort to sensation? Research has revealed quite a number of reasons but most fundamentally is the mercantilist or commercial motive. The media as private enterprises are expected to rise and fall by their own commercial wits. The owners argue that they have to make profit to ensure their survival in a liberal commercial environment where they are into competition between and within themselves. Yes they must survive, but to what detriment and at what cost? Should it be to the detriment of the many values in society including those that border on national security? In spite of the beautifully enunciated mission statements, the media are accused of frequently side tracking their self-engendered social goals in favour of expected revenue. This is an aspect which the Media seriously needs to look at especially in relation to the military.

Security considerations in reporting the Military

Security today, has broadened widely thus bringing about its many parameters – political, economic, social, environmental and so on. This chapter within context of the discourse limits its purview to military security which according to George Obiozor has to do with two-level interplay of the armed offensive and defensive capabilities of states and their perception of each other's intention[14]. Barry Buzan presents so many aspects to his discuss on security but of relevance here are his postulation that the distinction between threats and vulnerabilities points to a key divide in security policy. Units can seek to reduce their security either by reducing their vulnerability or by preventing or lessening threats. These alternatives underlie retrospectively, the ideas of national and international security[15]. The above postulations are obviously in tune with the realist conception of security and therefore, every nation seeks to undertake proactive security measures that would not make it vulnerable to security threats, and by seeking to prevent or lessen potential or emerging threats. These could be achieved through many means that includes those of overt and covert dimensions, psychological operations, misinformation, and disinformation and as well information denial among others. Journalists must take into consideration that in reporting for their media, any report that is capable of jeopardizing the national security interest must be handled with caution and most responsibly. But as Chijuka cautions, problems arise where the interest of the state and that of persons in power conflicts. Journalists must however, be very careful to discern between issues of genuine interest to national security and not those that may be camouflaged under the guise of national interest to justify personal interests. As he further noted, when such happens, the desires and ambitions of incumbent rulers may be mistaken for or regarded as synonymous with national interest[16].

Aiding media access to unclassified information

Information is a very critical tool required by journalists to be able to carry out the jobs assigned them by their organisations on daily basis. They thrive on the information they receive from their various sources to enable them meet up with their daily obligation of providing newsworthy information within stipulated deadlines for the media organisations. This, the journalist must continue to do to be able to keep his or her job. While journalists across several beats have their own unique and peculiar problems obtaining the right information at the right time to meet deadlines, journalists on the defence beat usually complain that the military most often times are not only stingy with information but that the military institution over classifies its information. While this may be true, the media often tends to forget that the information which journalists by their judgement think may be of public interest would not actually be of public interest as their release may injure or harm national security. While arguments about information that should be released or not released, classified or not classified would always exist between the media and the military, the point needs be taken that for mutual institutional and indeed national interest, ways must be evolved by which to aid media access to unclassified information about the military. This is very necessary as the military need to show greater regard for the right of the media to as much information as possible in the public interest. In relation to sustenance of Nigerian democracy, it must be recognised that the better informed the Nigerian public is about the operations of government including those of security and military affairs, the greater will be the health of Nigerian democracy[17]. The media conversely should reciprocate such gesture and ensure it does not indulge in anything that may compromise the security of military operations and indeed national security. The military through its Public Relations branches can best assist the media to do their job through prompt release of information, taking the media into confidence through improved access, pre-operational briefing where necessary, regular interaction and capacity building. The military needs to be able to do this to disabuse the minds of civilians who feel that the military classifies a lot of information just to cover up embarrassing cases of maladministration and corruption[18].

Fostering a Culture of Cordial Media-Military Relationship

There is no doubt from the foregoing analysis that ensuring true, accurate and balanced reporting of security and military affairs are mutually exclusive responsibilities of the military and the media and there is the need especially on the part of the military to continue to foster and ensure a culture of strengthening civic Media-Military relationship. This can only be achieved through application of a realistic and robust Public Relations approach. In carrying out these mutually exclusive roles and responsibility, the two institutions could achieve success through mapping out of appropriate strategies. As for the military, Pyper, suggests that there are ways in which the military can legitimately influence public opinion to support its conception of any conflict without resorting to manipulation of news. The first is the long-term application of good PR techniques to build up the image and the reputation of the Armed Forces[19].

Strategic PR must be designed to instil confidence in the public. In a sense, strategic PR is the progressive accumulation of influence against a time when things go wrong and military image comes under attack. Strategic Public Relations must also be accompanied by tactical Public Relations. This is a kind of PR that is deliberately targeted, during the build-up and conduct of hostilities, at winning the battle for the hearts and minds of the public[20]. He also suggests to the military that in course of any conflict when mistakes are made, attempts must not be made to disguise them by any means. As for the media, what could be done is a trend which is already being practiced in many media establishments globally. For example, specialized reporting by which many papers today have defence reporters accredited to Defence Beats and other military establishments, and equally of embedding journalists during exercises and operations as practised in modern militaries.

Conclusion

For the Nigerian military and indeed national armed forces across the world, military public relations as in the Americas should be taken as compelling necessity that requires every support especially in this age of globalization which demands conformity to global benchmarks. The Military should realise that unrestricted flow of information is the lifeblood of any democracy. Public control of government institutions especially depends on truthful accounting of activities conducted in the name of the citizenry. Military Public affairs is the effort of the military as an institution of government to identify with the citizens' interest, seek informed support, and render accounts of work performed. The power of public opinion and the need to maintain public favour are concepts that have long been appreciated throughout history[21]. The Nigerian Army and indeed the military can learn, borrow as well as imbibe the US Military Public Affairs Philosophy at the core of which mission emphasizes that both soldiers and citizens should understand the role of the institution. Informed soldiers are more likely to survive and win if they know why they fight and how well they are doing it. At the same time, informed citizens are more likely to give soldiers their sympathy and support. Battles are won, disasters are averted, and rescues accomplished when there is favourable public opinion. When people don't understand what their soldiers do for them, there is scepticism and distrust. Rumour fills the vacuum when there are no facts[22].

By the same token and within that frame of reference, military doctrine based on lessons learned defines US public affairs philosophy and practice. It guides commanders and public affairs officers (PAOs) on how they should treat information they collect and pass on to both the public and soldiers. Opposing forces or adversaries might lie or disinform, but the American military must speak only the truth. Information, whether complimentary or embarrassing, is freely passed through internal channels and given to the news media for public dissemination within the constraints of military security and public law. Generally four doctrinal concepts guide U.S. military public affairs practice namely; the public's right to know; maximum disclosure with minimum delay; information must come from a trusted source; and internal news comes from the commander first[23]. The Nigerian Military, I believe would greatly benefit if it learns, borrows and imbibe such a philosophy and doctrine.

References

1. Michael Kingsley, **Mass media and Politics**, Encarta Premium, 2006.
2. Cited in Bamba Diao "Media in Modern Conflicts: Effects on Military Operations in Senegal", Project submitted to National War College, June 2006.
3. Hugh Beach, "News Management in Conventional War"
4. S.F. Crozier, cited in Alan Hooper, (1982) **The Military and the Media** (Aldershot, Gower Pub P. 3
5. Ibid, P.3
6. Ibid
7. Ibid
8. Ibid
9. Agim, J.A. (2004) **The Principles and Practice of Public Relations in the Military and the Police**, Enugu, Ultimate Publishers, P. 146
10. H.H. Pyper "The Media in Modern Warfare- Friend or Foe?" in Hawk, Bracknell RAF Staff College, 1992
11. Ibid
12. Ibid
13. Alan Hooper, **The Military and the Media,** Op cit
14. George Obiozor, cited in Adache JEA **Regional Integration in Africa: The ECOWAS Experience**, (UNIABUJA, PhD Dissertation 2006, P.47)
15. Barry Buzan, cited in Adache JEA – Ibid
16. Fred Chijuka "Nigerian Media: Balanced Reporting Versus Sensationalism and National Security", Paper presented at Defence Information Seminar, Abuja, 12 march 2007
17. Ibid
18. Mahmud Jega, Media Access to Unclassified Military Information", Paper presented at Capacity building Workshop for Defence Correspondents at Yenagoa, May 2007
19. H.H. Pyper, "The Media in Modern Warfare", Op cit
20. Ibid
21. Stephen Johnson, "Military Public Relations in the Americas: Learning to Promote the Flow", A Research and Education in Defence Studies paper, Washington DC, May 22-25, 2001 (Posted on the web)
22. Ibid
23. Ibid (Cited from US Public Affairs Document)

CHAPTER SIXTEEN

SECURITY THREATS, CRISIS MANAGEMENT AND THE ROLE OF COMMUNICATION

Introduction

The notion of security globally has several dimensions which all bother on the peace and survival of individuals, groups and organizations in society. Security is a first order priority of all human societies and constitutes one primary determinant of what a person or group can do[1]. For Barry Buzan, security of people involves factors such as life, health, status, wealth and freedom all of which are beset by the contradictions between objective and subjective evolution[2]. Dimensions of security as generally recognized in the world today include political security which has to do with the manner by which states organize themselves, and their system of governments which provides basis for their legitimacy; economic security which is about access to resources, finance and markets that are necessary to sustain acceptable levels of welfare and state power. Environmental security concerns the maintenance of the local and planetary biosphere as the essential support system on which all other human enterprises depend[3].

Security indeed has to do with all these but more than this, it is about people and their ways of life as well as their values which must at all times be protected from intrusion as well as harm of any nature or form. Anything therefore that would constitute harm in any way or has the capacity and potential to constitute danger can be viewed as a threat. In the world today, there are so many forms of security threats as individuals, groups, organizations and even nations come under one form of security threat or the other. Very frequently, corporations and organizations come under siege either internally or externally. Such threats which could either be real or imagined, natural or man-made, complex and dangerous. The threats keep workers and especially senior executives very concerned, worried, and restless as the very survival of the firm or organization, not just its profitability is at stake. Therefore by confronting threats and limiting risk, particularly through robust security and business community systems, the company can assure its survival, gain a competitive edge and enhance shareholder value[4]. Where however, a threat or potential threat could not be prevented or contained through proactive measures, the situation no doubt will lead to crisis situations of great magnitudes. A security situation that degenerates into threat of whatever magnitude certainly would require to be managed by communication among other measures.

Communications as a process of expressing ideas and feelings or of providing information from one person to another or from one source to another or groups of people through selected channels is very critical in the management of crisis situations. This is applicable to all segments or organizations in society including the military. Communication serves the end of an information goal or objective. In public relations, communications is the process and means by which public relations objectives are achieved. It may take the form of news releases, press conferences, special events, brochures, speeches, bumper stickers, newsletters, parades, posters and the like[5].

Key Concepts and their Meanings

Security

By one of its definition, security is defined as the degree of protection against danger, damage, loss, and crime. Security as a form of protection is structures and processes that provide or improve security as a condition. The Institute for Security and Open Methodologies defines security as "a form of protection where a separation is created between the assets and the threat". This includes but is not limited to the elimination of either the asset or the threat. The military has its angle to the definition of security seen along background of scholars and differences in the security interests of nations around the world. Two schools of thought – the realists and the idealists are however, prominent. To the realist school of thought to which Bellamy belongs, he sees national security as relative freedom from war coupled with relatively high expectation that defeat will not be a consequence of any war that should occur[6].Lippman reinforces this view as he sees national security as the ability of a nation to maintain its core values and avoid war, and if challenged, to maintain such core values by victories in war[7]. The realist school believes that military might, is the fundamental requirement for national security. Scholars who belong to the idealist school of thought however, see security differently from another perspective.

A prominent member of the Idealist School is Robert McNamara, a one-time secretary of State of the United States who sees security through the prism of development. According to him, security is not military force though it may involve it, security is not military activity though it may encompass it, and security is not military hardware though it may include it. Security is development and without development, there is no security[8].

For organizational crisis situations there is a school of thought that sees it as any emotionally charged situation that, once it becomes public, invites negative stakeholder reaction and thereby has the potential to threaten the financial well-being, reputation, or survival of the firm or some portion thereof.

Security Threat:

A security threat can be taken to be any incident or situation that jeopardizes the security of an individual, group, organization or country. Waever associates the concept of security threat to security problems that undermine the security of any nation or community, and relates it to: ...developments that threaten the sovereignty or independence of a state in a particularly rapid or dramatic fashion, and deprive it of the capacity to manage itself. This, in turn, undercuts the political order. Such a threat must therefore be met with the mobilization of the maximum effort[9]. Similarly, security threat can be described as capacity of any human and non-human elements to destroy the vital interests of other considered targets. Often a weapon is used. Examples are robbery, kidnapping, hijacking, extortion and blackmail. A dissection of the concept of security threat shows that it covers all aspects of any malicious intention or action or occurrence geared towards making a party vulnerable and exposed to security risk. Security threat can be simply divided into two, namely, natural and man-made threats. The former are usually generated by nature while the latter involve cruel attacks arising from human actions and behaviour. The manmade threats involve malicious activities of man, which may include armed robbery, assassination, computer intrusion, information hacking and corruption, violent behaviour, ethnocentrism, religious bigotry and terrorism[10].

Crisis:

Crisis is a term that can be referred to as occurrences leading to serious or great danger, or an unstable situation of extreme danger or difficulty. It is also a time of difficulty or confusion when problems must be solved or important decisions must be made. This could be the period when a problem or situation is at its worse point. Crisis therefore portends the presence of instability in society. Crisis is thus a violent behaviour intended to hurt, injure, destroy or kill, being one of the various forms through which conflict is manifested. Crisis can occur on personal or social level. It may be an unstable or dangerous social situation in political, economic, military or on a large scale environmental event or community especially one involving an impending abrupt change. More loosely, it is term relating to a testing of time or emergency event[11]. Crisis can therefore be taken as a substantial unforeseen circumstance that can potentially jeopardize organizations employees, the customers, products, services and even reputation. It follows therefore that immediate decisions and actions from people are required.

Seeger et al, point to four defining characteristics of crisis. They are: specific, unexpected, and non – routine events or series of events that create high level of uncertainty and threat or perceived threat to an organization's high priority goals. Thus the first three characteristics are that the event is unexpected – i.e. a surprise, creates uncertainty and is seen as a threat to important goals[12].

Crisis Management

Crisis Management denotes the process by which an organization deals with a major event that threatens to harm the organization, its stakeholders, or the general public. The study of crisis management originated with the large scale industrial and environmental disasters in the 1980's. Three elements are common to most definitions of crisis: (a) a threat to the organization, (b) the element of surprise, and (c) a short decision time In contrast to risk management, which involves assessing potential threats and finding the best ways to avoid those threats, crisis management involves dealing with threats after they have occurred. It is a discipline within the broader context of management consisting of skills and techniques required to identify, assess, understand, and cope with a serious situation, especially from the moment it first occurs to the point that recovery procedures start[13]. Crisis Management by this diagnosis thus means the process of preparing for, and responding to unpredictable negative event so as to prevent it from escalating into an even bigger problem or worse of all, exploding into a full blown, widespread, life threatening disaster. It thus involves the execution of well-coordinated actions to control the damage and preserve or restore public confidence in the system under crisis.

Communications:

A simple and basic definition of communication denotes it as the exchange of thoughts, messages or information, as by speech, signals, writing or behaviour. Dennis Wilcox et al, see communication as the act of transmitting information, ideas and attitudes from one person to another. Communication can take place, however, only if the speaker and the listener (called the sender and the receiver) have a common understanding of the symbols being used. Words are the most common symbols. The degree to which two people understand each other is heavily dependent upon their common knowledge of word symbols... An important aspect of communication is the opportunity for feedback, or response from the listener to the speaker. Feedback is just as important as the dissemination of the message itself, because it tells the sender whether he or she is being understood[14].

Communication Channels

The communication process utilizes communication channels. Apart from the well-known traditional channels of communication especially of the print and electronic media, there are other channels such as news releases, press conferences, special events, brochures, speeches, bumper stickers, newsletters, and posters. An organization may create a separate web site for the crisis or designate a section of its current web site for the purpose of the crisis. Having a crisis web site is now a common best practice. An organization may however, not want to publicize a crisis by placing information about it on the web site.

Types of Security Threats/Crisis

There are many types of security threats/crisis situations. Some of them include the following.

- Natural crisis also referred to as natural disasters are most often considered as acts of God examples of which include earthquakes, volcanic eruptions, tornadoes and hurricanes, floods, landslides, tsunamis, storms, storms and droughts. A prominent example of tsunami is the 2004 Indian Ocean Earthquake.
- Technological crises on the other hand are caused by human application of science and technology when especially they become very complex. Examples cited include software failures, industrial accidents as well as oil spills.
- Confrontation crisis occur when discontented individuals/or groups fight businesses, government and various interest groups to win acceptance of their demands and expectations. Examples cited include, picketing, sit-ins, ultimatum to those in authority, blockade or occupation of buildings, and resisting or disobeying police.
- Crises of Malevolence are said to occur when opponents of an organization or miscreant individuals use unorthodox means or extreme tactics for the purpose of expressing hostility or anger toward a company, country or economic system with the aim of destabilizing or destroying it. Examples include product tampering, kidnapping, malicious rumours, terrorism and espionage.
- Workplace violence or Crises occur when an employee or former employee commits violence against other employees on organizational grounds.
- Rumours: False information about an organization or its products creates crises hurting the organization's reputation. A rumour that links an organization to radical groups or stories that their products are contaminated are typical examples.
- Sudden crises are circumstances that occur without warning and beyond an institution's control. Consequently, sudden crises are most often situations for which the institution and its leadership are not blamed.
- Smouldering crises differ from sudden crises in that they begin as minor internal issues that, due to manager's negligence, develop to crisis status. These are situations when leaders are blamed for the crisis and its subsequent effect on the institution in question. James categorizes five phases of crisis that require specific crisis leadership competencies. These include Signal detection, Preparation and prevention, Containment and damage control, Business recovery, and Learning[15]. These are aspects that put to test the leadership qualities that exist in an organization. The point to note however about most of these crisis forms is that most often, they remain extant or potential crisis situations which most often exist as threats until full manifestation into one form of crisis or another.

THE MILITARY AND PUBLIC RELATIONS – Issues, Strategies and Challenges

Elements of Crisis Management.

These consist of:

- Methods used to respond to both the reality and perception of crises.
- Establishing matrics to define what scenarios constitute a crisis and should consequently trigger the necessary response mechanisms.
- Communication that occurs within the response phase of emergency management scenarios [16].

Crisis management methods of a business or an organization are called Crisis Management Plan. The credibility and reputation of organizations is heavily influenced by the perception of their responses during crisis situations. The organization and communication involved in responding to a crisis in a timely fashion makes for a challenge in businesses. There must be open and consistent communication throughout the hierarchy to contribute to a successful crisis communication process.

Models and theories associated with crisis management

Crisis Management Model:

Successfully defusing a crisis requires an understanding of how to handle a crisis – before they occur. Gonzalez-Herrero and Pratt categorized them into three phases :

- The diagnosis of the impending trouble or the danger signals.
- Choosing appropriate Turnaround Strategy and
- Implementation of the change process and its monitoring[17].

Management Crisis Planning

No corporation looks forward to facing a situation that causes a significant disruption to their business, especially one that stimulates extensive media coverage. Public scrutiny can result in a negative financial, political, legal and government impact. Crisis management planning deals with providing the best response to a crisis and includes.

Contingency planning

Preparing contingency plans in advance, as part of a crisis management plan, is the first step to ensuring that an organization is appropriately prepared for a crisis. Crisis management teams can rehearse a crisis plan by developing a simulated scenario to use as a drill. The plan should clearly stipulate that the only people to speak publicly about the crisis are the designated persons, such as the company spokesperson or crisis team members. The first hours after a crisis breaks are the most crucial, so working with speed and efficiency is important, and the plan should indicate how quickly each function should be performed. When preparing to offer a statement externally as well as internally, information should be accurate. Providing incorrect or manipulated information has a tendency to backfire and will greatly exacerbate the situation. The contingency plan should contain information and guidance that will help decision makers to consider not only the short-term consequences, but the long-term effects of every decision[18].

Crisis Management Planning and Action: Contingency Planning Processes

Organizations prepare contingency plans in recognition of the fact that things go wrong from time to time. Contingency planning as experts outline thus involves:

- Preparing for predictable and quantifiable crises
- Preparing for unexpected and unwelcome events

The aim is to minimize the impact of a foreseeable event and to plan for how the organization will resume normal operations after the crisis. Contingency plan for crisis management planning and action accordingly seeks to:

- Identify alternative courses of action that can be taken if circumstances change with time
- Detailed standby procedures to enable continuation of essential activities and services during the period of emergency
- Includes programmes for improving the business in the longer term once the immediate situation has been resolved.

After contingency planning, the crisis management process involves

- Identifying Crisis
- Planning a response
- Responding to limit the damage
- Selecting a team and leader to deal with the crisis
- Resolving the crisis

The role of the Crisis Manager here is very crucial and include

- Crisis Assessment
- Event tracking
- Managing Human Considerations
- Damage Assessment as well as assessments of resources and options
- Development of Contingencies
- Managing Communications
- Coordinating with external bodies
- Controlling Information
- Controlling expectations

- Managing Legal requirements

Tips on Handling a Crisis

- Appoint a Crisis Manager
- Recognize that the Crisis Manager is likely to adopt a more authoritarian style than is normal
- Do an objective Assessment of the cause(s) of the crisis
- Determine whether the cause(s) will have a long term effect or whether it will be a short term phenomenon
- Project the most likely cause of events
- Focus on activities that will mitigate or eliminate the problem

Dealing with the People Aspects of a Crisis

- Form A Crisis Team
- Designate one person only to speak about the crisis to the outside world
- Act to prevent or counter the spread of negative information
- Make use of the media to provide counter argument

Do not cover up or tell untruths – trying to manipulate or distort information will backfire

The Role of Leadership in Crisis Management

Crisis leadership research concludes that leadership action in crisis reflects the competency of an organization, because the test of crisis demonstrates how well the institution's leadership structure serves the organization's goals and withstands crisis. Developing effective human resources is vital when building organizational capabilities through crisis management executive leadership.

Communications in Crisis Management

Crisis response is what management does and says after the crisis occurs. It involves essentially the communication process. Crisis management is a very critical organizational function failure of which could cause serious harm to an organization and may adversely affect it. Public relations play a critical role in the crisis response by helping to develop the messages that are sent to various publics. A communications expert, James Lukaszewski, asserts that the most challenging part of crisis communication management is reacting - with the right response - quickly. This is because behaviour always precedes communication. Non-behaviour or inappropriate behaviour leads to spin, not communication. In emergencies, it's the non-action and the resulting spins that cause embarrassment, humiliation, prolonged visibility, and unnecessary litigation[19]. Communication is thus crucial in among others. Its functions include:

- Helping management understand the impact of inappropriate or poorly thought out crisis response as one of the most important strategic services the public relations practitioner can provide. To have a strategic discussion requires a tool that has value without insulting the executive's intelligence, has impact without belabouring the obvious, inspires action without over-simplifying, and illustrates options and choices without teaching unnecessary, ill-advised lessons in public relations.
- Examining the dimensions of a crisis, which executives can clearly recognize and relate to, helps the public relations counsellor provide truly meaningful, strategic advice. It is this kind of analytical approach that helps senior management avoid career-defining moments, unless the moments are deserved[20].

For the purpose of communication in a crisis a crisis management team, Barton identifies the common members of the crisis team as public relations, legal, security, operations, finance, and human resources. However, the composition will vary based on the nature of the crisis. For instance, information technology would be required if the crisis involved the computer system.

Spokesperson

A key component of crisis team training is spokesperson training. Organizational members must be prepared to talk to the news media during a crisis. Media training should be provided before a crisis occurs. In the process of communication, the spokesperson should endeavour to appear pleasant on camera by avoiding nervous habits that people interpret as deception. He should have strong eye contact and avoid irritating mannerisms and other distracting nervous gestures. He should present information clearly by avoiding jargon or technical terms. Lack of clarity makes people think the organization is purposefully being confusing in order to hide something.

The Role of Media Relations

Media relations during crisis are an aspect of the communication process. It involves working with various media for the purpose of informing the public of an organization's mission, policies and practices in a positive, consistent and credible manner. Typically, this means coordinating directly with the people responsible for producing the news and features in the mass media. The goal of media relations is to maximize positive coverage in the mass media without paying for it directly through advertising[21]. As institutions and organizations function and operate especially in the modern times, there is the compelling need for establishment and maintenance of several modes of relations,- media relations being one of them. Media relations in today's world has become a very essential kernel and fundamental aspect of public relations practice in view of the very crucial position of the Mass Media as bridge between peoples, sectors and many other segments in society. The Mass media represent the most economic and effective channel of communication with the general public for the purpose of information dissemination and publicity. The Mass media reach into nearly every home and work place in society with heaps of information on a daily basis. The media thus governs the way in which people deal and relate with each other across distances. According to Cutlip and Center, the media constitute a nations public information system – a system in which public relations men and women play an important role[22]. Military Services all over the world have elaborate public information branches with extensive media relations networks. Their principal functions are "to provide information about military policy and operations, encourage recruitment, and maintain good relations between military establishments and their surrounding communities[23].

The Geneva centre for the Democratic Control of Armed Forces, DCAF affirms that independent media generally help the public and their political representatives in the task of informed decision making. They contribute to overseeing the action of the branches of state and may influence the content and quality of issues raised in public debates which in turn, influences government and parliaments to explain their decisions and policies to the citizens and to enhance positive participation in the political process. They can further disseminate information about those who hold public office in the security field, the kind of security policy adopted, deployment of troops abroad, military doctrine, procurement and treaties[24], and other security challenges.

Media Relations in Crisis Situations

During crisis, the public depends almost totally entirely on the media for news that may be vital for survival and for important messages from public and private authorities. The mass media are the only institution that can collect massive amount of information and disseminate quickly[25]. The Armed Forces by their nature are the legitimate managers of the instruments of violence on behalf of the state. To that extent, their roles as defined by the constitution places them at the very epicentre of crisis whenever the need arises. Warfare is a grave crisis situation in which the Armed Forces would always be involved as they are established among others to fight war and restore peace or, to prevent war through deterrence. As various branches in the armed forces have their roles, military PR personnel have the responsibility of managing media relations during crisis in peace and in war, through proper information management. The success of any crisis management drive however, depends on the availability of a crisis plan meant to mitigate an impending situation.

The Crisis Plan

In the same manner as the "teeth arms" train in peace time preparatory to war, PR personnel as a service arm must have their crisis management plan. It is said that an organization with a crisis plan stands better chance of coping with any crisis situation or accident with full confidence. A crisis situation that is not well prepared for and not well managed can bring an organization into disrepute and lower its image before the public[26]. It is therefore pertinent from the foregoing that that the articulation of a proper PR plan embedded with a sound media relations strategy must be at the heart of every corporate public relations policy[27]. Crisis situations that are peculiar to the military include war, border incursions, air crash involving military personnel, death and casualty of military personnel in operations, a ship running aground, border clashes, military - civilian confrontation, bomb scare and bomb blasts, mutiny, dramatic retirements especially of senior military officers, rumours of fraud in military establishments, etc. It should be borne in mind that during crisis, whatever information that is given out must be very timely to avoid rumour mongering and publication of false or wrong information by scoop chasing journalists whose nose for news most often leads them to publishing sensational stories.

References

1. S.A Ochoche, "Changing Concepts of International Peace & Security in Garuba Chris International Peace & Security": The 'Nigerian Contribution, Lecture delivered at the National War College, April, 1996
2. BarryBuzan, **People, States and Fears: The National Security Problem in International Relations** (London, Harvester Wheatshef 1983) Pg. 44.
3. Obiozor GA et al, **Nigeria and ECOWAS since 1985: Towards a Dynamic Regional Integration** (Enugu,Fourth Dimension Publishers, 1991) Pg. 2.
4. Refer: http://www.slideshare.net/nostrad/corporate - security - business – continuity – and – management – 3899328
5. Dennis Wilcox et al, Public Relations, Strategies and Tactics (New York, Harper & row 1989) PP 185 - 186
6. I. Bellamy, People States And& Fear: An Agenda For International Security in Post – Cold War Era (Colorado: Reiner Publishers 1991) Pg.7.
7. W. Lipmann, **United States Foreign Policy, Shield of the Republic**, (Boston, Little Brum& Co 1943) Pg. 51
8. R. Mcnamara, **The Essence of Security**, (USA: Harper & Row 1978) Pg.29
9. Weaver Cited at http://www.ehow.com/facts_648845_definition-security-threat.html
10. http://www.knowledgerush.com/kr/encyclopedia/threat
11. Abitsokwa, Tanko Sallah, "Resolving Communual Crisis in Nigeria: Challenges and Prospects" Thesis Submitted to National Open University of Nigeria, March 2010, Pg.10
12. Seegar et al Cited in AbitsokwaTanko(Ibid).
13. http://en.wikipedia.org/wiki/crisis_management
14. Dennis Wilcox et al, Public Relations, Strategies and Tactics, Op cit
15. Lerbinger @ http://en.wikipedia.org/wiki/crisis_management
16. Ibid
17. Ibid
18. Ibid
19. Ibid
20. James E. Lukaszenski @ http://en.wikipedia.org/wiki/crisis_management
21. http://en.wikipedia.org/wiki/Media_Relations
22. Cutlip, Center and Broom (1985) Effective Public Relations (New Jersey, Prentice Hall) P. 359
23. Wilcox, D.L. et al (1989) Public Relations: Strategies and Tactics (New York, Harper and Row) P. 256

24. Hans, B. et al, Parliamentary Oversight of the Security Sector (Geneva, IPU, DCAF) P. 39
25. Graber, D.A. (1984) Mass Media and American Politics (Chicago, Univ of Ilinois Press) P. 289
26. Oladimeji O.A. Effective Public Relations and Information in Military Operations. Paper presented at Directorate of Army Public Relations Training Period, 1991.
27. Ibid

CHAPTER SEVENTEEN

CHALLENGES TO MILITARY PUBLIC RELATIONS PRACTICE

Introduction

Public relations as its exponents acclaim, has become generally accepted as an important element of business and other aspects of human interaction for simple, complex organizations as well as governments. Sam Black, a well-known PR exponent attests to this fact by his assertion that there is no mystique in public relations. It is an integral part of the effective management of any organized activity but requires training and experience, common sense and application[1]. From a marketing perspective as another exponent views it, public relations should play an important role as part of the marketing strategy. Public relations not only help position the company's brand or product and build brand equity, but also make the entire communications programme more effective. Through public relations, the company can identify key audiences and design programmes to reach them through publicity and other tactics that go beyond paid advertising. Proactive public relations will support the launch of a new product in an overseas market or help maintain the company's product in the news through positive publicity. Effective public relations can also counteract negative impressions about your product and foster goodwill for the company and towards the company's products[2]. Public relations practice, spans several sectors including business and industry, trade associations, professional societies and labour unions, voluntary agencies, health care institutions, the arts and religious institutions. Its application is suitable to politics, government and government agencies, educational institutions as well as the armed forces.

Since its evolution, the practice of public relations within and across cultures in many facets of human endeavour has added tremendous value to organizations and invariably to society. James Grunig posits that when the public relations department helps an organization build good relationships with publics, it has added value to society as well as to the organization. Organizations practice social responsibility when they take the Interests of publics into account as well as their self-interests. When an organization ignores or opposes the interests of publics, they typically will organize into activist groups to confront and challenge the organization. The result is conflict. Public relations serve society, then, by working with publics to resolve the conflicts that tear societies apart[3.] Thus by ensuring free flow of communication, public relations practitioners help to reduce conflict and misunderstanding in society. Public relations has facilitated positive branding for many organizations, products and services, it has helped to shape organizational messages to the right audiences, generated favourable leads for organizations and their products and services, placed them in the best media spot light as well as enhanced their ratings immensely.

The achievements of public relations in all these sectors through the efforts of its practitioners are however, not without challenges that are intrinsic and peculiar to the varied sectors of practice. Such challenges peculiar as they may be are not even universal as they vary from country to country, organization to organization. However, in relation to the military which is the focus of this discuss, some of the challenges which face the practice of public relations in the military but which however, are by no means universal to all militaries globally are examined below.

The Legal Challenge

The issue of the military's 'competence' to conduct public relations as pointed out in chapter 5 is one which essentially questions the legality of such activity without any prior political authority. It is an issue that obtains within countries under the liberal democratic model of civil military relations within Europe and especially the United States of America. By its nature, political power within such a system is attained through competitive struggle in an open electorate. The implementation of policy is placed on bureaucratic and military elites who are subordinate to a central political authority. That same authority oversees the formation and implementation of the national defence policy. The military under this system operates in a manner that is similar to civil servants in obeisance to the directives of the political masters. By such operation, the military is made wholly accountable to the political authority with "civil control" of all military affairs from the commitment of troops to battle in time of war to the conduct of military public relations and information programmes in peace. Notwithstanding however, the charge of its "consistent violation of the law" and the "persistence of its illegal propaganda", through public relations, the military, however, strongly believes in the rightness of its actions. John Swomley pointed this out in relation to the US Military by his expression that the military had "asserted its right to propagandize civilians against the expressed will of Congress. No President or Secretary of Defence has been able to stop it except temporarily and then only at a few specific points in the interests of coordinating military policy with the State Department's policy"[4]. While this opposition to military PR by western democracies has however not curtailed or impinged on its practice, it nevertheless remains a legal and moral dilemma.

Recognition and Acknowledgement of the Importance of Public Relations

The recognition as well as acknowledgement of the importance of PR in many armed forces constitutes a very serious challenge. This is not limited to developing countries as similar experience had obtained in Britain. According to Hooper, the speed of recognition and the acknowledgement of the importance of public relations vary between the three Services and there is even a variation of attitude within each service... the promotion prospects for those serving in PR appointments are not thought to be good[5]. Similarly, Oladimeji, a retired Navy Commodore and a respected and experienced former Director of Naval Information lamented in relation to the Nigerian military that, in spite of their training, the Nigerian Armed Forces did not take full advantage of public relations techniques to solve problems of public opinion and attitude towards the military. This was because, the top hierarchy of the military don't accord it priority; it is misunderstood at heavy cost to the image of the armed forces[6]. He avers further that the specialist public relations officers in the military were always swimming against the heavy tide of prejudice. Rank ceilings for them were low; the best and brightest professional could not be attracted; funding was ridiculously low for the job at hand. This was why the public relations departments in the Armed Forces had to cope with ups and downs in their fortunes[7] Lack of appreciation of the place of public relations in the Nigerian military could be attributed to ignorance or misunderstanding of its potential. There is therefore the need for change of attitude as the job in fact, provides an exciting and stimulating challenge for an officer who has the imagination to seize upon its importance and its opportunities. It will open up a new dimension in his understanding of what really matters most in modern conflict[8].

Public Relations in Management Function of the Military

Public Relations is a management function. This is an aspect which its practitioners and experts have over time always harped upon. It is a generally established aspect of its benchmark by which the PR Manager is considered part of top or decision level making management. The hierarchy at which organizations place recognition on their PR establishments and indeed their PR managers goes a long way to reveal the esteem to which they place public relations. The Public relations profession thus places great premium on status rating of its practitioners in view of the important role of the PR manager to every organization. He should usually be a very visible personality within the organization and outside of it with unhindered access to the chief executive and other top level personalities. He advises and makes contributions to management as well as policy issues from the view point of public relations. Many organizations fail to accord PR this recognition and would rather see PR by its "gin and tonic" image. According to Coulson – Thomas: While some public relations officials are accepted as an indispensable part of the boardroom team others still man the press and do little else. The gap between best and worst practice is wide[9].

The United States gives a very high premium to military public relations. "Public Affairs" is the military designation for public relations at the Department of Defence level. Under direction of an Assistant Secretary of Defence, trained information officers of the Army, Navy, Marine Corps and Air Force are assigned to the Office of Public Affairs at the Pentagon in Washington. Along with civil service public relations specialists, they are responsible for producing and releasing all military news at the seat of government. The office is a central point for handling public information and related activities concerning the department of defence, including the three military departments. Its basic function is to assure prompt and accurate response to enquiries concerning the department of defence, DoD, to provide public understanding of DoD's aims, activities and needs; and to provide liaison and cooperation with information media representatives. With this as the main outlet to the public for national defence news, the operations function is as important as the advisory one. Facts must be released as soon as possible within the large general outline of national security. This top level direction and operations are handled by Public Affairs four offices – News Services, Public services, Security Review, and Plans and programmes. A fifth, Declassification Policy, also functions within the Office of Public Affairs but is not directly involved in the military public relations activity[10]. About the same premium is placed on military public relations in the United Kingdom and other developed nations of the West.

The situations in the militaries of most developing nations including Nigeria are however, not the same. While in these nations the military seem to appreciate the role and value of public relations, much consideration and recognition is not given to public relations at the higher military command hierarchies. Agim in relation to Nigeria conveys the vivid dilemma of the military public relations or Information officers. As he put it, in the absence of open door media policy, the military high commands erroneously treat their public relations or information officers as outsiders. They are not sure whether certain information is safe with their information officers... there is a high level of uncertainty among the information officers on what they may say that may invoke displeasure in the military. This is because public relations in the military are not yet a management function. Public relations and information officers are not part of important decision making that affect their organization and nobody bothers to communicate to them even on some basic issues[11].

Distrust between the Military and the Media

A lingering but persistent challenge to military public relations practice is that of the well-known distrust between the military and the media even as both institutions require each other in the national interest. Alluding to the situation in Nigeria, General Agwai, a former Nigerian Military Chief of Defence Staff said that media disposition towards the military in Nigeria has historically been adversarial. The military at the advent of democratic governance came under unimaginable bout of media antagonism, understandably because of its repressive experience under military governance. Without questioning the inability of the media to distinguish military governance from the military institution itself, the military has gone ahead to commendably forge a working relationship with the media. Although cooperation has improved, there still exist some levels of frost in relations which could be traced to the nature and goals of both institutions that appear fundamentally opposed to each other.

The military often finds itself at cross purpose with the press because by its constitutional role, it is the guardian and protector of the state, a responsibility it guides jealously. The media on the other hand prides itself as the watchdog of society with the duty to foist accountability on all public institutions... The Nigerian military in its campaign for transformation has no greater tool to winning the hearts and minds of the nation than the news media[12]. Equally on the aspect of military-media distrust, Cutlip, Center and Broom aver in relation to the United states that the military PR practitioner faces some difficult problems as he or she is caught in the middle between military leaders who distrust the media and resent their intrusions and journalists who are constantly frustrated in "the right to know" by military security or deception[13]. Veteran... Pentagon journalist thinks "hostility of the military toward the press has deepened in recent years". On the other hand, another observer sees the media as patsies for the Pentagon, a journalism bristling with "strident, frustrated chauvinism[14].

Public Relations Education and Training

Another critical challenge to public relations practice in the military is of appropriate public relations education and training. In recognition of its essence, the Public Relations Society of America had noted that the growth, evolution and maturation of public relations are sure to continue. Elements are in place for impressive incremental growth and change in the next century: the spread of democratic institutions around the world; the growing importance of communicating with internal as well as external publics; the veritable explosion of one-to-one communication and the technology to implement it; and the steady advance of the public relations body of knowledge, especially analysis of public awareness and change in attitudes and behaviour[15], demands proper acquisition of the right education including further training. Public relations practitioners the Commission noted, should be grounded in the liberal arts and sciences. Well-prepared in public relations theory and practice, tested not only in the classroom but in the field; understanding the inherent connection between public relations and management, sociology and the many other pillars of modern society; but also with the necessary skills-writing, analysing, thinking- sharpened and ready for use[16].

This is the quality of education recommended and provided for PR practitioners in the US to which the US Military Public Affairs conforms in standard. About the same standard applies in the United Kingdom and other developed nations. The level however, of PR training in many developing countries are inadequate and below the required standard. Agim identifies training as one of the most serious problems of PR in the military. The Nigerian Army which he noted seems to have a more organized PR department in all major formations and units does not have any training for officers and soldiers. The few personnel that are desirous of self-development are left on their own to fight for such courses in civil institutions. The same problem applies to the Navy and the Air Force. They even have fewer trained personnel. The rest are appointment by respective commanders without any formal training[17]. The Nigerian Army has however, recently established a School of Public relations and Information for its personnel.

Low level of ICT Knowledge, Application and Infrastructure

Information Communication Technology (ICT) is the processing and maintenance of information, and the use of all forms of computer, communication, network and mobile technologies to mediate information. Communication technologies include all media employed in transmitting audio, video, data or multimedia such as cable, satellite, fibre optics, wireless (radio, infra-red, Bluetooth, Wi-Fi). Network technologies include personal area networks (PAN), campus area network (CAN), intranets, extranets, LANs, WANs, MANs and the internet. Computer technologies include all removable media such as optical discs, disks, flash memories, and video books, multimedia projectors, interactive electronic boards, and continuously emerging state-of-the-art PCs. Mobile technologies comprises mobile phones, PDAs, palmtops, etc. These technologies have information as their material object. Information is not reserved for use in isolation, but, rather communicated among users. ICT applied to education enhances the delivery and access to knowledge, and improves the curriculum. It produces richer learning outcomes compared to education without ICT. It encourages critical thinking and offers unlimited means of achieving educational goals.

A basic understanding of ICT in education is vital in keeping abreast of rapidly changing technologies[18]. While in the military of the advanced western world, the knowledge, use, application and even availability of ICT infrastructure are taken for granted, it is not so in militaries of developing countries especially Nigeria where, as rightly observed, in educational institutions, especially higher institutions, the mode of delivery of knowledge and curriculum are not yet ICT enhanced. It is obvious that ICT is still in the emerging phase in Nigerian educational system[19]. While this challenge persists, studies on the other hand have shown that internet is becoming increasingly popular with availability mainly in towns and cities. Most Nigerians access the internet at cybercafés where they pay between US 50 cents to US $1 per hour for the service. While only a small proportion of the population has internet at home, most offices are equipped with computers with relatively high internet connection. Mobile phones have increased internet access options, but the potential impact is restrained by the high costs associated with this access[20].

The above picture presents the larger picture of the level of understanding, knowledge and application of ICT in the larger Nigerian society beginning especially with the education sector which provides the basic foundation for such knowledge. With such a picture, the level could only be imagined as to extent of similar understanding, knowledge and application of ICT in the Nigerian military. The situation is certainly reflective of what obtains in the larger Nigerian society as the level of ICT development in the military does not have any appreciable rating. The same rating applies to the development of ICT infrastructure which is no doubt quite poor.

Other challenges to military public relations practice especially in relation to the Nigerian military include inadequate public relations tools and standard equipment, inadequate logistics, encroachment on public relations functions, poor community relations as well as poor media relations and lack of functional library and internet services.

References

1. Black, Sam, (1989) **Introduction to Public Relations, London,** TheModino Press, P.xiii
2. Veronica Diaz, "Challenges in the Practice of Public Relations across Cultures" @ http://www.bing.com/ search?q=challenges+in+the+practice+of+public+relations+across+frontiers
3. James E. Grunig, "The Role of Public Relations in Management and its Contribution to Organizational and Societal Effectiveness" @ http://www. instituteforpr.org/wp-content/uploads/2001_PRManagement.pdf
4. Swomley, J., (1967) **The Military Establishment,** Boston, Beacon press, P. 127
5. Allan Hooper (1982) **The Military and the Media,** Aldershot 1982, P. 4
6. Oladimeji, O. (2001) **Military Image and Media Message,** Lagos, Miral Press, P. 1x
7. Ibid
8. Ibid
9. Colin Coulson Thomas (1979) **Public Relations: A Practical Guide**, Plymouth, Macdonald and Evans,
10. Arthur Dreyer, "Functions and Responsibilities in the Departments of Defense, Army, Navy, Marine corps and Air Force Information Services in Military Public Affairs" in Stephenson, H. (1960) **Handbook of Public Relations** New York, McGraw-Hill, P. 775
11. Agim, J.A. (2004) **The Principles and Practice of Public Relations in the Military and the Police**, Enugu, Ultimate Publishers, P. 145
12. Agwai, M. L.," The Need for Closer Cooperation between the Nigerian Military and the Media" in M. D. Yusuf, **The Military, The Media and Nigeria's National Security**, Ibadan, Gold Press Ltd P. 22
13. Cutlip, S.M. et al (1985) **Effective Public Relations** 6th ed New Jersey, Prentice Hall Englewood Cliffs, P. 584
14. Roger Morris, "Reporting for Duty- the Pentagon and the Press", cited in Cutlip, S.M. et al (Ibid)
15. PRSA committee on PR education @ http://work.colum.edu/amilier/pr-education.htm
16. Ibid
17. Agim, J.A. (2004), Op cit P. 12

18. N. OgechukwuIloanusiand,C.CharlesOsuagwu,@ http://www.worldwidelearn. com/elearning-essentials/elearning-benefits.htm (2009)
19. Ibid
20. Friedrich-Ebert-Stiftung, (2012) **African Media Barometer: Nigeria 2011**, P. 21

CHAPTER EIGHTEEN

MILITARY PUBLIC RELATIONS, EFFECTIVE COMMUNICATIONS AND INTERPERSONAL SKILLS

Introduction

The view has often been expressed by public relations and communication specialists that given its unique position, no organization more than the military require the services of professionally competent public relations men to put its view across. For its existence and the effectiveness of its operations in war and in peace time, the military needs public understanding and support. As Oladimeji asserts in relation to the Nigerian Military, public relations imperatives becomes more crucial because of the huge national resources involved in defence efforts, the need to repair the battered image of the odious decades of military rule and the imperative of new democratic setting. If public relations are a priority, getting all levels of the military to acquire appropriate skills in media relations so as to get the best out of the news media for the Armed Forces is an urgent task[1]. Given this position therefore for the Military PR practitioner, the significance of effective communications and interpersonal skills among other skills is indeed significant.

Communication in today's world is no doubt, central to all human activities, including social processes and interaction, interchange of thoughts, ideas and opinions. Experts uphold communication as the interpretation, transmission and receiving of ideas and information, indeed a transaction. It would be difficult to think of anything that takes place, that makes a sound or gesture, which does not in some way communicate. Our social life abounds with communication, some of it overt, much of it unverbalized[2]. Communication arguably, is the greatest enhancer and facilitator of Globalization. It is the central element, the interconnection between peoples and cultures. Communication technology facilitated especially through international computer networks are now an integral part of global communication. They form part of the great precipitate to globalization; the central crux to McLuhan's concept of Global Village. Indeed, there have been strong assertions that globalization may not have come to being without the help of communication.

Communication according to Agim, is central to every social interaction. Everyone can communicate, to a greater or lesser extent. And every one can understand the importance of this ability. Difficulties however, arise when the experts or communicators assume that communication is no more than a natural ability. In reality, communication is a sophisticated and complex process[3]. Haywood sees it as a discipline and can be practiced well or badly. As with any discipline, it has rules; can be tested; measured; learnt and examined[4]. Communication helps in the establishment of regular relationships, the creating and reduction of tensions, the setting and the measuring of achievements and the acquisition of skills. We know, we feel, and are actively involved in communications every moment of our lives. But to define this all important phenomenon is a difficult task[5]. People communicate with the objective of achieving set communication goals. A communication that achieves its objectives can be taken to be an effective communication. By another view, communication is said to be effective if the aggregate effort to share meaning by the communicator is proportionate to the meaning received by the communicatee[6].

Interpersonal skills on the other hand, are very critical to the communication process and helps in the achievement of effective communication. Interpersonal skills are means of interaction often referred to as communication or people skills. They are characteristic traits that a person uses to interact with other people. They include body language such as behavior and posture and a knack for listening and understanding. Communicating with a constructive and respectful tone of voice is a critical interpersonal skill to making a favorable impression. Mastering the use of interpersonal skills can influence both professional and personal lives for some people. Accomplished users of interpersonal skills, use them to achieve certain effects or results in formal and informal social circumstances. For business environments these skills may increase productivity with an encouraging approach of communications, which should be clearly administered with specific objectives. In personal settings where emotions are generally involved, the tone used can manage and control the sensitivity that is usually involved with feelings[7]. Communication skills are very essential for conveying people's thoughts, ideas, opinions and arguments to others with whom they interact on an on-going basis. The role of communication in people's personal as well as professional life is quite invaluable. Good interpersonal communication enhances the resolution of conflicts, the nurturing of relationships and in the creation of positive environment for mutual interaction.

Definition of Key Terms

Communication:

A simple and basic definition of communication denotes it as the exchange of thoughts, messages or information, as by speech, signals, writing or behaviour. Dennis Wilcox et al, see communication as the act of transmitting information, ideas and attitudes from one person to another. Communication can take place, however, only if the speaker and the listener (called the sender and the receiver) have a common understanding of the symbols being used. Words are the most common symbols. The degree to which two people understand each other is heavily dependent upon their common knowledge of word symbols... An important aspect of communication is the opportunity for feedback, or response from the listener to the speaker. Feedback is just as important as the dissemination of the message itself, because it tells the sender whether he or she is being understood[8]. Shannon denotes communication as all the procedures by which one mind may influence another. This involves not only written and oral speech, but also music, pictorials, arts, the theatre and ballet, These, too, affect human behaviour[9].

Effective Communication:

Barbara Brown's definition of effective communication holds that while Communication is the process of sharing information, thoughts and feelings between people through speaking, writing or body language, effective communication extends the concept to require that transmitted content is received and understood by someone in the way it was intended. The goals of effective communication include creating a common perception, changing behaviors and acquiring information[10]. There are 7 C's of effective communication which are applicable to both written as well as oral communication. They include[11]:

- Completeness - The communication must be complete. It should convey all facts required by the audience. The sender of the message must take into consideration the receiver's mind set and convey the message accordingly.
- Conciseness - Conciseness means communicating what you want to convey in least possible words without forgoing the other C's of communication.
- Consideration - Consideration implies "stepping into the shoes of others". Effective communication must take the audience into consideration, i.e, the audience's view points, background, mind-set, education level, etc. Make an attempt to envisage your audience, their requirements, emotions as well as problems. Ensure that the self-respect of the audience is maintained and their emotions are not at harm. Modify your words in message to suit the audience's needs while making your message complete.
- Clarity - Clarity implies emphasizing on a specific message or goal at a time, rather than trying to achieve too much at once. Clarity in communication makes understanding easier. Complete clarity of thoughts and ideas enhances the meaning of message.
- Concreteness - Concrete communication implies being particular and clear rather than fuzzy and general. Concreteness strengthens the confidence. Concrete message is supported with specific facts and figures. It makes use of words that are clear and that build the reputation.
- Courtesy - Courtesy in message implies the message should show the sender's expression as well as should respect the receiver. The sender of the message should be sincerely polite, judicious, reflective and enthusiastic.
- Correctness - Correctness in communication implies that there are no grammatical errors in communication. It among others makes use of appropriate and correct language in the message. It is important to note that awareness of these 7 C's of communication makes you an effective communicator.

Skills:

The Business Dictionary defines skill as ability and capacity acquired through deliberate, systematic, and sustained effort to smoothly and adaptively carry out complex activities or job functions involving ideas (cognitive skills), things (technical skills), and/or people[12]. The Free Online Dictionary also defines skills as proficiency, facility, or dexterity that is acquired or developed through training or experience. It is an art, trade, or technique, particularly one requiring use of the hands or body. A developed talent or ability[13].

Interpersonal Skills:

These are skills used by a person to properly interact with others. In the business domain, the term generally refers to an employee's ability to get along with others while getting the job done. Interpersonal skills include everything from communication and listening skills to attitude and deportment. Good interpersonal skills are a prerequisite for many positions in an organization[14]. Interpersonal communication skills are a collection of processes that are used to interact with other people, and they are an important component of the relationship building process. These skills include transmitting coherent language in both oral and verbal form, reading of written language produced by others, and listening to others when they are transmitting information orally. These skills are developed and improved over time. Having good interpersonal skills will help in every situation that life has to offer, whether the experience is one-on-one or within a group atmosphere. Being effective takes time and effort in learning, improving and practicing how interpersonal skills work best. If you watch the reaction and response of people, their behavior will always tell what is working and what is not working.

Objectives of Communication

Every mode of communication has its goals or objectives. An individual or organization that puts out a message across to a target audience has specified objectives that among others may include the following:

- To be understood by its target audience
- To be accepted by the audience
- For the purpose of getting something done
- To cultivate the understanding of others

While these may constitute the communication objective among others, the achievement of such objectives could be for the following purposes:

- To enhance increased productivity
- To bring about achievement of steadier work flow
- To establish strong business relationships & enhanced professional image

- For deliverance of clearer promotional materials
- To offer advice or give an order or warning
- To offer suggestion
- To persuade or convince
- To provide education or enlightenment
- To give and receive information
- To provide counseling, raise morale and motivation and
- To improve discipline

Types of Communication and Communication Skills

The main types of communication identified include the following:

- Nonverbal Communication. This describes the process of conveying meaning in the form of non-word messages. Research shows that the majority of our communication is non-verbal, also known as body language. Some of non-verbal communication includes gestures, body language or posture; facial expression and eye contact.
- Oral communication. This is carried out through the verbal process. Oral communication includes speeches, presentations, discussions, and aspects of interpersonal communication.
- Written communication. This is carried out through the written process through meaningful combination of alphabets or other discernible symbols of communication. The first stage of written communication emerged through the use of pictographs. The pictograms were made in stone. During the second stage, writing began to appear on paper, papyrus, clay, wax, etc. Common alphabets were introduced and allowed for the uniformity of language across large distances. A leap in technology occurred when the Gutenberg printing-press was invented in the 15th century. The third stage is characterized by the transfer of information through controlled waves and electronic signals.

Communication Skills:

There are four types of communication skills and these include:

- Reading Skills
- Writing Skills
- Speaking Skills and
- Listening Skills

Each of these skills are by themselves specialist areas that need to be individually improved upon on consistently so as to master and become adept at them for greater success.

Communication Process and Channels of Communication

Nick Sanchez in a research on the communication process denotes it as follows[15]:

The communication process is the guide toward realizing effective communication. It is through the communication process that the sharing of a common meaning between the sender and the receiver takes place. While effective communication is the most critical component of total quality management, the manner in which individuals perceive and talk to each other at work about different issues is a major determinant of the business success. Individuals that follow the communication process will have the opportunity to become more productive in every aspect of their profession. Effective communication leads to understanding.

The communication process is made up of four key components. The components include encoding, medium of transmission, decoding, and feedback. There are also two other factors in the process, and those two factors are present in the form of the sender and the receiver. The communication process begins with the sender and ends with the receiver. The sender is an individual, group, or organization who initiates the communication. This source is initially responsible for the success of the message. The sender's experiences, attitudes, knowledge, skill, perceptions, and culture influence the message. "The written words, spoken words, and nonverbal language selected are paramount in ensuring the receiver interprets the message as intended by the sender" (Burnett & Dollar, 1989). All communication begins with the sender.

The first step the sender is faced with involves the encoding process. In order to convey meaning, the sender must begin encoding, which means translating information into a message in the form of symbols that represent ideas or concepts. This process translates the ideas or concepts into the coded message that will be communicated. The symbols can take on numerous forms such as, languages, words, or gestures. These symbols are used to encode ideas into messages that others can understand.

To begin transmitting the message, the sender uses some kind of channel (also called a medium). The communication process utilizes communication channels. The channel is the means used to convey the message to an audience. Apart from the well-known traditional channels of communication especially of the print and electronic media, there are other channels such as news releases, press conferences, special events, brochures, speeches, bumper stickers, newsletters, and posters. Other channels include the telephone and a variety of written forms such as memos, letters, and reports. The effectiveness of the various channels fluctuates depending on the characteristics of the communication. For example, when immediate feedback is necessary, oral communication channels are more effective because any uncertainties can be cleared up on the spot. In a situation where the message must be delivered to more than a small group of people, written channels are often more effective. Although in many cases, both oral and written channels should be used because one supplements the other.

After the appropriate channel or channels are selected, the message enters the decoding stage of the communication process. Decoding is conducted by the receiver. Once the message is received and examined, the stimulus is sent to the brain for interpreting, in order to assign some type of meaning to it. It is this processing stage that constitutes decoding. The receiver begins to interpret the symbols sent by the sender, translating the message to their own set of experiences in order to make the symbols meaningful. Successful communication takes place when the receiver correctly interprets the sender's message. The receiver is the individual or individuals to whom the message is directed.

Feedback:

In the communication process, feedback refers to a response from the receiver be it an individual or audience, which gives the communicator an idea of how the message is being received and whether it needs to be modified for better understanding or comprehension. Feedback to a communication can be verbal or non-verbal. Feedback is the final link in the chain of the communication process. After receiving a message, the receiver responds in some way and signals that response to the sender. The signal may take the form of a spoken comment, a long sigh, a written message, a smile, or some other action. Without feedback, the sender cannot confirm that the receiver has interpreted the message correctly. It is the key component in the communication process because it allows the sender to evaluate the effectiveness of the message. Feedback ultimately provides an opportunity for the sender to take corrective action to clarify a misunderstood message. "Feedback plays an important role by indicating significant communication barriers: differences in background, different interpretations of words, and differing emotional reactions".

Illustration of a Communication Model

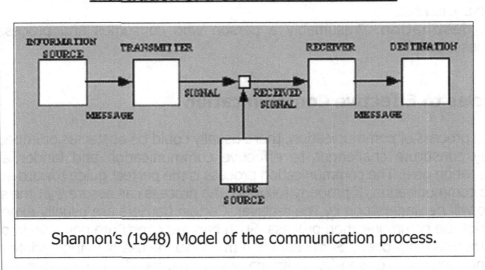

Shannon's (1948) Model of the communication process.

Shannon's model, as shown above, breaks the process of communication down into eight discrete components: (Adapted from Davis Foulger's Impression)

- An information **source**. Presumably a person who creates a message.
- The **message**, which is both sent by the information source and received by the destination.

- A **transmitter.** For Shannon's immediate purpose a telephone instrument that captures an audio signal, converts it into an electronic signal, and amplifies it for transmission through the telephone network. Transmission is readily generalized within Shannon's information theory to encompass a wide range of transmitters. The **signal**, which flows through a channel. There may be multiple parallel signals, as is the case in face-to-face interaction where sound and gesture involve different signal systems that depend on different channels and modes of transmission. There may be multiple serial signals, with sound and/or gesture turned into electronic signals, radio waves, or words and pictures in a book.
- A carrier or **channel**, which is represented by the small unlabelled box in the middle of the model. The most commonly used channels include air, light, electricity, radio waves, paper, and postal systems. Note that there may be multiple channels associated with the multiple layers of transmission, as described above.
- **Noise**, in the form of secondary signals that obscure or confuse the signal carried. Given Shannon's focus on telephone transmission, carriers, and reception, it should not be surprising that noise is restricted to noise that obscures or obliterates some portion of the signal within the channel. This is a fairly restrictive notion of noise, by current standards, and a somewhat misleading one.
- A **receiver**. In Shannon's conception, the receiving is through the telephone instrument. In face to face communication a set of ears (sound) and eyes (gesture). In television, several layers of receiver, including an antenna and a television set.
- A **destination**. Presumably a person who consumes and processes the message[16].

Obstacles to Effective Communication

In the process of communication, there usually could be obstacles or impediments that may constitute challenges to effective communication and hinder effective communication goal. The communication process is the perfect guide toward achieving effective communication. If properly followed, the process can assure that the sender's message will be understood by the receiver. Certain barriers are usually experienced throughout the communication process. Such barriers constitute negative impacts on the communication process. Some common them include use of inappropriate medium or channel, incorrect grammar, inflammatory words, words that conflict with body language, and technical jargon. Noise is also a common impediment. Noise essentially is anything that distorts a message by interfering with the communication process. It can occur during any stage of the process. Noise can take many forms, including a radio playing in the background, another person trying to enter your conversation, and any other distractions that prevent the receiver from paying attention. Some other barriers include the following[17]:

Physical Barriers:

One of the major barriers of communication in a workplace is the physical barrier. Physical barriers in an organization include large working areas that are physically separated from others. Other distractions that could cause a physical barrier in an organization are environmental factors such as background noise.

Language:

Inability to converse in a language that is known by both the sender and receiver is the greatest barrier to effective communication. When a person uses inappropriate words while conversing or writing, it could lead to misunderstanding between the sender and a receiver. It is not only the difference in language that causes a barrier to effective communication. People speaking the same language can sometimes find it difficult to comprehend what is being said.

Emotions:

Your emotions could be a barrier to communication if you are engrossed in them for some reason. In such cases, you tend to have trouble listening to others or understanding the message conveyed to you. A few of the emotional interferences include hostility, anger, resentfulness and fear. People, who suffer from ailments such as anxiety and depression, tend to misconstrue what is being said about them. Also, as they are battling something in their head, they may or may not be able to pay full attention to the speaker, which may make them appear disinterested and spaced-out.

Lack of Subject Knowledge:

If a person who sends a message lacks subject knowledge then he may not be able to convey his message clearly. The receiver could misunderstand his message and this could become a barrier to effective communication. This is visible in cases where people may try to cover-up their ignorance with some unverified facts. This creates confusion in the mind of the listener and creates a barrier to communication.

Overdose of Information:

It is always better to select appropriate and relevant points from the mass of information for presentation to the audience rather than allow yourself to be inundated with an overdose of information from which to pick relevant ones for presentation. Your guide should always be conciseness, accuracy and simplicity. Overdose of information leads to confusion and ambiguity. When too much of information is conveyed in a short period it is very likely to be misunderstood.

Developing Effective Communication Skills

The development of interpersonal communication skills takes patience and practice. It also takes time as well and there is need to develop positive attitude in doing so. There are so many tips or rather guidelines for effective interpersonal communications that have been provided by experts and authors in the field. Some of them include the following[18]:

Making Eye Contact:

Making eye contact in the process of communication is very critical as nothing builds rapport more than direct eye contact. It is a key component of interpersonal communication. If you are communicating to a large group, you need to survey all areas of the room and prove to your audience that you are comfortable speaking to them. It makes them feel that you are genuinely interested in your subject and the responses that may come forth from them. It also enhances your personal credibility as well as develops your confidence.

Mind Your Body Language:

Effective communication is more than just the words that come out of your mouth - it's also the attitude and feelings that you convey through your body. Since much of what you communicate to others is conveyed in your physical posture and mannerisms, it's important that you avoid such behaviors as "crossing your arms in front of your chest". This nonverbal cue may contradict what you are saying. Instead, sit up straight and lean in toward the person you are talking to. Since much of what you communicate to others is conveyed in your physical posture, it's important that you avoid such mannerisms that may tend to contradict what you are saying or suggest something otherwise. A posture of sitting up straight or leaning towards the person you are talking to makes individuals look approachable and can encourage smooth conversation. Mirroring another person's body language is also a useful tool when attempting to build a rapport.

Be an Active Listener:

A key element to effective communication is being an active listener. Practice active listening as it is not only habit-forming, but it is also one of the most significant pieces to the communication puzzle. Being an active listener requires focus and a clear mind. Avoid jumping to conclusions, making premature judgments, agreements, comparisons, or criticisms. Seek the reasons behind the comments or statements of those with whom you are speaking by asking, "Why?" Remember that you are only hearing or may have heard only one side to the story. Emphasize the facts and seek to gather objective information. Do not try to solve a problem until facts on all sides are available. Be consistent and ask for help from knowledgeable people. Speak loudly, but confidently:

An effective communicator is heard, but not misunderstood because of tone or inflection. He must always speak audibly enough. Speak at an appropriate volume so your entire audience can hear your thoughts and ideas. Present a tone of confidence and understanding. This tells your audience that you are worth hearing.

Share your opinions:

It is always better to share ideas and opinions. Telling someone what you truly believe is important; however, you should make sure such is done in a well-informed, prepared manner. An effective communicator should sound intelligent and convey meaning with their opinions. Make sure the other person will find meaning in your ideas and opinions.

Cultivate the Habit of Practice or Rehearsal:

Becoming an effective communicator takes practice. Spend time each day listening to a colleague and engaging in meaningful conversation. Rehearse speaking in a confident tone and making valuable points to your listener. If you are engaged to go and deliver a lecture, it will serve you better to rehearse such a process. The practice will better prepare you and refine your skills as an effective communicator.

Demonstrate Respect:

Respecting the ideas and opinions of others can help to foster an environment that allows you to share your own personal ideas and opinions. Demonstrating respect encourages a safe forum in which to present the ideas and opinions of all parties involved. That does not necessarily mean that you must agree with them. It simply means that you are respecting the space in which you are sharing them. Don't embarrass others, especially in public. Don't misdirect your anger. Act thoughtfully and carefully — don't react offensively. Pausing after speaking may encourage the person to absorb the information and to provide you with more information. You should however avoid jumping to conclusions and rushing to judgments.

Behave professionally:

You could do this by making the other person or audience feel that you do not make that other person feel you alone have monopoly of knowledge in that field even if you are the expert. Seek their views and make them feel relevant. You do not want to be, or appear to be, an advocate or adversary. You can validate a person's feelings without agreeing or disagreeing with the content of their concerns through basic acknowledgement with nodding of head, or with expressions of concurrence like " I see", or through eye contact, as appropriate within the person's cultural norms.

Pose Questions:

Don't be afraid to ask questions in order to better clarify the issue or business that is on the table. It is important to pose questions that will help to give you a better understanding of what is being communicated to you, as well as to propel the dialogue forward.

Ensure Feedback:

Be sure you are understood through a proper appraisal of the feedback process. Feedback closes the communication loop and confirms that the message was received clearly. Asking questions or repeating the message accurately allows further clarification of the information if necessary, and tells the communicator the communication process was successful.

Significance of Effective Communication to Military Public Relations

Military Public Relations Officers, Public Affairs, and Information Officers are very important staffs of Military Public Relations or Public Affairs Departments worldwide. They carry out crucial roles and form a very important component of the military establishment. In the United States, the Public Affairs Officer (PAO) is responsible for developing a working relationship with reporters and other media representatives, maintaining a robust community relations program, keeping contact with other government agencies, and keeping internal and external publics informed on issues that may affect them. Known as "PA's" for short, they are expected to coordinate with the appropriate agencies prior to contacting and releasing information to the media on conditions that might result in favorable or unfavorable public reaction, including releases and public statements involving local, regional and national news[19].

Public Affairs Officers are responsible for preparing information relative to unit participation in military operations, world events, and environmental matters through news releases, special activities, photographs, radio and television, and other informational material. They also review materials such as speeches, news articles, and radio and television shows for security review and integration with the objectives of the military, and determine appropriate topics. They produce speeches and act as ghost writers for commanders, often completely developing a commander's public persona. These duties are virtually the same in most military public relations branches globally[20].

The duties enumerated above all have bearing on communication. They are enormous and demand that the Military PR or PAO must be experts or versatile in so many areas most importantly, communication as it is at the very heart of Public relations practice. He or she must therefore possess all the required skills of communication namely: Reading Skills, Writing Skills, Speaking Skills and Listening Skills. He or she must above all be friendly, patient and approachable at all times.

All of these skills come into play and have bearing on every of the above aspects of communication with the public especially spokesman ship.

Spokesman ship:

A spokesman or spokesperson is one who speaks as the representative of another person, group or corporate body often in a professional capacity. NATO Military Policy on Public Affairs describes Spokespersons as any uniformed member of NATO regardless of rank who responds to media or speaks publicly about an issue... Official spokespersons are those persons who by virtue of their position Or appointment are expected to speak to the media, the public, or internally about NATO military affairs. This includes the Chairman of the Military Committee, Strategic Commanders, Force and Operational Commanders, and the Chief PAOs of all those organisations[21]. Spokesman ship according to Oladimeji, is part science, part art. It is a mix of theory and practice techniques that you must learn and sharpen... spokesmen should not speak above their level of knowledge, competence or authority. A military public speaker, he adds, needs not be a polished orator. However, he must be able to present facts simply, fluently and coherently. He must have first-hand knowledge of the military and his or her command. An interview or briefing is not a verbal duel between you and the reporter. It is an opportunity to tell your story to convince the listener or reader[22]. Oladimeji sees every military personnel as a potential spokesperson. It is in that regard that he advises the military to always keep its men happy and informed as every member is a potential spokesperson. Enthusiastic and well-motivated employees (men) can become positive spokesmen for you. Ill-treated men will become ill-motivated and your most negative spokespeople[23].

Qualities of a Good Spokesperson:

Oladimeji further lists the qualities of a good spokesperson to among others include the following:

- The three-Cs – common sense, common courtesy and communication skills.
- In-depth knowledge of the organization or profession you speak for.
- Working knowledge of news media
- Sales skills – Salesman's skills and contact management of media men.
- Interpersonal relations to coordinate information of public interest with all departments
- Resourcefulness to get informed on topical issues of public interest.
- Verbal communication skills – Needs not be an orator; should be able to communicate in simple straight forward style.
- Writing Skills.
- Information processing skills to make to make information available instantly as needed[24].

In the modern military, public information, communication and indeed spokesman ship has become a job for all personnel given the dynamics of modern day military operations. All military personnel essentially require public relations skills many aspects of which are communications and interpersonal skills. Rear Admiral J. Holland emphasized this much when he said that: from now on, wars (and war for budgetary allocations) will be fought in the public view. All officers will have to learn how to "meet the press", and public affairs officers will no longer suffice as the mouth pieces[25].

References

1. Oladimeji, O.A. (2000) Military Image and Media Message Lagos, Miral Miral Press) P. 85
2. Cutlip, E. et al, (1985) Effective Public Relations (New Jersey, Prentice Hall Inc) P. 260
3. Agim, J. (2010) Image Communication and Reputation Management (Owwerri, Ultimate Books) P. 1
4. Haywood, quoted in Agim, J. (Ibid)
5. Agim, J. Ibid
6. Ibid
7. Michaels S.J. @ http://ezinearticles.com/?Interpersonal-Skills&id=6248306
8. Dennis Wilcox et al, Public Relations, Strategies and Tactics (New York, Harper & Row 1989) PP 185 – 186
9. Cutlip, et al (1985) Effective Public Relations, (New Jersey, Prentice Hall) P. 359
10. BarbaraBrown http://www.livestrong.com/article/69309-effective-communication/
11. http://www.managementstudyguide.com/seven-cs-of-effective-communication.htm
12. http://www.businessdictionary.com/definition/skill.html
13. http://www.thefreedictionary.com/Skills
14. http://www.investopedia.com/terms/i/interpersonal-skills.asp#axzz1t3sQjPw1
15. http://web.njit.edu/~lipuma/352comproc/comproc.htm
16. http://davis.foulger.info/research/unifiedModelOfCommunication.htm
17. MayaPillai@http://www.buzzle.com/articles/barriers-to-effective-communication.html
18. http://www.ehow.com/how_4546032_developing-effective-communication-skills.html
19. http://en.wikipedia.org/wiki/Public_affairs_(military)
20. Ibid
21. http://www.nato.int/ims/docu/mc0457_en.pdf
22. Oladimeji, O.A. PP. 95 - 96
23. Ibid, P. 98
24. Ibid, PP 107 – 108
25. Rear Admiral J. Holland, cited in Oladimeji O.A. P. 67

CHAPTER NINETEEN

CONCLUSION: THE IMPORTANCE OF MILITARY PUBLIC RELATIONS IN DEMOCRATIC SOCIETY

It is perhaps, appropriate to premise the discussion of the importance of military public relations in a democratic society on the observation by Samuel Huntington in an article, "The Soldier and the State in the 1970's", which was an update of his well-known original seminal work. He stated that,"...In modern, developed societies,... characterised by relatively highly institutionalized political structures and patterns of role... and by relatively highly institutionalized and professionalized officer corps, the central problem of civil military relations thus becomes the relationship between the military professionals and the political leadership[1]".

Given, as implied in the statement that the major problem of civil military relations centres on the relationship between the military and political leadership, the conduct of public relations by the military without prior political authority as by especially western democratic precepts is probably one aspect of such problem. As analysed in chapter five, this is an issue that is particularly prevalent in the United States where the 'competence' of the military to conduct public relations had been questioned by Government and the Congress.

In the light of the central focal theme of this work on the importance of public relations to the Armed Forces, the discussion, in chapter four which analysed the role and function of military public relations in the interface of military and society, and also, the objectives enunciated as to the purpose of military public relations in chapter six, jointly provide a clue to the necessity for military public relations in the society. If, as has been established, the analysis in those two chapters have been able to answer the question: "Why are Public Relations necessary to the Armed Forces?", it then also follows, judging from the analysis, that public relations is relevant to the military not only from the point of view of its "self-interest", but also most importantly, that it is an important element that helps to explain its role in the various aspects of its interplay with society. This probably explains why the military, in conducting its public relations, takes time to identify properly its various targets, and is very careful to map out appropriate public relations strategies and tactics that will help achieve the public relations objectives.

The overall relevance of public relations in society be they for industries, communities, non-profit organisations, the military and even government, within a democratic society may be seen from the increasing importance which the various organisations continue to attach to public relations activities. Perhaps, a statement which summarises its values within a democratic context is that once prepared by a Task Force appointed by the Public Relations Society of America (PRSA), which examined the stature and role of public relations. It noted:

"Public relations is a means for the public to have its desires and interests felt by the institutions in society. It interprets and speaks for the public to otherwise unresponsive organisations, as well as speaking for those organisations to the public. Public relations is a means to achieve mutual adjustment between institutions and groups, establishing smoother relationships that benefit the public. Public relations are a safety valve for freedom. By providing means of working out accommodations, it makes arbitrary actions or coercion less likely. Public relations is an essential element in the communication system that enables individuals to be informed on many aspects of subjects that affects their lives. Public relations personnel can help activate the organisation's social conscience. Public relations (either systematic or unconscious) are a universal activity. It functions in all aspects of life. Everyone practices principles of public relations in seeking acceptance, cooperation or affection of others[2]".

It is out of such a broad framework that an understanding and support of the various services' role in the national defence of the United States are fostered through programmes for disseminating public information, and, for improving community relations. The US Armed Services have public relations objectives that are similar to those of the army which specify the following missions:

- Organization-Develop a public affairs organization that is recognized for its excellence, responsiveness, foresight, and dedication to the goals of the Total Army.
- Personnel Army Public Affairs personnel must be professional, well trained, highly motivated, and have confidence of the public, their colleagues, and their superiors.
- Internal Affairs - Maintain an internal information effort that fulfils the information wants and needs of the Total Army's internal audience inorder to sustain an effective motivated and loyal force.
- External Affairs_ Promote clear and open channels of communication between the Total Army and its external publics[3]".

On the basis of these objectives, it is therefore relevant, as Lowndes F. Stephens, pointed out on the essence of professional orientation of military public affairs officers that, "these goals reflect what Feld calls the "open equality" relationship of the U.S. armed forces with other institutions in American society. Under an "open equality" system, the military alone are not responsible for decisions regarding national defence. The armed forces must be "ready on Call", responsive and accountable to a political regime which includes a civilian Commander-in-Chief, civilian technicians, and a political community of voters and public interest groups[4]".

Given that public relations is one avenue through which the military is able to be accountable to society, it is, essential that this is a function that must always be taken seriously if public support is to be guaranteed. The force of public opinion, in an ever advancing world, has continued to be well recognized by various institutions in society. In this regard, Robert Reilly, appropriately hit the nail on the head with his observation that: "In this era of rapid communication and shifting alliances, public opinion has become a dominant factor. The late Harry Truman said no man could function any longer as president without the support of public opinion. We've seen public opinion cut short a war in Vietnam, topple an American President, help oust the Shah of Iran, provoke tax reforms, elect more conservative leadership, and support a growing fitness. Public opinion is a bit like the wind; we observe its effects even when we can't pinpoint its source. It is also unstable, changing periodically to reflect new information, new thinking or the result of fresh events[5]".

The recognition of the importance of public opinion in society is such that it excites various comments from different persons. It is an issue which, in relation to the essence of military public relations, Morris Janowitz had posed a question to which he also attempted an answer. He said: "It remains outside the capacity of social research even with the most elaborate field techniques available to give a clear answer to the question: What are the consequences of these public information programmes on public attitudes and political decisions? "Available research knowledge suggests that mass communications can be decisive in moments of crisis and tension, but that, in general, their influence is limited and has effect gradually, over a long period of time". The influence of the mass media, supported by networks of interpersonal contacts among opinion leaders, is not in dramatic conversion of public opinion, but rather in setting the limits within which public debate on controversial issues takes place. To this end, the public information programme of the military establishment are important, even though it is impossible to say how important[6]".

Public information programmes constitute a vital aspect of military public relations. It may therefore be said in conclusion, that, military public relations is certainly very important in a democratic society. This is recognized by the military, and even by governments, especially, Britain and the United States which are two nations that are usually cited to approximating as well as upholding of liberal democratic principles. This, however, is in spite of the fact that the military's 'competence' to conduct public relations is consistently put to question, especially the United States. If democracy does not recognize the value and importance of military public relations in peace and in war, the British parliament, in 1982, would not have set up a committee to investigate an issue that relates to the "The handling of press and public information during the Falklands conflict", which was an aspect of military public relations.

Finally, it may be reiterated, based on the overall analysis that military public relations are important in democratic society. Its overall advantage may lie more with the military, but the public also derive its benefits in many ways. Public relations afford the public, knowledge about the military and its role in society. Through it they are made aware that the military considers the people as supreme in a nation. Furthermore assurance is provided through public relations that the military is in no way a threat institution to society either by its performance of obligatory internal security duties to providing also, the assurance that it is no threat to the peoples elected governments.

References

1. Huntington, Samuel. "The Soldier and the State in the 1970's", in Margiotta, F.D. (1978) **The Changing World of the American Military**, Colorado, Westview, P.15-16
2. Dennis Wilcox, et al (1989) **Public Relations: Strategies and Tactics**, New York, Harper and Row,, pp.17-18
3. Lowndes, F. Stephens, "The Professional Orientation of Military Public Affairs Officers" in Public Relations Quarterly, vol. 23, 1978, p. 19-23
4. Ibid
5. Reilly, R. (1987) **Public Relations in Action** 2nd ed, Englewood Cliffs, New Jersey, p. 35-36
6. Janowitz, Morris. (1964) **The Professional Soldier**, New york, The Free Press, pp.401-402

BIBLIOGRAPHY

Books

Ackroyd, C. et al (1974) **The Technology of Political Control**, London, Penguin Books

AjaAkpuru–Aja,(1999) **Policy & Strategic Studies**, Abakaliki, Willy – Rose Publishers

Agim, J.A. (2004) **The Principles and Practice of Public Relations in the Military and the Police**, Enugu, Ultimate Publishers

Arthur Dreyer, "Functions and Responsibilities in the Departments of Defense,

Army, Navy, Marine corps and Air Force Information Services in Military Public

Affairs" in Stephenson, H. (1960) **Handbook of Public Relations** New York, McGraw-Hill

Awad, J. (1985) **The Power of Public Relations**, New York, PraegerPublishers

Barry Buzan (1983) **People, States and Fears: The National Security Problem in International Relations** (London, Harvester Wheatshef

Bellamy I (1991) **People States and Fear: An Agenda For International Security in Post – Cold War Era** (Colorado: Reiner Publishers).

Baynes, J.C.M. (1972)**The Soldier in Modern Society, London Eyre Methuen**

Black, Sam, (1966) **Practical Public Relations**, London Sir Isaac Pitman

Black, Sam, (1989) **Introduction to Public Relations, London** The Modino Press

Bowman and Ellis, (1969) **Manual of Public Relations,** London Heinemann

Capitanchik and Eichenberg **(1983) Defence and Public Opinion** London Rouledge

Childs, H. (1982)**An Introduction to Public Opinion, New York:** John Wiley and Sons Inc,

Clotfelter, J., (1973)**The Military in American Politics,** NewYork, Harper & Row

Cochran,L. C, (1974) **Civil Military Relations, London, The Free Press**

Cochran, L.C. (ed) (1974) **Civil Military Relations,** London, Collier Macmillan

Collin Coulson–Thomas, (1979) **Public Relations: A Practical Guide** (New York: Bath Macdonald and Evans

Cutlip, S.M. et al (1985) **Effective Public Relations** 6th ed New Jersey, Prentice Hall Englewood Cliffs

Edmonds, M., (1988) **Armed Services and Society,** Leicester University press

Frank Jefkins, (1991) **Public Relations**, Plymouth, M&E Publishers

Graber, D.A. (1984) **Mass Media and American Politics,** Chicago, Univ of Ilinois Press

Hans, B. et al, **Parliamentary Oversight of the Security Sector** (Geneva, IPU, DCAF)

Haywood, R. (1990) **All About Public Relations** 2nd ed, London, McGraw-Hill

Hooper, A., (1982) **The Military and the Media,** Aldershot, Gower Publishers

Howard, S., (1960) **Handbook of Public Relations** New York, McGraw-Hill

Huntington, S.P. (1957) **The Soldier and the State,** Harvard University Press

Huntington, S.P. (1961)**The Common Defence** New York, Columbia University Press

Huntington, S. "The Soldier and the State in the 1970's", in Margiotta, F.D.'s (1978) **The Changing World of the American Military,**Colorado, Westview

Kurt Lang, (1972) **Military Institutions and the Sociology of War** London, Sage

Kurkeja, V. (1990) (1990)**Civil_Military Relations in South East Asia,** New Delhi Sage

Lipmann W. (1943) **United States Foreign Policy, Shield of the Republic**, Boston Little Brum& Co

Mcnamara R. (1978) **The Essence of Security,** (USA: Harper & Row

Margiota, F.D. (1978) **The Changing World of the American Military,** Colorado, Westview

Nigerian Institute of Public Relations Lagos (2008) Professional Development Programme

Obiozor GA et al (1991) **Nigeria and ECOWAS since 1985: Towards a Dynamic Regional Integration** Enugu, Fourth Dimension Publishers

Oladimeji, O. (2001) **Military Image and Media Message,** Lagos: Miral Press

Onwudiwe E. &Osaghae (eds) (2010) **Winning Hearts and Minds: A Community Relations Approach for the Nigerian Military,** Ibadan, John Archer Publishers

Raymond,J., (1964) **Power at the Pentagon,** London, Heinemann

Reilly, R., (1987) **Public Relations in Action,** New Jersey,   Englewood Cliffs

Sani L. Mohammed (ed) (2006) **Civil and Security Agencies Relationship: Role of the Military in Consolidating Democracy in Nigeria** Abuja: **the Military in Consolidating Democracy in Nigeria** Abuja: Friedrich Ebert Stiftung

Stanhope, H., (1979)**The Soldiers,** London Hamish Hamilton

Stephenson, H. (1960) **Handbook of Public Relations** New York, McGraw-Hill

Swomley, J. M., (1964) **The Military Establishment,** Boston, Beacon Press

Taylor, P.M. (1992) **War and the Media: Propaganda and Persuasion in the Gulf**

War, Manchester University press

Wilcox, D.L. et al (1989) **Public Relations: Strategies and Tactics,**New York, Harper&& Row,

Yusuf M.D., (2010) **The Military, The Media and Nigeria's National Security,** Ibadan, Gold Press

Published Articles

Agbambu, Chris, "Strengthening the Cord that Binds Civil Military Relationship" in Nigerian Tribune, Monday 29 March 2010

Beach, H. (General) "News management in conventional war" in British Army Review, vol 87, December, 1987

Gene, K. "Informing the public on national security" in Air Force Magazine, June 1984 and Defence Journal vol.115, no. 4, October 1985

Hasek, J, "Military Isolation and the Media: The Vietnam Case" in The Army Quarterly College, 1992

Hyper, H. "The Media in modern warfare: friend or foe?" in Hawk, Bracknell RAF

Humphries, A.A., "Two Routes to the Wrong Destination: Public Affairs in the South Atlantic War" in Naval War College Review

James E, and Philip, S. "Army Public Affairs Officers as perceived by Press and Military Colleagues" in Public Relations Quarterly Spring 1983

Lowndes,F. Stephens, "Professionalism of Army Public Affairs Personnel" in Public Relations Review vol. 7, Summer 1981

Lowndes F. Stephens, "The professional orientation of military public affairs officers" in Public. Relations Quarterly, vol 23 1978

Mungan, G,"The Eternal Triangle: Relations between Governments, Armed Services and the Media" in The Army Quarterly and Defence Journal, vol. 115, no.1, January 1985

Pockock, T., "Defence and Public Relations" in RUSSI Journal, September 1969 West Africa Magazine, 10-16 August 1992

Siddle, W., "The Military and the Press" in Army Journal, February 1985

Unpublished Works

Adache John "Regional Integration in Africa: The ECOWAS Experience" University of Abuja PhD Dissertation, 2006

Adache John Keeping the Armed Services in Public Eye: The Relevance of Military Public Relations in Modern Society, M.A. Dissertation submitted to Department of Politics and International Relations, Lancaster University for the Award of MA in Defence and Security Analysis July 1992

Olukolade, C.A., Mobilization of Public Support for Nigerias Military Operations: A Framework for Public Information Management", Research Project submitted to National Institute for Policy and Strategic Studies, Kuru, November 2011

Tanko Abitsokwa, Sallah, "Resolving Communual Crisis in Nigeria: Challenges and Prospects" Thesis Submitted to National Open University of Nigeria, March 2010

Tokoya, O.O. Public Relations Practice in the Nigerian Army: Challenges and Prospects. Research Project submitted to the National Defence College, Abuja, August 2009

Bamba Diao "Media in Modern Conflicts: Effects on Military Operations in Senegal", Project submitted to National War College, June 2006.

Report of Nigerian Army Public Relations training seminar, 1987

Lectures and Seminar Papers

Adache John, "Improving the Image of the Army in a Democratic Dispensation: Significance", Presentation at Capacity Building Workshop for Defence Correspondents at Yenagoa, BayelsaState, 16-18 May, 2007

Adache John, "Public Relations: Its Role in Political and Legislative Matters", Lecture Delivered to Legislative Aides of National Assembly, Abuja, 16 & 17 November, 2009

Adache John, "Security and Technology", lecture delivered at Defence and Security Management Course 4, National Defence College, Abuja, October 2011

Adamolekun Wole, "Sustainable Public Relations Strategies to Enhance the Operations of the Nigerian Air Force", Lecture delivered at Nigerian Air Force Training Seminar Nigerian Air Force Seminar on proactive public relations in the NAF in July 2010

Adediji, Tola, "Improving the Image of the Armed Forces through Public Relations", Lecture Delivered at Nigerian Army Public Relations Training Seminar, Lagos, 29-30 Dec 1987

Chijukka Fred, Opening Address at Nigerian Army Public Relations Training Seminar, Lagos, 29-30 Dec 1987

Chijuka Fred "Nigerian Media: Balanced Reporting Versus Sensationalism and National Security", Paper presented at Defence Information Seminar, Abuja, 12 March 2007

Fashina, Reuben, "Reflections on Army Public Relations Department since its Inception" in Report of Training Seminar organized by Nigerian Army Public Relations Department held at Command Officers Mess 1 Marina-Lagos, 29-30 December1987

Giwa, A. "Reflections on Army Public Relations Department Since its Inception" in Report of Training Seminar (Ibid)

Mahmud Jega, Media Access to Unclassified Military Information", Paper presented at Capacity building Workshop for Defence Correspondents at Yenagoa, May 2007

Nwolise, O.B.C. "Public Relations Tools for Maximising Objectives in the Nigerian Army", Lecture delivered at Directorate of Army Public Relations Training Period, Ibadan, 22-27 December, 1991.

Ibid

Ochoche S.A. "Changing Concepts of International Peace & Security in Garuba Chris International Peace & Security": The 'Nigerian Contribution, Lecture delivered at National War College, April, 1996

Oladimeji O.A. Effective Public Relations and Information in Military Operations. Paper presented at Directorate of Army Public Relations Training Period, 1991.

Ogbomoh, V.L. "Acceptability of Public Relations Practice" in Report of Training Seminar Organized by Nigerian Army Public Relations Department held at Command Officers Mess 1 Marina-Lagos, 29-30 December1987

Zabadi, I.S. "Public Perception of the Nigerian Army in a Democracy: The Way Forward" Paper presented at the Nigerian Army Workshop on "Enhancing Civil-Military Relations to Meet Contemporary Challenges of the Nigerian Army in a Democratic Environment", held at the Headquarters of 2 Division, Nigerian Army, Ibadan, 11 - 13 June 2011

Newspapers and Magazines

Air Force Magazine (UK) June 1984
Thisday 16 September 2010

Nigerian Forum, NIIA vol 23
Nigerian Tribune, Monday 29 March 2010
The Sunday Times (of London) 24 February, 1991

RUSSI Journal, September 1969
West Africa Magazine, 10-16 August 1992

Documents

Army Public Relations Officers Handbook, HQ APRD Lagos, 1973

Challenge and Commitment – A Defence Policy for Canada (Ottawa, Canadian Govt Pub 1987)
Constitution of the Federal Republic of Nigeria 1999
National Defence Policy of Nigeria, 2006

Manual of the Directorate of Army Public Relations 1991

Ministry of Defence Diary, 1999

Nigerian Army Diary 2002
The House of Commons Command paper on the handling of Press   and   public information during the Falklands War MOD London, Working Arrangement with the Media in Time of Tension and War

Internet Sources

RonSmithPublicRelationsHistoryathttp:// faculty.buffalostate.edu/smithrd/PR/history.htm

USArmyPublicAffairsHallofFameathttp://www.army.mil/institution/armypublicaffairs/hof/
Don Bates, *"Mini-Me History"* at www.instituteforpr.org
http://wiki.answers.com/Q/
What is the history and evolution of public relations#ixzz1aOE0KgjI
Grunig and Hunt's (1984) cited in OlutayoOtubanjo, "150 Years 0f Modern Public Relations Practices in Nigeria" at http://ssm.com/abstract=13727042
Stephen Johnson, "Military Public Relations in the Americas: Learning to Promote the Flow www.au.af.mil/au/awc/awcgate/ndu/military_media_in_americas.doc
Admiral Giampaolo di Paola, Foreword to NATO Military policy on public affairs @ http://www.nato.int/ims/docu/mil-publ-aff-policy.htm

Nowa A. Omoigui @ http;//www.dawodu.com/soja.htm

Orend Brian, "War", http://plato.stanford.edu/entries/war/
http://en.wikipedia.org.wiki/Military_Aid_to_the

Nelson O. Michael,"Reforms in Nigeria: the Place of Public Relations" http://www. articlesbase.com/organizational-articles/reforms-in-nigeria-the-place-of-public-relations-145498.html

Susan Jan "The Important Role of Public Relations" http://ezinearticles. com/?The-Important-Role-Of-Public-Relations&id=198392

Tony Jaques, "Issue and Crisis Management: Quicksand in the Definitional Landscape" in "Public Relations Review, 2009, 35(3) 280-286" cited at http://www.issueoutcomes. com.au/Websites/issueoutcomes/Images/Definitional-quicksand-PRR.pdf

Heidi Cohen, "31 public relations definition" @ http://heidicohen.com/public-relations-definition/2.

http://sbr.com.sg/media-marketing/commentary/public-relations-in-era-social-media

http://www.virtualsocialmedia.com/social-media-the-best-public-relations-tool/

http://www.prsa.org/SearchResults/view/6D-020203/0/How Blogs and social Media are Changing Public Relations

James Dao @ http://atwar.blogs.nytimes.com/2010/02/26/military-announces-new-social-media-policy/ http://atwar.blogs.nytimes.com/2010/02/26/military-announces-new-social-media-policy/

http://www.military.com/news/article/air-force-news/military-leaders-embrace-social-media

http://gulfnews.com/news/gulf/oman/listen-to-people-s-voice-says-former-african-military-ruler-1.963086

http://www.bbc.co.uk/news/

http://africanurbanism.blogspot.com/2012/01/protests-ignite-across-nigeria-against.html

Andrew Marshal, cited athttp://www.iwar.org.uk/rma/resources/nato/ar299stc-e.html

http://www.iwar.org.uk/rma/resources/nato/ar299stc-e.html

Dennis L. Wilcox et al (1989) Public Relations – Strategies and Tactics, (New York, Harper & Row Pub) P 530

http://education.ezine9.com/impact-of-globalization-146d7d24cc.html

Daniel Nation @ http://webtrends.about.com/OD/web20/a/social-media.htm

http://en.wikipedia.org/wiki/social_media

http://networkconference.netstudies.org/2010/04/social-media-and-globalisation/

DaveRoos @http://communication.howstuffworks.com/how-public-relations-works5.htm

See http://www.dinfos.osd.mil/DinfosWeb/About_main.aspx

Welcome to LSPR – PR and Beyond @ http://www.pr-school-london.com/

http://www.businessdictionary.com/definition/organized.html

ReubenBuhari,"DanmbazauHarpsonCivilMilitaryRelations" http://www.
nigerianbestforum.com/blog

http://en.wikipedia.org/wiki/perception_management

http://www.hyperdictionary.com/dictionary/perception

http:/en.wikipedia.org/wiki/perception

http://www.wisegeek.com/what-is-public-perception.htm

Wisegeek, "Public Perception", http://www.wisegeek.com/what-is-public-perception.htm
http://en.wikipedia.org/wiki/perception_management

http://www.nato.int/ims/docu/mil-publ-aff-policy.htm
www.terena.org/activities/tf-pr/

Weaver Cited at http://www.ehow.com/facts_648845_definition-security-threat.html

http://www.knowledgerush.com/kr/encyclopedia/threat

http://en.wikipedia.org/wiki/crisis_management

Lerbinger @ http://en.wikipedia.org/wiki/crisis_management

James E. Lukaszenski @ http://en.wikipedia.org/wiki/crisis_management

http://en.wikipedia.org/wiki/Media_Relations

INDEX